THE GREATNESS OF ELITES

THE GREATNESS OF ELITES

MAURICE MURET

TRANSLATED WITH AN INTRODUCTION
BY ALEXANDER JACOB

ARKTOS
LONDON 2022

Copyright © 2022 by Arktos Media Ltd.

All rights reserved. No part of this book may be reproduced or utilised in any form or by any means (whether electronic or mechanical), including photocopying, recording or by any information storage and retrieval system, without permission in writing from the publisher.

ISBN	978-1-914208-92-8 (Paperback)
	978-1-914208-93-5 (Hardback)
	978-1-914208-94-2 (Ebook)
TRANSLATION	Alexander Jacob
EDITING	Constantin von Hoffmeister
COVER & LAYOUT	Tor Westman

🌐 Arktos.com   fb.com/Arktos   @arktosmedia   arktosmedia

CONTENTS

Introduction by Alexander Jacob vii
Foreword xxi

I. The Handsome and Good Athenian 1
II. The Roman Citizen 33
III. The Renaissance Man 67
IV. The French Gentleman 99
V. The English Gentleman 139
VI. What Conclusion Do We Draw from the Preceding? 183

Bibliography 197

INTRODUCTION

BY ALEXANDER JACOB

MAURICE MURET (1870–1954) was a Swiss journalist and author who studied in Lausanne, Leipzig, Paris and Munich. He became editor of the *Journal des débats* in 1895 and contributed to the Foreign Affairs section of the *Gazette de Lausanne* from 1909. Muret was an anti-Dreyfusard and follower of Charles Maurras and the Action française. He published a book on *L'esprit juif* (The Jewish mind) in 1901 and disseminated German and Italian literature in France. During the First World War, Muret was decidedly Francophile and wrote two works condemning Germany's role in starting the war, *L'orgueil allemand* (German arrogance) (1915) and *L'évolution belliqueuse de Guillaume II* (The belligerent development of Wilhelm II) (1917). He published a work entitled *Le crépuscule des nations blanches* in 1925, which was translated into English by his American wife, Charlotte Touzalin, as *The Twilight of the White Races* (1926). His next works included *L'Archiduc François-Ferdinand* (1932) and *Guillaume II* (1940). His defence of aristocratic and heroic cultures was crystallised in two further works, *Grandeur des élites* (Paris, Albin Michel, 1939) and *France héroïque* (1943), whose heroes range from Vercingétorix to Maréchal Pétain.

*

Muret's book on the elites is a social history in the form of a shimmering tapestry of characters, both historical and fictional, who exemplify the elites of the cultured societies of Western Europe from ancient Greece to early twentieth-century Britain. Thomas Carlyle had maintained that great historic periods are propelled by heroic individuals, who give their life to the realisation of an ideal while Marx put forward the contrary theory that it was not individuals who led the masses but the masses that led the individuals. Rejecting both these notions, Muret insists that it is elites that constitute the essence of a great period of history. He gainsays Carlyle by pointing out that '[t]he great man has something immoderate and excessive whereas the Western genius, considered in its most noble creations, always contains something measured, tempered, balanced'. In other words, it is not sufficient to have enlightened personages to direct the affairs of an entire nation in a particular direction but there must be an elite class, or caste, that is capable of moulding society in its image. The essential basis of the elites of Europe is identified by Muret as the humanist ideal, and it is this that constitutes the strongest bulwark against the rising tide of the mass mentality emerging from Bolshevist Russia.

Muret notes that, even though the decline of the European aristocracy began with the French Revolution, the individual was still glorified in Western Europe and the concept of mass rule did not fully arise until the advent of Marxism. The Russian Revolution thus was a more alarming manifestation of the rise of the masses and the proletariat and this, Muret surmises, is partly because the aristocracy in Russia was not a very enlightened one and its loss was not felt by the Russian people as a very deleterious event. However, in its glorification of the proletarian, Bolshevism remains an extreme danger to the traditionally elitist societies of Western Europe since, according to Muret, hierarchical societies cannot be abruptly dismantled in order to make way for the rule of the lowest elements of the population. Rather, such societies should be preserved in an organic manner by a social mobility that allows upward movement only in carefully graded stages. Now that the mass ethos of Bolshevism was threatening the Western countries as well, Muret believes that only the Western ideal of humanism could offer an effective resistance to the Asiatic invasion from Russia.

Humanism is essentially a Graeco-Roman phenomenon that was revived in Italy during the Renaissance and further developed in the court of Louis XIV in the seventeenth century. Although it underwent a relative decay in the eighteenth century under the pressure of the Englightenment's adoration of reason and empiricism, it was restored in a striking manner in the English ideal of the gentleman that rose to prominence in the Victorian Age. In the aftermath of the devastating First World War, both Italy and Germany turned to statism as a political bulwark against Bolshevism. But Muret considers statism as not sufficiently related to society to be able to create the elites necessary to counter the Bolshevist rulers of the future society. Germany's racialism too is opposed to humanism and to Christianity, which Muret sees as the indispensable foundation of European morality and culture. He therefore hopes that France and England will be able, through their existing elites, to continue the humanistic social paradigm that alone can resist the Bolshevist propaganda of the dictatorship of the proletariat. While the British are not naturally part of the Graeco-Latin humanist culture — even though they still study it carefully in their schools — the French indeed have a longer traditional affiliation with it. As he says, 'Hellenism and Latinism have entered the blood of France to such an extent, the prestige of Classicism and the elites that it engendered remains so strong in this country that they try more to hoard its advantages for the benefit of the masses than to suppress them radically.'

*

Muret believed that elites are formed initially under enlightened autocrats such as Pericles in fifth century B.C. Greece and Louis XIV in seventeenth-century France. The original formation of an elite in the classical world is identified by Muret in the aristocratic democracy of Periclean Greece. Here the Greek adoration of beauty combined with virtue resulted in the cultivation of what was called *kalokagathia*, or the combined beauty of mind and body in the well-formed Greek aristocrat. The Greek civilisation was essentially an urban one, even though it benefited from maritime trade as well. Athenian culture was centred around the *polis*, or city, with the *agora*,[1] or public square, serving as the open-air meeting place for talented young men and their philosophical masters. Its generous humanism was devoted to the cultivation of literary eloquence and artistic excellence and, like its leader Pericles himself, it was opposed to both Spartan chauvinism and militarism.

The democracy of Athens was an aristocratic one insofar as its government was constituted of *eupatrides*, or men of good Greek ancestry, and only Athenian citizens voted in the assemblies to the exclusion of slaves and immigrants. Pericles embodied all the virtues of an aristocratic Greek, having first served in the army and then devoted his life to the public service of Athens, which he fulfilled with astonishing taste and judgement as patron of the imposing public works and arts that fill even modern minds with awe. His demagogic opponent, Cleon, on the other hand, was a symptom of the decay that Greece was soon to suffer with the decline of the aristocratic democratic government of Athens. Cleon was opposed to the Athenian aristocracy and when he took over the leadership on Pericles' death in 429 B.C., his reign was marked by bad government as well as bad manners. This decay was accelerated by the Hellenic expansion of Greece under the Macedonians and the substitution of Eastern luxury for the older *kalokagathia* civic virtues of Athens.

*

---

1 Marketplace.

With the rise of Rome, a new variant of aristocracy emerged in the West that was to have a lasting impact on the whole of Western European culture. Roman aristocracy was in its origins a rustic and military one. The original patricians were, rather like the later English squires, raised on estates in the country and served in the army, as the legendary figure of Cincinnatus, for example, did in the fifth century B.C. Although Rome began as a monarchy, it was, in 510 B.C., replaced by an aristocratic Republic ruled by patricians. The patricians were at first clearly distinguished from the commoners, or plebeians. However, gradually the two were increasingly intermixed. The aristocratic ethos was a rather austere one and practical. The hatred that Cato the Elder manifested for Carthage in the second century B.C. ('*Carthago delenda est*') was the hatred of a Roman peasant-soldier for the mercantile luxury of the Carthaginians. It was also the hatred of a land-based civilisation for the maritime one of the Phoenician. The Romans were also not a particularly scientific people and their devotion to the arts was not so original as that of the Greeks. However, the discipline that marked the Roman aristocracy was extremely impressive and constituted the foundation of the laws that were formulated in the Twelve Tables of the fifth century B.C. and later extended over the empire as Roman Law. Muret points out that the Romans were preoccupied with laws because they loved justice for its own sake and not, like the Hebrews, in order to foster petty tribalistic chauvinism.

Rome was distinguished in its developed phase by imperialism and the imposition of systematic laws both in Italy and in the expanding colonies of the Roman Empire. The Roman conquests were, to be sure, marked by cruelty and celebrated in triumphs that were humiliating for the conquered princes and armies. But the subsequent rule of the Romans in the colonies did not disturb the local traditions of the colonised but instead incorporated these nations systematically, under the Roman Law, into the famous *pax romana*. In fact, some defeated princes even voluntarily gave up their kingdoms to Rome and its superior legal and adminstrative organisation.

The rule of the colonies by the governors was generally honest but, with the increasing wealth acquired through Rome's colonial possessions, the gap between the rich and the poor increased and the latter had to be pacified through the organisation of proletarian games, such as gladiatorial fights, which betrayed a vulgarity and brutality of taste that still shock modern historians. Finally, with the advent of Christianity and its personal as opposed to state religion, Rome was undermined in its very foundations, which were the Roman 'polis' and the extended state. The Roman Empire was soon turned into a Christian one and the new religious empire was marked by Christian morality and its doctrine of Love. However, the Roman aristocratic imperium continued, in the subsequent centuries, to exercise a radiant influence over the whole of Europe through its stunning civilisatory achievements aptly crystallised in Pliny the Elder's words: 'May this divine benefit last forever which seems to have given to the world the Romans, like a second sun, in order to enlighten it!'

*

The revival of classical Graeco-Roman learning in the Renaissance was accompanied by a focus on individualism that acquires a bravado almost anticipatory of Nietzsche's 'superman'. However, unlike Nietzsche's ideal, the Renaissance man remains mostly Christian in his faith and achieves in the ideal of humanism a perfect blend of the classical sources of European culture with the Christian moral doctrines that had penetrated Europe since the early Middle Ages. There is no doubt that the Christian religion had assumed the mantle of the pagan Roman Empire with considerable ease and dignity and unified even greater expanses of Western Europe than the Roman Empire had done. It also exalted religion to the same level as politics in forming a dual reign of Emperor and Pope. And, just as it had absorbed several elements of the Graeco-Roman cults into its ritual and theological framework, it also accepted and codified the Germanic feudal system into an impressive hierarchical social institution. It thus succeeded in refining the Germanic knights through the chivalric institutions that came into the fore in the Middle Ages.

The earliest Renaissance poets, like Dante and Petrarch, are marked by their admiration of classical learning and focus on the Italian language and identity. In France too, ever since the High Middle Ages, there are signs of an impending change of worldview. The discovery of ancient Greek literature served to increase the scientific spirit just as the voyages of exploration expanded the horizons of the southern European princes. While it is true that mediaeval scholasticism too displayed elements of classical learning and even certain scientific formulations, it was confined mainly to the monasteries, and the antique ideas did not penetrate secular society until the Renaissance. The establishment of the Platonic Academy of Florence by Cosimo de' Medici in the fifteenth century is a significant landmark in Western European history in that it successfully combined classical learning with the Christian faith. Muret points particularly to Pico della Mirandola as a proponent of Renaissance individualism and humanism since his view of man was not confined to the traditional Christian one with its stress on the original sin of the first man. Rather, Pico focused on the free will innate in man, which allows him to choose between a debased earthly life and a spiritual godlike one. Apart from Pico, Muret adduces the example of Leon Battista Alberti, who was a typical Renaissance man talented in several disciplines, being 'a mathematician who was also a jurist, this moralist who was also a painter, a sculptor, an orator and a physician'. Alberti's most remarkable achievements were in architecture but he was, no less than Leonardo da Vinci, a polymath typical of his astonishingly creative age. Leonardo himself combined scientific curiosity with aesthetic feeling and it must be remembered that, in spite of his intensive scientific experimentations, he too died a Christian.

The Renaissance doubtless also suffered a weakening of the Christian spirit that had predominated in the Middle Ages. Thus Boccaccio reveals considerable impiety in his compositions and

Machiavelli's pragmatic cunning can clearly not be considered a model of Christian morality. Further, the unrestrained personality in the Italian Renaissance was often a surprising combination of aesthetic taste and judgement with amoral and even criminal social behaviour. Muret gives two brilliant examples of this apparent contradiction — that of Sigismondo Malatesta, who was at once utterly amoral in his personal life and one of the greatest patrons of the arts in the period, and of Benvenuto Cellini, who was not only a superlative sculptor and goldsmith but also a customary assassin.

The reactions against the untrammelled individualism of the Renaissance geniuses were not absent but unfortunately they were directed in a quasi-Protestant manner that did not make a serious effort to unify the classical outbursts of the Renaissance with Christian faith. Thus we have the example of Girolamo Savonarola, the proto-Protestant reformer who rebelled against the Medici rule in Florence but was not supported by Pope Alexander VI, who excommunicated and had him executed. Similarly, when the Italian Renaissance moved north through Johannes Reuchlin, who was deeply influenced by humanist learning, it did not succeed in establishing a unity of classical artistic exuberance with the Roman Catholic doctrines. Rather, the Germans who followed Luther tended to separate the classical world from their more Puritanical, iconoclastic view of Christianity. Thus the unity of Europe itself, which might have been achieved through a unity of the Renaissance ideals with a reformed Church, remained unaccomplished.

*

Muret's next exemplars of European elites are those of the high society of the time of Louis XIV, which, in the view of the Comte de Saint-Simon, was 'a long reign of the vile bourgeoisie'. Indeed, Louis XIV, in his opposition to the nobility (the '*gentilhommes*'), favoured members of the bourgeoisie who formed now a new class of gentlemen ('*honnêtes hommes*') and who sought to enter either the court or the high society of the reputable literary salons hosted by aristocrats like the marquise de Rambouillet. The world created by such hostesses was one of extreme refinement, where women were always present and it was the constant endeavour of the male guests to please them with their wit and gallantry. Pleasing thus became more important than edifying or moralising, even though the guests included great literary figures like Corneille and Boileau. What was cultivated in these salons was decorum, graciousness, gentility and a general light touch that abjured pedantry and scholarly erudition in favour of a more generous and liberal attitude to life and letters. The Chevalier de Méré thus declared that '[i]t is to be hoped, in order to be pleasant always, that one would excel in everything that suits gentlemen without however being too interested in anything, I mean, without doing anything that does not present itself of its own accord and without saying anything that might prove that one wants to assert oneself.' And La Rochefoucauld too advocates restraint in the expression of one's feelings so as to avoid confrontation with one's interlocutors. As Joseph Joubert put it, France in this century produced 'an uninterrupted succession of generations not scholarly but friends of knowledge and accustomed to the pleasures of the mind who multiplied in France, that country in the world where this education was best offered and perhaps best received.'

Though the *Grand Siècle* produced some of the finest literary products of France, the universal man of the French seventeenth century was gradually turning away from the asceticism and mysticism of the Middle Ages to a more reasonable, and sentimental, view of the world. However, the seventeenth century bourgeois was still ruled not by Reason itself but by Right Reason, which did not go beyond the limits of Christian morality. As Racine remarked to his son, 'one cannot be a gentleman without paying all one's debts first to God and then to men, and there is only religion that teaches us the methods and helps us to satisfy both men and God.' And in Madame de La Fayette's novel *La Princesse de Clèves,* one gets a moving example of the force of the right reason governing human relationships in this society in Monsieur de Clèves' words to the unfaithful princess: 'In the mood in which you are, by allowing you your liberty I set stricter restrictions than I could have imposed on you.'

The delicate balance between society manners and morality in the seventeenth century, however, was too fragile to be universally sustainable. Bossuet for one criticised the high society values of his time forcefully: 'The society people', he would say of the Chevalier de Méré and those who resemble him, 'lie to God and lie to themselves in claiming to conduct side by side a life of pleasure and true piety. These two things exclude each other absolutely.' The fascinating equilibrium represented by the high society of the seventeenth century could not be sustained with the growing rationalism and empiricism of the eighteenth century. In the eighteenth century, right reason was replaced by reason itself in the works of Voltaire and the Encylopedists, who rejected Christian morality, and of Rousseau, whose sentimentality even condoned the Terror of the French Revolution. As for the older aristocratic notion of honour, it was replaced by the more bourgeois one of 'conscience', which, being too personal and not associated with a whole class of people, could no longer serve as a foundation of social morality. Honour does reappear intermittently in the eighteenth and early nineteenth century but only in a military context, when Napoleon reorganised French society in an imperialistic fashion.

*

The ideal of refinement evident in the French bourgeois high society of the seventeenth century is evident also in England in the eighteenth century. But the British gentleman has a different origin than the French *honnête homme*. Derived from the warrior nobility, the British gentleman is less sociable than the French gentleman and more snobbish. Indeed, the upper class character of the gentleman was an accepted part of the traditionally hierarchical society of Britain that dates back to the Plantagenets — who were indeed, as Augustin Filon suggested,[2] the original founders of the British aristocratic culture. The social

---

2   A. Filon, *L'Angleterre d'Édouard VII* ('The England of Edward VII'), Paris, 1911.

strata below the nobles and the gentlemen—that is, the middle class not elevated through knighthoods, and the working class—aspired to the status of a gentleman and there was little criticism of his social eminence. However, the British nobles and gentlemen gradually lost their warrior affiliations with the entry into the peerage of wealthy members of the middle class. Unlike the Prussian nobility who retained their military character during most of their existence, the British gentleman turned, like his French counterpart, into a high society figure.

While the British gentleman was originally not particularly religious and even somewhat brutal in his manners, the eighteenth century infused a religious element into social life that is exemplified in Joseph Addison's fictional character Sir Roger de Coverley. Religion gained a greater foothold in gentlemanly society in the nineteenth century under the reign of Queen Victoria, who was essentially a 'bourgeois' sovereign. The Bible regained its importance after having lain dormant from the time of the Puritans, and sartorial style and church-going respectability were combined in the typical Victorian model of a gentleman. Muret gives as a prime example of the British gentleman of the Victorian age the Prince of Wales, the future Edward VII, who was considered the most elegant gentleman of his time.

Unlike the French gentleman, however, the British was not a particularly literary-minded one and showed less appreciation for the fine arts. He retained from his original warrior background the impassibility that marked the mediaeval knights and the traditionalism that became characteristic of the country squires. He also inherited from his warlike origins a taste for brutal team sports, like cricket and football, and willingly subjected himself to the harsh discipline of corporal punishment in the elite public schools of England. Yet, all this discipline was enforced on lives geared to monetary success in the Industrial Age, since Puritanical Christianity advocated not only hard work but also its material rewards. The original cast of the British gentleman, however, continued to survive in the soldierly gentleman of the British Empire, as evidenced, for example, in the characters depicted by Rudyard Kipling in his short story 'His Private Honour'.

After the Great War, the gentlemanly ideal suffered increasing attacks from socialistic fronts and authors like Arnold Bennett and H. G. Wells. While Wells criticised 'the aristocratic prejudice' of the English and hoped for a regeneration of English society through science and socialism, Bennett hoped for the destruction of the bourgeois order through 'the alliance of 'the intellectual and the proletarian'. Muret, however, brushes aside such socialistic criticisms and insists that the British gentleman still represents a valuable ideal of individual liberty since '[p]olitics, in his view, must not suffocate the human being for the benefit of a God or a king but make him serve both to the degree to which it is just while retaining his independence.' Muret is, in general, rather partial to the bourgeois, whom he considers to have been, at least in the nineteenth century, the successor of the aristocrat and propagator of traditional culture. But he does acknowledge the weakness of the ability of the bourgeoisie to withstand the assaults of the masses below it once the latter become aware of the exploitation to which they are subjected by the bourgeois:

> ... *demos* is in the process of making these classes, whose mastery they no longer wish to suffer, pay dearly for their faults. One could console oneself of this if all sorts of rules valid for all well-ordered societies were not in the process of perishing along with the bourgeoisie: the respect for tradition, the cult of the family, the spirit of order, prudence and economy. This entire bourgeois morality, a tested mixture of principles that were already dear to antiquity and of doctrines spread by the Gospel, is an execration to the masses because it imposes a brake on the naturally perverse instincts of man while the masses tend to shake off all manner of constraint.

He does not, however, like Willliam Lecky and Anthony Ludovici, denounce the bourgeois themselves for their plutocratic ambitions.[3]

---

3   See W. E. H. Lecky, *Democracy and Liberty*, Vol. I, Ch. 4 (quoted in A. Ludovici, *A Defence of Aristocracy: A Textbook for Tories*, London, 1915, p. 410): 'The worst aspect of plutocracy is the social and political influence of dishonestly acquired wealth. While the worst fields of patronage and professional life have been greatly purified during the present [nineteenth] century, the conditions of modern enterprise in the chief European countries, and still more in the

And the transformation of the Anglo-Saxon gentleman, British and American, in the Atlanticist empire of today, into a mercantile individualist hardly distinguishable in his taste and judgement from a proletarian is a prospect that Muret in 1939 obviously did not envision.

In his concluding chapter, Muret reiterates the importance of the gentlemanly ideal as exemplified in the French *Grand Siècle* and in the British Victorian Age as modern representatives of the ancient Greek notions of *kalokagathia* and of the Roman pride in Roman citizenship. However, the special merit of Muret's study of elites is indeed the stress he places in it on humanism as the essence of the high culture that they represent. He points out that, right from Graeco-Roman antiquity and through the Renaissance to the First World War, the greatest value of the elites has been their general devotion to humanism, for it is this that most fully embodies the glory of Western European civilisation. As Muret puts it:

> Humanism is the continuous and constant awareness of humanity. It invites us to know ourselves better, it invites us to love our neighbour better. It is at once the child of Plato and of Jesus Christ. It re-establishes man in his dignity, it gives him the knowledge of his duties. Between the past and the present it constructs a solid and safe bridge.

> United States, give much scope for kinds of speculation and financing which no honest man would pursue, and by which, in many conspicuous instances, colossal fortunes have been acquired. It is an evil omen for the future of a nation when men who have acquired such fortunes force their way into great social positions, and become the objects of admiration, adulation and imitation. One of the first duties, and one of the chief uses of courts and aristocracies is to guard the higher walks of society from this impure contact; and when courts and aristocracies betray their trust, and themselves bow before the golden idol, the period of their own downfall is not far distant.'

'History is a cemetery of aristocracies.'

— Vilfredo Pareto

FOREWORD

AN UNHEARD of distraction, but one which seems irresistible, seems to have taken hold of Europe and precipitates it into an indescribable distress. I wish to speak of this rising tide of the masses of which our times give a painful spectacle. It is not, besides, a new phenomenon. It has only been regrowing. We have seen antique societies dying of this disease. It has struck during the Middle Ages as well as in modern times. All through the nineteenth century, clear-visioned thinkers, free-minded, have seen the storm approaching and warned the holders of power of the lightning strike of the populace. Friedrich Nietzsche shines in the first rank of these critics and admonishers. Generalising, and beyond the limits of reason, an idea in which there was some truth, he attributed to the East, to the Eastern instincts, to the Eastern traditions, this moral revolution under which Europe was going to suffer cruelly. He saw it operating already from the fall of the ancient world but noticed its accelerated progress in the modern world. The entire historic part of the work of Friedrich Nietzsche is just the development of this idea, or as he called it, observation. Nietzsche characterised himself as an ecstatic Nihilist. Since then, another German has formulated a vision of the Western world rather similar in many aspects and not less depressing. One knows the theories of Oswald Spengler on the decline of the West, a fatal disaster appearing with a mathematical precision after the completion of the eternal cycle, at the moment determined by destiny, at the moment, in any case, foreseen by Oswald Spengler. Germany suffers, on account of its geographic position, the influence of the East as well as that of the West. It is natural that these prophets of misfortune emerged first there, determined to proclaim our eradication, perhaps our ruin.

The Great War contributed much to the success of the masses and their predominance. During the four years, the elites were eclipsed and the fate of the world rested on the masses, armed against one another. Victory, so dearly bought, was a victory of the masses over the elites. Something of that remains in the climate of our era. On this success of the armed masses another success was superimposed: that of the Soviet troop led by Lenin at the eastern extremity of Europe and which fascinated the proletariats at the end of the war. Was Bolshevism really the dictatorship of the working class? It is, in any case, in the name of this idea, this principle, that the revolution is taking place. The entire West was infected by it. It was really not until the Renaissance of the fifteenth and sixteenth centuries, this Renaissance that a famous historian characterised as 'the discovery of the individual' (at the end of the Middle Ages, which did not know of it, or denied it), that the superiority of the West became a dogma that was largely accepted, even outside Europe. Russia first began to undermine it at the start of this century in undertaking a battle in Manchuria.[1]

The Soviet Revolution, which appeared after, probably sounded the death-knell of this hegemony. Joseph de Maistre said of the violence of the passions of the Moscovites, 'If one could imprison a Russian desire in a fortress, it would bring the latter down.'[2] Russian Bolshevism and this divine right of the masses that it claims to establish will perhaps bring down the Western fortress founded, on the contrary, on the rights of the individual and whose essential merit consists — we shall

---

1   Russia invaded Chinese Manchuria in 1900 as part of its Eurasian imperialist ambitions and, by the end of that year, gained control of most of Manchuria. [All footnotes are by the translator.]

2   Joseph-Marie, Comte de Maistre (1753–1821), the monarchist counter-revolutionary, was the French ambassador to Russia from 1803 to 1817.

see this — in the production, through the centuries, of certain types of eminent individuals grouped in eminent elites.

Lenin said in a famous sentence: 'Let us turn towards Asia, we shall come to the ends of the West through the East.' And Zinoviev,[3] at the Congress of Baku in 1920,[4] believed he too had to declare: 'Russia offers its hand to Asia because the 800 million Asians are necessary for it to combat European imperialism and capitalism.' The predominance assumed in the East by Japan and the application that it makes for its own benefit of the methods typical of European imperialism throw a derisory light on words of this sort. It remains nevertheless true that Bolshevism has fascinated, let us repeat, certain Western minds, and not the least important. In Germany, on the morrow of the Russian Revolution, it had the benefit of an immense credit. It seduced even distinguished men who one would have thought would avoid this trap: 'Twilight falls on Europe', wrote Walter Rathenau a little before his tragic death, 'everything obliges us to look to the East. For us Germans it is a question of life or death but it is not without a horrible melancholy that people like us, with their past, their prejudices and their traditions, turn away from the West. A sentimental attraction that we do not have the right to feel or even to admit. Such is the great consequence of the war.'

Walther Rathenau[5] was a Jew, so to a certain degree, even if this degree is difficult to determine, Eastern in mentality. Is it because he is a Jew and of an Eastern mentality that he experienced the attraction of Bolshevism, of the dictatorship of the proletariat, the hegemony of the masses? The question is infinitely complex but it does seem that

---

3   Grigory Zinoviev (né Hirsch Apfelbaum) (1883–1936) was a Russian Jew who was closely allied with Lenin but was ousted from the Communist leadership in 1925 by Stalin.

4   The First Congress of the Peoples of the East was held in Baku (Azerbaijan) in 1920.

5   Walther Rathenau (1867–1922) was a German-Jewish businessman who served as Foreign Minister of the Weimar Republic in 1922.

one may affirm that Judaism, in its most typical representatives, has voluntarily espoused the quarrel of the multitudes against the leaders, of the masses against the elites.

One already finds, eloquently expressed in the Psalms of the Old Testament, this idea that the rich man is the wicked man, who exploits the poor, who is good and virtuous. Only the poor man practises justice and religion; only he has access to feelings of generosity. The idea of universal fraternity is very widespread among the prophets. And one knows what fascination it exercised when preached by the first Christians on the disinherited, bent under the Roman yoke, on the poor, the slaves. Nietzsche opposes too rigorously the morality of masters, the ideal of classical antiquity, to the morality of slaves, a Hebraic invention propagated by the Jews and that was increasingly imposed on the West. Nietzsche is wrong besides in not distinguishing between the Jewish morality of the biblical ages and the morality of the Christians, at least of the best among them. This is a capital mistake into which the theoreticians of the swastika fall again today, Mr. Alfred Rosenberg and the enemies of Christianity, so numerous in Germany. The Hebrews did not believe in the immortality of the soul, whence their fervour in claiming, here on earth, an ample part of temporal wealth. Jesus Christ and Christianity, propagating a belief in a future life transferring to almighty God in the beyond the application of perfect justice, invoked to repair all the iniquities committed on earth, perceptibly modified human mentality and fashioned a conscience superior to that of biblical times. The entire West has been affected, one can even say transformed, by this doctrine. The authors hostile to Christianity have not taken this metamorphosis sufficiently into account. It is, besides, accurate to affirm, as they do, that Judaism contains powerful seeds of the revolutionary and socialist mind that benefits the masses. Nothing surprising in the haste that the masses make, left to themselves, to make statesmen, Israelites, responsible for the defence of their temporal interests. It is a sure instinct that guides them in this action. They do not always show an equally subtle perspicacity.

It is possible that the rise of the masses in Russia and in the countries with Socialist leadership announces a new era of European humanity. In a book written much before the Great War, the philosopher Gustave le Bon[6] expressed his fear of seeing the rise of the masses coming 'to mark one of the last stages of Western civilisation' and serving as prelude to a long period of frightful anarchy. Social anarchy that foreign wars would aggravate. Dr. Le Bon recalled the spectacle offered by Europe at the moment of the French Revolution, when an entire nation keen on 'social equality, abstract rights and ideal freedoms' overturned the Western world in the name of a new gospel. It is possible that the Bolshevik Revolution may play in the Europe of today and tomorrow the 'mythic' role, as Georges Sorel would have said, played yesteryear by the French Revolution. The movement being today much more general in a West that has become singularly more permeable to all influences, and the masses being, on the other hand, infinitely better armed materially and morally than they ever were, the thrust risks also being much stronger. Oswald Spengler also foresaw, at a moment when Fascism and Hitlerism did not yet display their menace, bloody convulsions within a West tossed between the dictatorships of the proletariat, the caesarisms (one says today totalitarian regimes) and imperialist wars. One would like to believe that these prophets were mistaken in their sombre predictions. In any case, and no matter what the future has in store for the white nations, one takes pleasure, in the middle of such a disarray, in plunging oneself once again into the past and in examining more closely — that is the object of this book — what the individualist culture and the elites that

---

6   Gustave Le Bon (1841–1931) was an anthropologist, sociologist and psychologist who wrote several influential works on the psychological aspects of war, revolution and socialism. His most famous work is *La Psychologie des foules* ('The Psychology of Crowds'), published in 1895.

it formed have produced that is really beautiful, really good and really great for Western civilisation.

Only the respect for the individual, only the practice of individualism have allowed the formation of these elites, even more necessary for the ascent of humanity than those heroes in whom Carlyle saw the instruments par excellence of all progress,[7] but this notion of an elite, which supposes social classes, is unbearable to the pseudo-reformers infused with Marxism who dream of a society without categories and barriers where the individual, as he was conceived of in the past, would yield place to the 'collective individual', a strange term but one which one will find in the works of all the Bolshevist or Bolshevising authors: 'We Marxists', declares the historian Pokrovsky,[8] 'do not see in the individual the creator of history, he is for us the instrument through which history acts and perhaps one day we will construct these human instruments as we construct electric accumulator batteries today.' An absurd ideal, a monstrous ideal of a robot become a demi-god. An ideal, moreover, that has sprung from the brain stuffed with sophisms of these maniacs of materialism and mechanism who presided, at the dawn of 'the new age', over the destiny of unfortunate Russia. One could read in the *Pravda* of 17 May 1934: 'The new man is not formed of himself. It is the party that directs the entire process of social remoulding and of the re-education of the masses. The Communist must obey the party programme and its discipline', but this inhuman discipline was precisely so inhuman that it seems that in Russia itself a reaction, still timid, is in the process of being produced for the benefit of the classes and individuals. In a speech pronounced in January 1934, Stalin declared: 'Every Leninist knows that the levelling of needs and tastes is a petty bourgeois absurdity and is not at

---

7 Thomas Carlyle (1795–1881) was a Scottish historian who, in his work *On Heroes, Hero-worship and the Heroic in History* (1841) emphasised the pivotal role played by great men in history.

8 Mikhail Pokrovsky (1868–1932) was a Bolshevist historian who worked in the Soviet government's department of education.

all a fact of society organised according to Marxist methods, for one would not be able to demand of all men equality of tastes and needs nor uniformity of the conditions of their existence.'

According to certain historians of Bolshevism, it was under the pressure of the mass of Russian peasants that Stalin effected this significant redirection that constantly provides a reason for the reproaches of the Trotskyists accusing the dictator of the Kremlin of trampling down the pure doctrine of primitive maximalism.[9] It seemed that the Russian *mujik*,[10] forced into collectivism by the institution of the *mir* and so many other institutions of a communitarian sort, had to make himself the passionate propagator of the new system. On the contrary. It was he who rose first against the mirage of the collective man. The independent worker, that is, one not a member of the Communist Party, followed, timidly at first, resolutely afterwards. It was an 'independent' worker, Stakhanov,[11] who, on the night of 30 August 1935, imagined in the depths of a certain mine of the Donetz where he worked a new operation of the automatic hammer that allowed him to cut in six hours the enormous quantity of hundred and two tonnes of coal, an achievement that turned out to be a truly surprising glory for him.

Contrary to what had up to then been the rule, this exceptional worker, this individualist of the mine was officially celebrated and held up as an example. He was welcomed in Moscow with flowers and dithyrambs. Stalin went out of his way to receive him at the Kremlin, greeted him as a 'hero' of labour and declared that the movement which he had initiated and that was called after him 'Stakhanovism'

---

9   Maximalism is a Marxist term denoting a programme aimed at maximal change in society whereas the contrasting 'minimum programme' restricted itself to smaller, more immediate, social changes.

10 Peasant.

11 Alexey Stakhanov (1906–1977) was a Russian miner whose mining techniques helped increase worker productivity. From the forties he held important positions in the Ministry of the Coal Industry of the Soviet Union.

was produced 'from within the masses themselves in a spontaneous manner'. It seems that Stalin would have wished, at a certain point in his rule, to revisit the collectivist edifice and restore the honour of the individual, but this impetus was seriously contradicted again by the truly Communist workers, by the large mass of Bolshevist workers who had remained faithful to the original methods of the Party, to the gregarious ideal, to the discipline of the masses. Stalin, in any case, did not succeed in managing this mixture, delicately dosed, of the interest of the individual with the interest of society which he advocated in his speech of January 1934. This man, who crushes men around him like flies, was not able to crush the errors in which Lenin, besotted with Marxism, was complicit, like his successor, though he interpreted it differently, in a way, it seems, that was more clearly revolutionary, more orthodox. And it is Bolshevism in high dosage, without any notable concession to bourgeois or petty bourgeois individualism, to use the language of the Soviet authors, that the propaganda wished to impose on the European West. After twenty years of revolution, Russia has still not found its balance. And nobody knows what will emerge, finally, from the confusion of experiments to which it submits itself. Before even knowing the result of it, it intends besides to drag Europe into the tracks of its dangerous life. It dreams of imposing on the West, the corrupt West, as the Pan-Slavists said, its collective man, its government of the masses and other abominations.

*

Everything in modern life contributes, it must be recognised, to immolating the individual in the herd and to placing the masses in the forefront. Everything has become infused with an extreme complexity. It is becoming less and less possible for the human being to act in isolation. No matter what one undertakes, it is necessary to have diverse sorts of cooperation. Every action must be combined with that of other persons and other groups of persons. Every activity in modern life is more dependent than it ever was in the past. The multiplication of the means of communication and their growing speed, the progress of industrial concentration and economic concentration produce countless entanglements.

The autonomy of the existences dies, whereas the mechanisation of social life is enhanced every day with a new cog. The eighteenth century in its decline had cherished the dream of a state of nature, idyllic but utopic, which was like the swansong of the pride of the individual on the eve of his death. The French Revolution put a sudden and brutal end to this seductive dream. It gloried in proclaiming the Rights of Man, that is to say, the rights of the individual, raised against his masters, who ordered him from above. In fact, it unleashed those forces from below, latent forces that had been suppressed for a long time, that already bubbled within the masses and that had to give birth, to the benefit of revolutions and foreign wars, to collectivism, statism, socialism, which are today so alive under varying labels.

Wedged between the masses and the state, the two tyrants, the individual tried in vain to make himself small to be forgiven and to pass unobserved. He was tracked down, exploited and destroyed.

A hundred and fifty years ago, the crowds did not, or almost did not, count in the political, social and intellectual life of Europe. They played a role only accidentally when the elites, failing in their duty, had let slip from their hands what are today called the levers of command. Today, the masses play a preponderant role and that even in totalitarian regimes where the dictators suffer the masses as much as they rule them. What were the masses yesterday? Nothing. What have they become? Everything, or almost everything. One hardly exaggerates in writing that the divine right of kings, which was always combated, was substituted by the divine right of the masses and that questioning the excellence of this dogma becomes more and more rare. Through the economy the masses weigh on politics and give it an orientation corresponding to their desires, that is to say, to their material interests. Through the labour exchanges, the work confederations, through sit-down strikes, they impose their will on a minority of bosses subject to terror. In the totalitarian countries they do not even need these means of struggle. The right to strike is denied to the workers but the right to lock-out is at the same time denied to the bosses. The state arbitrates in conflicts and most often decides on litigations in favour of the class in which force, authority, prestige reside at present, that is to say, in the popular class, the masses.

Unless there is a reaction that can hardly be predicted and that will come at the critical moment, humanity will slide slowly towards this communitarian state that existed at the dawn of every society but, until the present, was considered a first stage, a point of departure and not a glorious consummation and an admirable crowning glory.

The rule of the masses signifies also a lowering of all the spiritual and moral values. And if one just thought of it, how could it be otherwise? A mass is always, in its entirety, inferior to the superior elements that may exist within it and that, mixed with it, is dissolved in it. A mass invariably finds its way to the lowest level, that is the truth of experience. The mass instinctively detests the superior man. It can tolerate it like a wild animal in a cage tolerates its master who gives it the whip and the bone methodically but it hardly likes him; it likes him in any case only for a limited time. At the first failure it frees itself of him by devouring him. The higher the man above it is, the more it detests him. And, as long as it is possible, it demands of him concessions, humiliations, denials. We have indeed seen the proof of what I suggest in the spectacle that intellectual Germany presents today. This nation was still, at the beginning of this century, one of the most cultivated and civilised of Europe. It counted in all fields scholars of a remarkable competence and a scrupulous conscience. A mass regime just had to install itself under a dictatorial mask in the country 'of thinkers and poets' and an official doctrine of an extravagant puerility — and a religious, social and political philosophy that was a veritable defiance of common sense and the historical past of the nation — immediately clouded the minds. The peasants of ancient Switzerland, rough individuals, robust and healthy mountain folk, refused to bend their knee before Gessler's hat.[12] The Germans of the Third Reich, deprived of personality and regimented, are less sparing in their genuflections.

It is true that the masses are capable of generous impulses. At the shout of '*Deus vult*' they join the Crusades, obeying the call of the fatherland in danger and enlist for a war of liberation with a disinterestedness that one should admire, but these enthusiasms are as ephemeral as they are violent and when they fall, they give place often to very low sentiments.

The masses were always envious and jealous. Today, they do not differ from what they were in the ancient cities, where their accession to power regularly sounded the death-knell of order and prosperity. Passionately egalitarian, they proclaim justice, but what is justice in the mind of the masses? It is too often through a hate-filled and mean equality that they claim to make equity prevail. Whether they be artificial or natural, all inequalities are suspect to them. A demagogy left to its instincts and left without a counterpoise abolishes monarchy, nobility, heritage. It then takes hold of the most intelligent, the most industrious, the cleverest. Natural inequality is more difficult to suppress than artificial inequality. Obstinate and relentless, demagogy, in the troubled times of social revolutions, nevertheless reaches its goal. It then throws down the competent people from power, of course not because they are competent but because they are unequal. And the result obtained is the same: 'Everywhere', writes Aristotle, 'that merit is not esteemed above everything else, one will not be able to have a solidly founded aristocratic constitution.' It follows logically that a mass regime hostile to every aristocratic constitution deprives itself voluntarily, in order to live according to its taste, of what is necessary for life. Property, the most tangible sign of all of an unequal society, receives the particular hatred of the masses. So they inveigh against property! Taxes, incessantly increased, will absorb the wealth of

---

12 Albrecht Gessler was a fourteenth-century Habsburg bailiff who ordered all the inhabitants of Altdorf to bow before his hat placed atop a pole in the market place. It was his cruel regime that led to the Wilhelm Tell rebellion.

the possessors and will make them the victims of their work, their economising spirit, their expertise. When the people are masters, the tax ceases to be a proportional or, if you wish, honestly progressive contribution to the public expenditures. It becomes an instrument of dispossession in the hands of those who have nothing or little to the detriment of the most detested among the unequal, those 'privileged' through wealth. Every popular revolution is accompanied, in the name of justice, by a transfer of public fortune and the wealth of the possessing class is not at all lost to everybody. At the speed with which the social revolutions take place at present, the *nouveaux riches* will hardly have the time to enjoy their wealth.

The dispossession of the majorities by the minorities henceforth has as an instrument: the popular vote. Contained for a long time by the restrictions of a prudent legislation, universal suffrage has broken its banks and threatens to wash away everything. Half of the citizens plus one, or the majority, makes the law for the other half minus one, or the minority. A conception that is at once naïve and cunning, of absolute truth, and the work of the majority attributes to the latter a rigorous right of coercion on the rest of the people. It is admitted that a majority could not be mistaken and that its decisions are without appeal. Like the British parliament, a majority can do everything except change a man into a woman. One puts the vote to the test on all occasions. Has one not seen a congress of free thinkers decree, after a vote, with a crushing majority, that 'God does not exist'? A congress of free thinkers is still a select group, if not a veritable elite. What should one think of the massive vote of an electoral body composed of all the confused citizens without any regard to education, instruction, aptitudes? It is, however, on herds formed in this manner that the task of determining the destinies of the greatest states is incumbent. The elector votes under the influence of hatred and envy, under the influence of an ill-satisfied rancour, of a discontent caused by adverse circumstances or by a troubled situation. It is exceptional for his vote to be inspired by an elevated ideal beyond his passions. How could deliberating assemblies formed in this manner merit the name of an elite and ensure their rights to the elites?

The Christian churches, which restrained demagogy for a long time, have their portion of responsibility for the present evils. They always took great care, under the pretext of granting to Caesar that which is Caesar's, to recognise the established governments as having come from God, which has often not failed to do a great injury to God. This complacency worsened as the clergies, all the clergies, began to recruit more and more from what is called the deep base of the people. The difference of quality between the herd and the cowherd began to be erased. To count on pastors to lead the sheep to social and philosophical truth would be to make a really rash calculation. The lay herd does not obey more wisely handled staffs.[13] Right from the school benches, the masses are formed by the school teacher, who has himself come from the ranks of the people and whose mission it is to inculcate in the children entrusted to his care this naïvely revolutionary mystique with which he is inflated. Equipped with a rudimentary instruction, the school teacher communicates to the pupil coarse convictions, which are, however, so much the more fervent.

'One does not convince a school teacher', said Émile Faguet.[14] The school teacher has become so much less easy to convince since the demagogic gospel that he has contributed so much to making prevalent has won the game and this victory has set him at the top along with his herd. The school teacher henceforth raises the child not for his parents, not for the city but, as he says, for the people. Should one celebrate the result?

All the modern inventions, all the scientific progress, contribute to found the rule of the masses to the detriment of individuals and of purely personal values. Machines, through their production in

---

13   The staff, or crook, is the stick which a shepherd uses to guide his flock. Bishops too carry a symbolic staff.

14   Émile Faguet (1847–1916) was a French author, literary critic and member of the Académie française.

series, debase individual taste, if they do not kill it entirely. The entertainments that fill the leisure of the people are of the same nature and on the same level. Pleasures will be more and more gregarious: sensational films that are, besides, vulgar, brutal sports, often barbaric and bloody, radio broadcasts of a sometimes disgusting baseness. What educational value can one attribute to these pastimes? The very individual pleasure of reading will disappear from a civilisation that is deadly to the human individual. Already books are on the wane. In order to be bought, to be read, to excuse themselves, books too have sacrificed to the instincts of the mass that are currently in fashion. They have lasted five hundred years. One would like to be sure that the spoken books and the shouted books that will succeed them will be worth more spiritually and morally. It is not likely.

It happens that the masses, purged of their illusions by such a collective movement of such a vast scope, end by following a minority that has no other merit than a more daring activity than the rest of the community. The dictatorship of an individual belonging to this daring minority generally ends revolutionary adventures. One then sees the ignorant and weary masses throwing themselves into the arms of a resolute and rough man. The dictator in his turn is supported by this mass and governs in its name and with it. In such a way that one finally does not know any longer if it is he that leads the masses or the masses that lead him. If he wishes to prolong his life, the dictator needs to cleverly flatter the collective passions. If he really knows his trade, he channels these passions and seizes them in his favour. If he allows himself to be pushed aside by them or if he fails to satisfy them, that is the end of his rule. It is rare that the affection of the masses for a leader outlives a great political or military disaster. And as for the leader, his hidden but true and deep feeling with regard to the hordes that he commands is nothing but a solid contempt. What should one think of this sentence from *Mein Kampf*, where Mr. Adolf Hitler formulated so far in advance that which would become the final end of his government: 'Propaganda does not have to look for an objective truth but to dictate to the masses in an authoritative manner the truth fashioned and adapted to the goal to be pursued.' Is it not distressing that the democratic momentum of the nineteenth century, after all generous, has failed to this degree? The totalitarian conception of the state, that is the price that the disempowered West pays today for its disregard, not to say its destruction, of the elites and its diabolical effort to remove them from power.

Perspicacious minds have for a long time foreseen this accident that is fatal to healthy societies. And not only the philosophers and sociologists whose trade, if one may say so, it was but certain authors with imagination and power of observation among those that one calls novelists announced the catastrophe. Contrary to Eugène Sue,[15] George Sand, Émile Zola, all infused with the mystique of the masses, Balzac, Mérimée and Flaubert, reasoning less as scientists than as men of experience, had foreseen the error into which the century rushed blindly. It is not uninteresting to reproduce their diagnostics today: 'If you call on the masses to make laws', wrote Balzac in *Le Médecin de Campagne*, 'can the masses act superior to themselves? No. The more the assembly represents faithfully the opinions of the crowds the less elevated their views will be and less accurate, and more vacillating their legislation, for the masses will always be what the masses are.' More categorically still, Prosper Mérimée declared before Mrs. Adam: 'When the masses are the sole masters of their destiny, they have only servants and no masters to govern them, and they will rediscover their brutal appetites and be seized once again by their tyrannical instincts. And the worst, the most insupportable of tyrannies is that of the masses. That is why I am afraid of universal suffrage without an authority that rules it. Universal suffrage, when it is master of the government, fights against freedom. We saw that indeed in 1848. It falls victim to agitators and excludes the level-headed element of the country from participation in the affairs of the state.'

---

15 Eugène Sue (1804–1857) was a French novelist.

One could not deny that these authors of yesterday and earlier had a clear view that allowed them to read clearly the destiny of Western humanity. At all times, from the dawn of civilised times, great minds have feared the masses and dreaded, for the general welfare, its accession to power. What is the Beast of the Apocalypse, relentless in blaspheming God and everything that is great and noble in the world, if it not be the collective consciousness taking the place of the individual? The vision of St. John at Patmos presents a terrifying but prophetic description of this monster. Leviathan is establishing and flaunting itself today. If the Westerners will not pull themselves together tomorrow, the monster will take possession of more.

*

If the elites disappear rapidly, it is also partially their fault. A well-formed society recognises the rights of the elites but prescribes duties to them too. An aristocracy, an elite, if it wishes to live, must serve. If they discard their role, they exercise a parasitical function to the detriment of the social body. And the people let them feel it. Then decadence watches out for them and their fate is accomplished. The nobles of the *ancien régime* signed their death warrant when they broke off all contact with the peasants, when they stopped living, or living any more, except to hunt, oppressing the farmers with useless vexations. The rule of the bourgeoisie established itself on the ruins of the deposed feudalism, but it seems to have lasted a shorter time. Its apogee coincided with the advent of big industry, which had grown too quickly. Pushed to the extent that one still observes, it causes more harm than it procures advantages. In an ambiance that has become hostile, it calls forth nationalisation and confiscation. Having wished to earn too much, the bourgeoisie risks losing everything. Under the mask of liberalism, it has treated the masses with a disdain and a cruelty unknown in older society. So *demos* is in the process of making these classes, whose mastery they no longer wish to suffer, pay dearly for their faults. One could console oneself of this if all sorts of rules valid for all well-ordered societies were not in the process of perishing along with the bourgeoisie: the respect for tradition, the cult of the family, the spirit of order, prudence and economy. This entire bourgeois morality, a tested mixture of principles that were already dear to antiquity and of doctrines spread by the Gospel, is an execration to the masses because it imposes a brake on the naturally perverse instincts of man while the masses tend to shake off all manner of constraint. Equality of enjoyment, thus equality of fortune, is the principal aspiration of the masses, now conscious of their strength and grouped in greedy trades unions. Our Western democracies might well have arrived at the stage of which Fustel de Coulanges traced in *Cité antique* the tragic picture that everybody knows.[16] Gratified by the right to vote, the masses, that is to say, the poor, have not seen their wealth growing through this fact alone but they have not been slow in understanding that the equality of rights, the first stage, might help them to make the conquest of wealth, which is the second stage. So we have entered once again (because there is nothing new under the sun) the era of confiscations and dispossessions or, if you like, 'individual recoveries', to use Bolshevist terms. Universal suffrage is of great help in historic periods of this sort and is manifested in excesses even more arbitrary than those of which the worst tyrannies ever provided an example. The state, the all-powerful Moloch and, ever since it acts in accord with the masses, untouchable, presides over the dispossession of those who still have possessions to the benefit of those who have nothing and who think less of possessing than of enjoying immediately the wealth of those that are robbed. Absurd pillage, extravagant waste, which destroys at will fortunes patiently acquired and, most often, through hard work, during stable and reasonable periods. A barbaric operation that does not really benefit anybody. It restricts itself to opening up the path to the dreary state of an ant-hill. The state,

---

16 Fustel de Coulanges (1830–1889) was a French historian whose first work, *La Cité antique* (1864, 'The Ancient City') was a remarkably original study of the religious origins of Graeco-Latin civilisation.

and more particularly the Communist state, is an insatiable glutton. The more one gives it, the more it demands. After being inclined towards this Soviet regime or what remains of it, in Russia itself, famous intellectuals who admired it from afar have returned horrified. Does their disappointment, which is expressed roughly, allow one to hope that the West will pull itself together? Or are our societies belonging to an ancient civilisation also ripe for atrocious experiments of this sort? That is the question that one returns to always. And all minds are oppressed by it.

However, we did not lack warnings. *Voces clamantium in deserto*, the voices shouting in the desert, perhaps eloquent voices nevertheless and how persuasive, provided that one does not refuse to let oneself be persuaded!

Two very great minds, a philosopher who was also a historian, Friedrich Nietzsche, and a historian who was also a philosopher, Ernest Renan, strictly warned their contemporaries at the moment that the storm was worsening against the turpitude of the rule of the masses and of the necessity of maintaining elites. At the beginning of this introduction, I pointed to the attitude adopted by Nietzsche with regard to the problem of the masses and the elite, a problem that virtually haunted him. The polemical part of his message is subject to caution and I would like the studies of which this book is constituted to make that clear. The distinction that the German philosopher makes once and for all between the morality of masters and the morality of slaves — the former triumphing among the Greeks and Romans of antiquity, the latter introduced into Europe by Christianity — is too absolute. I cannot repeat it too often because it is true and because the history of all the elites that we are going to review confirms it: Western civilisation, in the best that it has produced since antiquity, is an amalgam in which the antique philosophies and Christian doctrine have an almost equal share. Nietzsche is wrong to blaspheme against Christianity but he is right in revolting against this Hegelian doctrine of the godlike State that has seized Germany and made it, in

Europe, a very uncertain ally. Through its militarism and its absolutism Germany has contributed much to the exaltation of the masses, to the detriment of that respect for the individual that informed its classical literature. 'Höchstes Glück der Erdenkinder — Sey nur die Persönlichkeit',[17] exclaimed Goethe in a burst of emotion for which many people will be eternally grateful even while regretting that his exclamation was not listened to by his compatriots. For he restricted himself, in speaking in this way, to formulating what constituted, before the Prussian dominance, the true greatness, the true nobility, of the German spirit. With the support of his philosophy and as if to crown it, Nietzsche advocated what he called the good European. And what did he understand by this if not a 'gentleman' (the expression is his), the scion of those old Mediterranean cultures that the author of *Jenseits von Gut und Böse*[18] admired? Nietzsche loved Athens because it had 'thrown a bridge between Asia and Europe' but to the benefit of Europe. Singularly anxious about the immediate future of our civilisation, Nietzsche, resolute nevertheless in guarding the faith, attached himself to the ideal of the good European to which he gave some essential traits of his superman and especially — this fact is to be noted when the Germany of the swastika rejects with horror everything that is Latin — some French traits: 'One should see', wrote Nietzsche, 'in my book entitled *Jenseits von Gut und Böse* a breviary of the gentleman, taking this term in the most spiritual and radical sense.'[19]

Between an aristocracy and a civilisation there was for Nietzsche a close dependence. And the last really respectable form of European civilisation Nietzsche saw in the aristocratic civilisation of seventeenth-century France. The good European was not, according to

---

17 'The highest happiness of the children of the earth is personality' — a line from Goethe's collection of lyrical poems, *West-östlicher Divan*, Buch Suleika.

18 'Beyond Good and Evil'.

19 In the section entitled 'Völker und Vaterländer' (Peoples and Nations) of *Beyond Good and Evil*, however, Nietzsche denigrates the English for their mediocre intellect and lack of true philosophy or music.

Nietzsche, an international but a supra-national type. And that is why the French culture of the *Grand Siècle* seemed to him to realise, more than any other, that condition that he would have liked to see predominate in Europe. When the fine intelligence of Nietzsche fell into a frightful abyss, he was in the process of becoming increasingly more Mediterranean, increasingly more French, in his mind and in his heart. Did he not go so far as to write: 'I owe more to Montaigne than to Schopenhauer'? He appreciated fully the formal beauty of French art. 'As an artist', he said, 'one has only one fatherland: Paris.' Nothing more touching than this obstination shown by Friedrich Nietzsche, despairing of Europe, despairing of Germany, such as they were during his life, that they would ever surmount the gregarious ideal and the government of the masses. Among the good Europeans such as he imagined them, he cited as being the closest to his ideal Napoleon, Goethe, Beethoven, Stendhal, Heinrich Heine, Schopenhauer. There are a majority of Germans on this list, but these Germans whom he named distinguished themselves by the little consideration they had for that which is specifically Teutonic. Germany, according to Nietzsche, had not yet found its form and had not yet realised itself. Germany is, besides, more determined than ever not to go in the direction that Nietzsche tried to lead it in. The very categorical book of Mr. Friedrich Sieburg[20] on the defence of German nationalism rejects with bitterness 'the universal human ideal', the cult of Reason and other classical or Western nonsense. Mr. Sieburg prefers, along with his compatriots, what he calls 'the great seduction of the return to chaos'.

Though an independent thinker, one notes with pleasure — to the honour of Germany — a mind as superior as Mr. Thomas Mann deploring this attitude of the German youth: 'This generation', he writes, 'only wishes to absent itself for ever from its own self, what it wants,

---

20 Friedrich Sieburg (1893–1964) was a German journalist whose book *Es werde Deutschland* (1933) was translated into English by Winifred Ray as *Germany, My Country* (1933).

what it loves, is intoxication.' And again: 'The goal of the march is not of much importance to this youth, which only aspires to get lost among the masses. The only goal is drunkenness, they have to free themselves of their own self, of their own thought or, more precisely, morality and reason in general.'

What a sad ideal and what a sad spectacle! Germany deliberately rejecting this humanism of which it is now more important than ever to save the remnants!

But Germany, as a whole, has always kept itself away from Europe, from Western Europe and Mediterranean Europe. I cannot do anything if, in a gallery of Western elites such as this little book presents, the place of Germany is empty.

The aristocratic ideal of Ernest Renan, even if it was expressed with more discretion, that delicious discretion that he brought to everything, was not less strongly reasoned. For having lived in a country that had for a long time broken links with the tribulations of democracy, Ernest Renan cursed the masses and their growing influence more consistently even than the great German philosopher. Ernest Renan wrote 'superior man' where Friedrich Nietzsche wrote 'superman', but it is a similar ideal that both of them formulated under these diverse names. After some genuflexions before Science, this science which the nineteenth century made its new idol for so long, Ernest Renan turned away from it when he saw the demagogues make of it the instrument of their domination. More precisely, he dreamed of snatching from them this powerful and noble instrument for the benefit of the purely aristocratic ideal that was his. Renan had championed the universal suffrage, without success it goes without saying, but, having plunged into the abyss, he climbed out of it without being scorched. He had developed, with regard to this institution, a contempt that is reflected in all his politics and his sociology. *La Réforme intellectuel et morale*[21] contains, in its soft form, one of the most mor-

---

21 The intellectual and moral Reformation.

dant indictments against the natural equality of men that has ever been pronounced. The plays entitled *Caliban* and *L'eau de Jouvence* extol the role of the aristocracies, the *Dialogues philosophiques*, in the part entitled 'Rêves', propose for the salvation of humanity a coolly calculated plan of the domination of subhumans by supermen. This plan defied all the conquests of democracy. He demonstrated, on the contrary, the necessity of making an end of it. Theoctiste, describing the oligarchy of the future, imagines it consisted of learned scientists in possession of such formidable means of destruction that nobody would henceforth dare to challenge them: 'The forces of humanity', declares another personage who seems indeed to speak in the name of Renan himself, 'would in this way be concentrated in a small number of hands and would become the property of a league capable of disposing of the very existence of the planet and of terrorising the entire world.' What a disillusionment must Ernest Renan have felt to come to the formulation of this programme of brutal force. Was his ideal, besides, not rather fanciful? Everything becomes vulgarised when the masses have a say in the the matter. It is difficult to see the chemists and physicists of the committee of public health, imagined by the author of *L'Avenir de la Science*,[22] keeping for themselves their murders while they are secret benefactors. Insofar as science plays a role, it is in the destruction of the present society that it is employed rather more than in preserving it. Through the use of bombs, explosives, asphyxiating gas, through the game of terrorist attacks, the progress of science is, in the accepted sense of the term, eminently subversive. The oligarchs of the Renanesque committee would really risk arriving too late. They could indeed find nothing more to preserve than ruins. No, the salvation that can arrive, if it should arrive, will come from elsewhere. Those that I have attempted to describe in this volume represent what Europe and Western civilisation have produced that is most perfect and most worthy of imitation in their best moments. Is

---

22 Ernest Renan, *L'Avenir de la Science: Pensées de 1848* ('The Future of Science: Thoughts from 1848'), Paris, 1890.

there a link, a dependence among them, a rigorous connection of one to another? It would be rash to affirm it absolutely but one can admit, without risking being wrong, that it is the Greek civilisation, with its respect of the individual and its love of liberty, which began to create the European as opposed to the Asiatic, which fashioned the handsome and good Athenian, the sworn enemy of the Eastern barbarian, ugly and vile, destined to slavery.

At the same time, the *civis romanus*[23] develops fully in favour of his struggle for his free personality, in opposition to constraints no matter whence they may come. And is one not forced, finally, to maintain that the frankly individualistic ideal of the English evokes *mutatis mutandis* that of the Athenians and the Romans of the best epoch? The character of the English civilisation appears with the Magna Carta, is established with the revolt against the papacy, the destruction of the invincible Armada, the Cromwellian occurrence, the *habeas corpus*. What is the English civilisation if not a continuous and tenacious will to affirm the liberty of the individual against the encroachments of the state? The constitutional struggles of Great Britain all along the centuries do not have any other aim. Perhaps the private nature of the Englishman inclined in this direction but perhaps also the classical education assigned to the leaders, and this atmosphere of humanism, in which they spend their years of youth, have broadly contributed to this resemblance which will then be only a relationship. In any case, the relationship of the καλὸς κἀγαθός Greek and the *civis romanus* of the classical epoch and the English gentleman of yesterday and today seems to me undeniable.

I would, however, believe that I have deceived the reader and I would be afraid to construct my thesis on mere words by forcing myself to demonstrate the rigorous identity of these types or by trying to maintain that their difference is only that of the times in which they lived. I have preferred to consider successively the formation of these

---

23 Roman citizen.

elites as so many fortunate phenomena, giving them all their own physiognomy, sometimes similar, more often distinct. In short, it is to a rapid and synoptic review of the qualities of nobility of Western civilisation in its most successful aspects that I invite my readers. We shall see finally if it is possible to draw from this review some conclusions and of what sort. A great poet said in the past that nothing was sadder than the recollection of happy times in a moment of distress. To which another poet, not less great, replied that in recalling a happy past one felt, on the contrary, a gentle reassurance. Let us try to persuade ourselves that the latter opinion is the truer. The age in which we live suspects elites and tends to replace them once and for all with the better educated masses. By recalling the achievements of the elites, by refreshing the lustre that they cast on periods favoured by history I dare to hope that the reader will derive some pleasure and understand that it is the duty of humanity to persist on this path.

I

THE HANDSOME AND GOOD ATHENIAN

ALL THE CENTURIES have made of ancient Greece an image according to their own perception. So it is difficult to distinguish the most authentic among these images. What remains of the Hellenic civilisation is, anyway, admirable and the rest does not matter. Its temples, its statues, its literary works are of a beauty of which one can boldly affirm that they have rarely been equalled and never surpassed. It is as a creator of beauty and realiser of a splendid ideal that we revere, love, envy Greece. It represents to our eyes a golden age, raised at the dawn of conscious humanity, an age of happy childhood, which for its trial effort wanted a master stroke and on the whole achieved its goal. Ernest Renan has spoken of the Greek miracle.[1] He has placed it beside the Jewish miracle but the most recent archaeological discoveries have somewhat debilitated this notion. One is right in wondering at the Hellenic perfection but it was certainly less immediate and less spontaneous than it was imagined fifty years ago. Greek art seems to

---

1   Ernest Renan (1823–1892) was a French orientalist and biblical scholar. Renan refers to 'the Greek miracle' in 'Prière sur l'Acropole' (Prayer on the Acropolis), which forms the second chapter of his *Souvenirs d'enfance et de jeunesse* (1883, 'Memories of Childhoof and Youth') and describes the impression made by ancient Greek culture on the author during a visit to Greece in 1865.

have groped and restarted several times before producing those masterpieces whose sight dazzles us. The Greeks themselves knew what to expect. Thucydides betrayed an obscure sentiment of prehistory in his country when he wrote: 'Many things prove that the ancient fashion of living of the Greeks resembled that of the barbarians.'[2] It is through a slow and continuous effort that the Hellenes differentiated themselves from the barbarians whom they despised as much as they feared. And they did not place them all, besides, on the same footing. Aristotle distinguished at the gates of Hellas two barbarians, those of the north (the European barbarians) and those of the south (the Asiatic barbarians). The barbarians of the north were courageous and free but incapable of thinking, incapable of creating beautiful things, incapable of governing themselves wisely. Those of the south were cultivated and softened and lazy. Whence the enslavement that weighed upon them. Egypt played a role among these peoples that constituted the education of Greece and that Greece was to surpass but Greece in its classical period despised Egypt heartily: the Greeks boasted of drinking wine when the Egyptians drank beer. What a decisive proof of the superiority of the Hellenes!

Literature and *littérateurs* have contributed to travesting the true Greece under the pretext of showing it in all its splendour. When Michelet,[3] a rhetorician without equal, writes: 'The free child of Attica received religion, national history and the spirit of the city, the vital spirit of the law, in waves from his milk and honey, from the great font of Sophocles or Aeschylus', he gives proof of his poetic gifts but does not give a perfectly accurate idea of Athenian civilisation. 'If one has a heart, a soul and a mind, one cannot really speak of Athens without exaggerating', said Aeschylus. Athens elicits hyperboles. The most scrupulous historians have a tendency, if they are also artists, to further embellish all this fine history and civilisation. The *Prière*

---

2   See Thucydides, *History of the Peloponnesian War*, Bk. I, Ch. 1.

3   Jules Michelet (1798–1874) was a French historian.

sur l'Acropole is a superb piece, but did Athens always practise so jealously this cult of Reason, of beauty and wisdom which Renan — and Taine[4] — make its almost exclusive merit? One recalls the Greece of Leconte de Lisle,[5] solemn, stiff, somewhat pedantic, that of Anatole France,[6] affected in the style of declining classicism, that of Pierre Louÿs,[7] depraved and even corrupted. The legend of Phryne defending herself before her judges[8] served for a long time, in the eyes of certain Montmartre or — as one used to say in the past — boulevard authors, as a translation of what was most Greek in ancient Greece. Flaubert, in his sensual Romanticism, had besides given an example of this error when he showed Venus saying in his *Tentation de Saint Antoine*: 'I made the entire horizon of Hellas with my girdle, its fields shone with the roses of my cheeks, its shores were divided according to the form of my lips. One found my soul in the organisation of its festivals.' Nothing less founded than this manner of transforming the Greeks of the classical age into a people of refined gallants, confusing the practice of voluptuousness with the cult of that which is beautiful.

---

4   Hippolyte Taine (1828-1893) was a French literary critic and art historian famous for his *Histoire de la Littérature Anglaise* (1864, 'History of English Literature') and several volumes on the philosophy of art, including *Philosophie de l'art en Grèce* (1869).

5   Charles Leconte de Lisle (1818-1894) was a French poet noted for his collections of poems, *Poèmes antiques* (1852), *Poèmes barbares* (1862) and *Poèmes tragiques* (1884).

6   Anatole France (1844-1924) was a poet and novelist who won the Nobel Prize in 1921.

7   Pierre Louÿs (1870-1925) was a French poet and novelist who chose ancient Greek subjects for many of his works.

8   Phyrne was a Greek courtesan of the late fourth century B.C. who was defended at her trial for impiety by the orator Hypereides. According to a historically unverifiable account by Athenaeus of Naucratis (third century A.D.), Phyrne resorted to baring her breasts before the judges as a prophetess of Aphrodite when it became apparent that the verdict was going to be unfavourable to her and thereby obtained an acquittal.

The best of the Athenians were chaste and the debauched had a bad reputation.

These great civilisations of antiquity lack besides — and that is very striking — the divine stamp affixed on ours by the most noble of religions that ever drew man close to God, but one would be wrong in misunderstanding for that reason the moral greatness of Hellenism and the defence that it presented of human dignity. Did not the most illustrious Christian educators pay a brilliant homage to these exceptional merits of Hellenism when they gave to the humanities such a large place in the instruction of children and youth? There are profound differences between the honest man of Athens in the age of its finest effloresence and the honest man of the following centuries in Rome, Paris and London. This small book has for its goal precisely the observation of these characters and these differences but the Athenian ideal of the 'handsome and good' man, of the καλός κἀγαθός man, following the customary expression, can still be offered for our respect and even our imitation. The meaning of this well-known expression has varied slightly in the course of the ages. The καλοὶ κἀγαθοὶ were originally the gentlemen, the nobles, the well-born people. Later, these words designated simply a good man, a gallant man, a cultivated aristocrat. It was necessary for the Greeks, in order to be accomplished, to unite beauty with goodness. An admirable conception of the individual! What a perfect marriage this union of aesthetics and morality whence emerged the perfect man! Already Homer calls the elegant and rich men ἀγαθοὶ in contrast to the others, the κείρονες, the κέρηες.[9] This ideal persisted during the entire period when democracy was the dominant feature. Plotinus himself still confuses, or almost, the beautiful and the good which, uniting, form God Himself. 'The beautiful', he says, 'is like a radiation that the good projects before it'. Eudemus of Rhodes,[10] who was the most intimate friend of Aristotle

---

9   The bad.

10 Eudemus of Rhodes (fourth century B.C.) was a Greek philosopher who was a pupil of Aristotle. The work on ethics Muret refers to is the edition of Aristotle's

and his best pupil, devoted an entire chapter of his treatise on morality (chapter XV) to defining *kalokagathia*.[11] It is the virtue par excellence in which all the others end and come to merge: 'Now', he declares at the beginning of his dissertation, 'we must analyse the virtue that is formed by the unification of all the others and which we have called honesty, the perfect virtue, as beautiful as it is good.' One is, according to him, morally 'beautiful and virtuous, that is, perfectly honest' when one only seeks wealth that is beautiful in itself and when one only practises beautiful actions because they are beautiful. 'By beautiful actions', Eudemus writes further, 'I mean virtue and all the acts that virtue inspires.' Such was the *kalokagathia* taken to the extreme, but among other philosophers more immersed in the real world, the *kalokagathia* was presented in a less austere light. The 'beautiful and good' men were sometimes only the men of good society in contrast to the less good. They were not necessarily lightnings of virtue. When Bdelycleon, in *The Wasps* of Aristophanes, teaches his father how he should conduct himself in the society of beautiful and good people (ἤν ξυνῆς γ'ἀνδράσι καλοῖς τέ κἀγαθοῖς), he understands by this formula simply the social class which one would today call high society people. And when Plato points out Lysis in the gymnasium in such a beautiful posture,[12] he has less in view the moral comportment than the purely physical grace of this stripling: 'He held himself upright in a group of young men and children, with a coronet on his head, of a visage truly rare and worthy of being called not only handsome but handsome and good.' Thus every mortal who distinguished himself from the crowd by the physical qualities and moral virtues, harmoniously merged and measured out, was handsome and good (καλός κἀγαθός). Propitious circumstances would have been able to make of all the handsome and

---

Ethics attributed to Eudemus.

11 *Kalokagathia* is an abstract noun formed from the words *kalos kai agathos* (beautiful and good). This ideal of an aristocratic Greek gentleman is discussed by Aristotle/Eudemus in the *Eudemian Ethics,* Bk. VIII, Ch. 3.

12 See Plato, *Lysis*, 206.

good men one of those heroes of ancient Greece of whom one knows that they were hardly inferior to the gods. And what then were the immortal gods if not mortals who were stronger and more powerful but hardly more virtuous?

The *kalokagathia* was the tradition among the Greeks of the higher classes in the most classical periods of their history. It was the password that allowed them to recognise one another among themselves. In the name of this code of decorum, in the name of these rules of 'youthful and honest manners', as they were called for a long time, the beautiful and the good rejected those who were not. What a charming and severe lesson of *kalokagathia* Cleisthenes of Sicyon gave to a certain suitor for the hand of his daughter whose indignity he discovered after having had a soft spot for him? And could one find a more charming definition of this eminent quality than that which emerges from a narrative of Herodotus (VI, 130)?[13] I cite the text in the translation of Pierre Saliat, revised by Eugène Talbot and published in Paris in 1864. This testimony taken from life and reproduced in its antique form says more than a long dissertation: 'This Cleisthenes,[14] son of Aristonym, whose father was Myron, son of Andreas, having a daughter called Agariste, decided to give her only to the most valiant Greek that he would find. Thus, when the Olympics were being celebrated and someone won at the chariot race, he had it announced that the Greek who esteemed himself worthy of being his son-in-law should go in sixty days or earlier to Sicyon and, at the end of a year after the sixty days, he intended to give his daughter in marriage. On this announcement, all the young gentlemen of Greece who esteemed themselves either for their merits or for those of their parents went to Sicyon to marry the daughter of the potentate, who erected palisades and barriers to test the value of the candidates both in races and in fights.'

---

13   Herodotus, *Historiae*, Bk. VI, 126–130.

14   Cleisthenes (sixth c. B.C.) was the tyrant of Sicyon.

There came καλοὶ κἀγαθοὶ youths from all the neighbouring countries, from Sybaris and Italy, from Aetolia and the Peloponnese and from Trapezon. Athens sent Hippocleides, son of Tisander, of whom Herodotus says that 'his wealth and beauty' made him a magnificent match: 'So many were the suitors', reports Herodotus. When these came on the assigned day, Cleisthenes wished to know the country and race of everybody and then retained them for a year in order to test their values, customs and ambitions, taking them aside and sometimes communicating with all of them together. Further, he had games and hand-to-hand combat performed for the youngest but principally he noted their comportment at table. And in this way he studied them during the whole year that he retained them and treated them magnificently. Of all, the two Athenians pleased him and especially Hippocleides, son of Tisander, whom he judged on the basis of his worth and because he belonged to the Cypselides of Corinth. When the day arrived for the marriage when he had to name the one whom he wished as a son-in-law, he made a huge sacrifice of a hundred bulls and a very sumptuous feast for these foreign lords and all the Sicyonians. When the tables were cleared, the lovers made music for a long time, spoke (discoursed) together in front of all present, trying to say the best about the proposed topic. Continuing the festival and preferring Hippocleides much over the others, he ordered the bell-ringers to confer on him a *basse danse*, which they did, and he danced with great physical contentment. Seeing which Cleisthenes did not think less of him. After he had caught his breath a little, he ordered that a table be brought to him on which he danced first in the Lacedaimonian style, then in the Attic and thirdly, placing his head on the table and making a forked tree, danced and shook his legs as well as his arms and hands. Cleisthenes was satisfied with the first and second dance even though he felt a great regret in his heart if he would find it suitable to have a son-in-law who was not very shameful in his gestures and comportment, but when he saw his legs playing he could not help saying to him: 'Son of Tisander, you have danced away your marriage.' Hippocleides replied: 'Hippocleides does not care.' And from this comes the proverb: 'Hippocleides does not care.'

Then Cleisthenes spoke. He declared his regret at having only one daughter when so many suitors, 'persons of repute and singular recommendation' had presented themselves. To all he gave, for their travel expenses, a silver talent and his daughter Agariste to Megacles, son of Alcmeon.

Megacles, besides, showed himself worthy of the family that he entered into. He had from his marriage two sons and a daughter who received the same name as her mother, Agariste. The which Agariste, having married Xanthippe, son of Ariphron, and becoming pregnant, dreamed that she would give birth to a lion. Some days later, she gave birth to the wonderful child who would be Pericles and who, in an Athens where democracy began to establish itself, had to not only give an example of the most eminent virtues but also endow with an immortal glory the city whose mastery he had gained.

*

The Athenian ambiance favoured that refinement of the mind and customs that conduces to the flowering of an elite. The climate of Attica is of an extreme pleasantness. The air, charged with marine exhalations, is very subtle and sweet. The plains around the city are not very fertile. Everything contributed to make the inhabitant of Attica a city-dweller. And if the air of the country is favourable to certain honest and rough customs, that of the cities engenders by itself sociability, emulation among intellectuals and all those qualities that finally create a civilisation. The proximity of the sea encouraged the Athenian to voyage. He became very quickly a good merchant, a shrewd businessman. And the money earned in this way allowed him to build for himself a beautiful house and to decorate it in his style. His natural taste defended him against the extremes of luxury. The climate, never rigorous, never inclined him, as it does in the countries of the north, to feast on food and strong drinks. The Athenian of the classical period is frugal and sober. He eats especially cereals and fruits. He eats little meat. It is reserved for banquets. During the hunting season, the lovers of the hunt gave large dinners of game, whose reputation extended throughout Greece. In normal times it was customary to drink wine only after having diluted it with water. To drink pure wine was considered a breach of decorum. The Boeotians, who were besides not well recorded, were a little more censured for this bad habit. As for the Athenians, they crowned themselves with flowers when savouring their wine mixed with water, which refreshed them even while it stimulated their strength without distracting their mind.

Life was made easier for the Athenians by slavery. The slaves were recruited from among the prisoners of war, those Asiatics whom the Greeks rounded up after having defeated them on the battlefields. The victory of Salamis[15] had been for the Greek world something like the Battle of the Marne[16] for the Western world. Salamis had repulsed the Asiatic barbarism just as the victory of the Marne was to repulse for a while the pan-Germanic barbarism. Slavery seemed something absolutely natural and legitimate to the Athenians of the classical period. The idea did not arise to them, in spite of the rapid progresses accomplished by democracy, that there could be a common standard between themselves and the barbarians of Asia, but the proprietors of slaves treated the latter with humanity. Aristotle speaks even of friendship (φιλὶα) existing between the masters and the servants. It happened that the slaves were subjected to torture for serious faults, but they were never tortured for nothing, for pleasure, or 'to pass time'. The Athenian was not cruel. He did not have any of those refined tortures in which, not far from them, the Eastern tyrants delighted.

One could reproach the Athenians for not being brave, for training in the gymnasium to make their body more supple and formed

---

15 The Battle of Salamis (480 B.C.) was fought between the Greek city-states under Themistocles and the Persian Empire under King Xerxes.

16 Both the first Battle of the Marne (September 1914) and the second (July–August 1918) were won by the Allied forces against Germany.

rather than practising a sort of boxing with bloody pugilists. One could censure them for neglecting the actual military virtues. It is in this that Lacedaimonia distinguished itself absolutely from Athens. Lycurgus, or the one who was called thus, made Sparta an entrenched camp both of Spartans and of soldiers. It was forbidden to the Lacedaimonians to undertake commerce. Commerce renders wealthy and wealth softens. Solon, in whom Mr. Werner Jaeger[17] sees the true initiator of the παιδεία and the properly Greek ideal, demanded, on the contrary, of all the Athenians that they practise a trade and teach one to their sons. To make of the Lacedaimonian a model soldier Lycurgus had broken the family bonds. The Athenian legislators, on the contrary, allowed the family to survive and founded on it the city. The Athenian was at once a father and a citizen. Athens placed the civic virtues and the family virtues on the same footing. Less imperious and less implacable than at Sparta, the laws of Athens allowed the sons of Pallas a liberty that did not exist in the ancient customs. Plato, who knew how to observe and compare, noted this phenomenon which he honours in his city. He observes that the honest people at Athens seemed more honest than elsewhere because nothing but their conscience forced them to be virtuous. If they were not military like the Lacedaimonians, they did not indulge in outdoor life less and the physical exercises that it consists of. They tasted the benefits of cold water and hot water, they wanted their bodies to be both clean and supple and muscled: 'Under the splendid air of your heavens', said an Athenian poet,[18] 'where the nine sacred Muses nourished golden-haired Harmony, you walk endlessly with delight.' The public life took place in the open air. The agora was accessible to everybody. All the citizens mingled there in a hearty confusion. Groups formed here and there, where they commented on a new girl or discussed a

---

17 Werner Jaeger (1888–1961) was a German classical scholar who produced several important studies on Aristotle and the Church Fathers as well as a treatise on classical education called *Paideia: The Ideals of Greek Culture*, 1945.

18 Euripides, *Medea*.

new candidature. The *corso*,[19] which is still held in the majority of the cities of the Mediterranean and Adriatic shore, must be a heritage of these distant times. People trained quite naturally for politics through conversations which took place during these promenades in company. The mind was formed at the same time as the body. Between the former and the latter, the masters of the youth took care to see that the healthy balance was not broken. Among the handsome and good men of the upper class horse-riding was strongly favoured. In the book full of Attic refinements, 'about a horse', where Cherbuliez[20] produced a very delicate eulogy of Athenian civilisation, one can read the following which must be accurate: 'To be admitted into a fashionable club, to frequent the school of Gorgias and run races, such were the marks by which the gentle and well-born were recognised, the horse being considered as efficacious a means of shining as a political club and as an animal that was not less aristocratic than a sophist.' Fortunate age, when the effort of centuries had not yet accumulated so many books full of lifeless wisdom that one should however know in order to create another! These hours, these months, these years that the youth today spends bent over powdery books, the young Athenian lived them in the public square, the gymnasium, the spas, in the gardens where he met other young people and where he was instructed at the feet of beloved masters. One should not forget that Greek philosophy was born thanks to the conversations in large parks, planted with trees and watered by brooks. It did not arise, like that of modern times, from the crammed and tortuous brains of solitary thinkers, often deprived of all contact with the external world. Zeno was to give as a motto to the Stoics, 'Live according to Nature'.

Nature was the educator par excellence of the Greeks, their mistress in thought and conduct: 'To place man in accord with Nature', wrote Charles Maurras, 'without exhausting Nature and without

---

19 A street for social promenades where races were also held.
20 Victor Cherbuliez (1829–1899) was a Swiss-French novelist whose first book was a study of Athenian art called *Un cheval de Phidias* (1864).

overwhelming man', such was the goal that the best Greeks proposed to themselves in their best period. And one cannot deny the fortunate result of such an effort. Did not Rabelais and Rousseau have to limit themselves to reconnecting with this tradition?

Philosophy and politics 'chatted' at Athens before inspiring the works of thinkers and the acts of leaders. Athens was a small city. The Hellenes never surpassed five or six million, ten million with their colonies, and this explains the facility and importance of personal contacts, especially in the capital whose primacy was not contested: Athens. People spoke a lot in Athens, perhaps too much. The fine speakers enjoyed, on account of just the fact that they spoke well, a prestige that events did not always justify. The handsome and good man was such only if he expressed himself, besides, with facility and elegance. He had at his disposition, besides, the most accomplished idiom that the instinctive genius of a people had ever created. Ancient Greek had a sonority, a harmony, a suppleness that no language has ever surpassed. These particles which we had so much difficulty on the school benches in translating and which make a Greek sentence like an exquisite mosaic, all had their reason, all added a nuance to the most nuanced, the most subtle, the most elegant language that has ever resonated and fluttered on the lips of man. Conscious of this wonder, the Athenians treat their language with infinite respect. They had too many rhetoricians, of course, but it is the perfection of the instrument that stimulated this abundance. Could one resist this appeal? And is there, besides, anything more touching than the training to which Demosthenes subjected himself to render himself worthy of Athens and its love of fine language? He shut himself at home for weeks, declaimed aloud. And in order not to be tempted to go out, he shaved half of his head. If he had showed himself in this guise, he would have been covered with ridicule. Thanks to his perseverance he overcame defects of elocution that were serious. He even overcame a stammer that drove him to despair. The eloquence of the great orators presents the same essential characteristics as the architecture and statuary of Athens: taste and finesse when necessary, majesty and solemnity when it impresses. It is in Rome that an orator was defined as a good man who knows how to speak. The best Greek orators were also good people, honourable men expert in the art of fine speech. The eloquence of Demosthenes especially supports this formula: he pleaded with passion for reason.

The peoples of the pre-Hellenic antiquity did not separate their cause from that of their gods. The Jewish people themselves, having become monotheistic and thus morally superior to the others, professed a rather crude and primitive religion. Their strong and jealous Jehovah did not have much in common with Christianity. The Hebrews did not believe in the immortality of the soul and all their manner of thought and acting reflected that. The learned, specialised in the origins of the Greek gods, are agreed today in supposing that the Hellenes also at first had only vague notions about the immortality of the soul, but the finest period of the Athenian civilisation, the sixth and fifth centuries, witnessed the development of this idea of immortality. It became at least, as Plato must have said, a fine hope.

The Greeks made death an ideal exempt from this fear that accompanies it among the Christians. They did not see in it, as the Gospel teaches us, the wages of sin. Profoundly rationalist, very little mystical, the Greek envisages death if not with serenity at least without excessive anguish. It is not difficult for him to arrange things with his gods and he is also not obsessed, as the Christian of the Middle Ages was, with the perspective of horrible punishments, the fruits of impiety. It was less the obedience to the gods than the obedience to the voice of reason that guided the honest Athenian man in his daily conduct. Had not his gods, besides, shown him some very piteous examples? Were they not subject to all the weaknesses to which mortals often succumb? What was their authority to demand from poor men the rigorous cult of virtue? In the final analysis, the true divinity of the Athenians was Reason, the Reason that they perceived under all the traits of Pallas, goddess of sagacity and protector of their sons. The barbarians adored strength, but the Athenians divinised wisdom. They had the very clear sentiment of the superiority of their religion over that of the other peoples but, not any more than their neighbours, they did not rise to the notion of one universal God, father of the entire human race. It is true that this notion, even today, has few followers. '*Gesta Dei per Francos*[21]' said the French Middle Ages and what an abuse did the Germany of the Great War not make of its old German god! The elite of the Athenians limited themselves to believing in national, if not local, gods and to honouring them. The good citizen arranged their statues in his home, offered them prayers and sacrifices, and took great care not to be wanting with regard to them and especially not to excite their jealousy, but it does not seem that he professed great love for them. The gods of Olympus did not inspire martyrs. They hardly deserved, besides, to be loved to the death. Jupiter, tormenting Prometheus for having wished to bring the benefit of fire to men, gives a rather poor idea of the sentiments of the Immortals towards men. It would have been paradoxical if the Greeks, as a whole, did not take this fact into account. Morality among them resulted especially from the polis, this public and civic life so developed among the Athenians of the classical period. It did not have much to do with religion. The latter did not include any dogma among the Greeks. And never would the idea have come to the Greeks of creating a tribunal of Inquisition or to throw a citizen to the flames, guilty of having expressed some peculiar ideas on the nature of the gods. Socrates was condemned to drink hemlock (which, besides, produced a relatively gentle death) much less for having outraged God than for having taught principles supposed to be harmful to the city. The Greek who had divinised Reason pushed rationalism to its final consequences. He adopted very quickly a sceptical if not rebellious attitude with regard to all of this Olympus of which Musset said rather lightly that it did not include a single atheist. That sentiment which

---

21   *Dei gesta per Francos* ('The Deeds of God through the Franks') is a chronicle of the First Crusade by Guibert de Nogent (1108).

has been called piety without faith and which is the characteristic of a refined civilisation had to exist among those Athenians of the elite, among those handsome and good Athenians whose essential traits I attempt to depict here. They respected religion as the basis of the state but they would not have guaranteed the absolute truth of all those myths where Zeus, Aphrodite and Dionysos sometimes played an equivocal role. How many 'Christians' maintain the same attitude today with regard to the Christian religion and the Christian culture!

Aristotle reports that the honest people of his time treated their slaves with kindness. But this kindness had nothing in common with the ideal of charity that Christianity was to proclaim. The handsome and good Athenian could open his doors to the shipwrecked person and his purse to the poor ruined by the bankruptcy of his enterprises, but he did not go farther. And his soul must have been insensitive to the distresses that he comforted. Pity, in the sense in which we understand it, was a condemnable weakness. It was reserved for Jesus Christ to pronounce the sublime words: 'Love one another'. The supreme wisdom for the Greek resided in these words, beautiful also but less beautiful, that he could read on the pediment of the Temple of Delphi: 'Know yourself'. Thence flowed all his morality, thence were derived all his duties.

It was necessary, in order to remain wise, to avoid all excess. Fanaticism was unheard of, even despised by the Athenians of good birth and good company. Nothing excessive, μηδέν ἄγαν. Solon, travelling in Asia Minor, did not lack the opportunity to give a lesson in moderation to King Croesus who had shown himself to be excessively proud at the risk of drawing the wrath of the gods upon his head. Had not Croesus, who was lavish, tried to dazzle with the display of his wealth that illustrious Athenian who presented himself in the guise of a modest tourist? But Solon was not enchanted and even tried to prove to Croesus that certain virtuous exploits that he narrated to him excelled, and by far, the benefits of fortune. Then Croesus went into a livid rage and, according to Plutarch, bitterly reproached Solon.

Upon which, Solon, without losing his calm, said to the king of the Lydians: 'The Greeks have been given, among other divine favours, a share of the virtue of maintaining moderation in all things. We have a firm, simple and, as it were, popular wisdom that has nothing royal or brilliant about it but that results from this moderation itself. It notes that human life is agitated by continual vicissitudes. It does not permit us either to boast about our own wealth nor admire in another a happiness exposed to the changes of fortune. The future prepares for every man a thousand unexpected events. The one therefore to whom god accords until the end a prosperous fate we esteem happy. But the happiness of the man who is still alive and is exposed to all the perils of life is, as for the athlete who is still wrestling, an uncertain stroke of luck that one cannot take for granted.' Croesus, still following Plutarch's account, persisted in his anger but one can be sure that Solon withdrew more convinced than ever of the moral superiority of the Greeks to those barbarians of Asia. The sequel of events was, besides, to prove him right. Croesus ended badly.

*

The authors devoted to democracy have liked to maintain that Greece always had only democracy and the republic. That is just fine words. The Greek republic and democracy hardly resembled ours. And then Greece had gone through in its origins a monarchic period. During the time of Homer and Hesiod, supremacy belonged to princes reigning over a clan and very jealous of their authority. Ulysses was the king of Ithaca; Sparta, during the period of its splendour, was an oligarchy. Athens boasted, already before Pericles, under Pericles, and under his successors, of being a democracy but, I repeat, of a very special sort. Athens too had begun, besides, with an aristocratic government. It obeyed leaders who were *eupatridae*,[22] that is, well-born. In the course of the seventh century, the free citizens were divided into four tenant

---

22 The population of ancient Attica was divided by Theseus into *eupatridae* (those born of noble fathers), *geomori* (peasants) and *demiurgi* (craftsmen).

classes. This state of affairs gave birth to an aristocracy of wealth from which emerged later this aristocracy of handsome and good people who were recruited both from those who enjoyed the benefits of fortune and those who enjoyed superiority of intellect. Solon[23] contributed powerfully to making Athens the mother of this civilisation, whose memory still fills with fragrance the history of humanity. His legislative work, his economic work, his political work betray that ideal of moderation and balance to which Greece owes a part of its renown. Solon, one of the 'Seven Sages'[24] (happy time when the people suffered a sage as their leader!) reveals in his poems — for he was also a poet — an ardent love of justice. When he died, he left to his age an ideal of reason and justice and a feeling of adoration for beauty that was to greatly facilitate the task of a Pericles. Certain authors have maintained that it is indeed falsely that so many historians, distracted by their love, have celebrated the liberalism of Athens at its apogee. I would take care to disregard the merits of Fustel de Coulanges[25] but did he not too deliberately deny taste and the sense of freedom in the Athenians? The thesis of Fustel de Coulanges consists in maintaining that the citizen of antiquity, whether he lived in a monarchy or in a republic, was not at all master of his own movements, that all his activity was subordinated to the state, that he was immeasurably small before this implacable despot. It seems that more recent researches have allowed one to affirm that the Greeks of Athens, if not all Greeks, maintained a broad independence with regard to the governments. This seems true especially of the elite minds with whom we are concerned. 'Our city', exclaims an Athenian poet of the fifth century, 'no

---

23   Solon (ca. 630 B.C.–ca. 560 B.C.) was an Athenian statesman noted for the legal reforms that he instituted.

24   The seven philosophers and statesmen of sixth century B.C. Greece called the Seven Sages included Thales of Miletus, Pittacus of Mytilene, Bias of Priene, Solon of Athens, Periander of Corinth, Cleobolus of Lindos, and Chilon of Sparta.

25   See above, p. xxxvii, fn. 16.

longer has power over a single man', and one feels to what extent he appreciates this atmosphere of proud independence and free discussion which made Athens' glory. The Athenians passionately loved their fatherland; one could even maintain that patriotism, in the sense in which we understand it, is a creation of the Hellenic genius, and more especially of the Athenian genius, but civic dedication, in this era, did not oppress the individual as it did since that time. People attended with full devotion those religious festivals that glorified the gods under the auspices of the state and the state under the auspices of the gods but, once the procession was finished, every citizen assumed his liberty of thought again. Born subtle and insubordinate, the Greek had a great deal of the critical spirit. He expended it generously at every opportunity.

One would like to create, in order to designate this form of ancient society, a term like aristo-democracy or demo-aristocracy. The citizens were apparently equal among themselves. A potter or a vegetable seller could call out on the street to the highest magistrate and all the big decisions belonged to the assembly of the people, but this people did not include either slaves or immigrants. The fate of Athens rested fundamentally in the hands of thirty or forty thousand individuals. And among this number the best trained and best educated pronounced the decisive words. At least it was so in those periods of the sixth, fifth and fourth century before the Christian era that are considered by all to be apogee of Athens. When the lower part of the nation succeeds in gaining the upper hand, troubles result, civil wars, finally decadence. Athens experienced all the misery of class hatreds and ferocious jealousies of the poorer classes against the rich but it also went through the finest periods of its history when the masses bowed before the mind, taste and talent. Egalitarian, the people of Athens, however, admitted certain superiorities. Anaxagoras, the friend of Pericles, liked to say of the mind (νοῦς) 'that it is absolute virtue'. Pericles himself, who was called the Olympian — which did not prevent him from establishing one of the most popular regimes that the world has ever known — came from a noble family and was not ashamed of it, unlike certain modern politicians. He let people call him Pericles, son of Xanthippe. Which did not prevent him, I repeat, from attaching his name to a constitution of which it has been said that it was a preview of the Declaration of the Rights of Man.[26]

Restrained, held in check in this way by immutable principles based, besides, on a society that, through the implementation of slavery, had largely facilitated the solution of the economic problems, the Athenian aristo-democracy offered to the cultivation of the human plant the most propitious soil. Handsome and good men rarely found better conditions in which to be born and shine.

*

Athens not only symbolised reason and wisdom, it glorified beauty and offered imperishable models of it. Other peoples, at other times, have loved that which pleases the eyes but the aesthetic sense was, at Athens, during the great centuries, a collective sentiment, an ideal in which all communicated. Does one exaggerate in alleging that the least sailor in the port understood beauty, enjoyed it, honoured it, and that it formed in some way the true national religion? The cult of beauty was expressed first through those magnificent temples where gods reigned who were only the most beautiful of the children of men. What difference between these splendid gods and, for example, the monstrous idols of the Hindu religion! Never would a Greek knee have been bent before such gods good for barbarian Asia. The Athenians loved their temples just as the people of the Middle Ages did their cathedrals, and with greater reason. Of those faults of taste that mar the most beautiful mediaeval churches one would seek in vain traces in the sanctuaries of Greece. Art inspired the religion. Its secrets were transmitted from father to son, piously, in certain families devoted to the maintenance of altars. It is under the vaults of the

---

26 *The Declaration of the Rights of Man and of the Citizen* was drafted by the marquis de Lafayette and adopted by the National Constituent Assembly in 1789.

Greek temples that the odes of Pindar and the *Oresteia* of Aeschylus resonated and that the Hermes of Praxiteles[27] offered the spectacle of its dazzling perfection. The Parthenon was born out of the love of the Athenians for gods for whom they had to provide a refuge that was suited to their image. The Altis of Olympia[28] also emerged from a brain full of the divine spirit. Absolute beauty, eternal beauty found an unequalled expression in the principal monuments of Athens: 'O beauty, o simple and true nobility!', murmured Ernest Renan in his *Prière sur l'Acropole*. He continued addressing Pallas: 'Goddess whose cult signifies Reason and Wisdom, you whose temple is an eternal lesson of conscience and sincerity!' and he ended his long prayer with this shorter prayer which will no longer be answered: 'Democracy, teach us to extract a diamond from the impure crowds!' This prayer will no longer be answered because the Athenian democracy was not, as we have observed, a democracy in the modern sense of the word. Ernest Renan, besides, hardly had any illusions, or else would he have added that the Athenian nation was a nation of aristocrats, a public composed entirely of connoisseurs, a democracy 'that captures nuances so fine that our refined persons hardly perceive them?' I know that Ernest Renan had adhered, as I thought I had to observe, to the 'Greek partiality' born of the philhellenism that his youth was nourished on, but he is basically not less right about it. The love of beauty in all its forms has never been the privilege of an entire nation as it was at Athens for two or three centuries.

The bold gesture that one attributes to Phryne is perhaps only a weak fancy but the anecdote that shows Sophocles accused of senility by his children and reciting to his judges his tragedy of *Oedipus at Colonus*, in order to justify himself, seems quite authentic. Does one see a modern author employing today the same method to obtain his

---

27   Praxiteles (fourth-century-B.C.) was the most famous of the ancient Attic sculptors.

28   The Altis of Olympia was the sacred grove of Zeus in Olympia, where the Olympic Games were held.

acquittal in a press trial or any other affair? The idea would not even come to him, or else it would sink in ridicule. What masterpiece could influence a contemporary jury in favour of a defendant?

No, the admiration of fine forms no longer arouses those natural outbursts that seemed natural to the Athenians. The love of beauty is no longer taken for granted, men no longer imbibe it with their mother's milk. Manual work and intellectual work such as they are practised in contemporary society deform bodies too quickly and too completely. Beauty no longer exists except on faces. It was not so among the Greeks of the past, a free race, a relaxed race whose physical work consisted essentially in rendering supple, embellishing, the human being in the gymnasiums. With what respect the ancient authors spoke of beauty, of manly beauty as well as of feminine! And in these words that I comment on and that are the inspiration of these pages, in this formula of the handsome and good Athenian, is it not significant that beauty comes even before goodness? Let us listen to Plato celebrating the young men whose education he was pleased to undertake: 'He seemed to me', he writes of Charmides, 'admirable in his size and beauty. Everybody was struck and stirred when he entered. That he made this impression on us men was not so surprising but I noticed that, among the children too, none looked elsewhere, not even the smallest, and everybody contemplated him like a statue.' Let us listen to Socrates explaining, with a genealogy of a rigour that would please the eugenicists, the exceptional merit of this perfectly beautiful and good young man: 'It is natural, Charmides, that you excel all the others because nobody here, I think, could show in Athens two other families whose alliance could produce someone more handsome and better than those whence you have issued. In fact, your paternal family, that of Critias, son of Drapide, was celebrated by Anacreon, Solon and many other poets as excelling in beauty, virtue and in all the other riches which constitute one's happiness. And likewise that of your mother, for nobody appeared more handsome or taller than your uncle Pyrilampes every time that he was sent as ambassador to the

Great King or to any other on the continent. This other family does not yield in any aspect to the other. Being born of such parents it is natural that you are the best in everything.'

All the modern theories on heredity, atavism, selection, are they not presupposed, as it were, in this text? Has one ever celebrated more worthily divine youth allied to divine beauty? Today, however, the fine head of a handsome man is for the most artistic of modern authors 'a fine pianist's head', and he ridicules it.

It was in the fifth century that the classical type of Greek beauty was formed. Polykleitos[29] gave its manifest laws in his *Doryphoros*.[30] Up to the time of Alexander, all the Greek sculptors were inspired by this model and were faithful to it. The handsome man, according to Polykleitos, has a body seven or eight times longer than his head, a rather short brow, well-groomed hair, eyes slightly sunken, a small mouth, thin lips, an unobtrusive chin, a regular nose and forming almost a straight line with the brow. A bearing that is natural and with a grace that does not exclude robustness completes this ensemble. It is perhaps the Hermes of Praxiteles that has best realised the masculine ideal of the Greeks and the Aphrodite of Milo the ideal woman. Since that time nothing has been imagined and much less executed that is more perfect.

Athens and the *kalokagathia* are marvellously summed up in the personage of Pericles.[31] Plutarch demonstrates through the example of this leader that virtuous men form the happiness of the people that they happen to rule. Athens was already a democracy when Pericles

---

29 Polykleitos was a sculptor in bronze of the fifth century B.C. who wrote a 'Canon' on the art of sculptural representation.

30 *Doryphoros* was a sculpture of a male by Polykleitos exemplifying his sculptural ideal.

31 Pericles (ca. 495–429 B.C.) was an Athenian general and statesman who expanded the Delian League of city-states led by Athens, which was founded in 478 B.C., into an Athenian Empire in 454 B.C. He was also a patron of the arts and helped make Athens the cultural capital of the Greek world.

took charge of public affairs, but one cannot repeat too often that democracy was at that time not at all what it became later. Thucydides, whose testimony is not suspect, observes that Athens was a democracy only 'in name' and that it was in fact 'a monarchy in the hands of the leading citizen'. Pericles did not raise himself, besides, to supreme power in one stroke. Born indeed of an illustrious family, he nevertheless had to conquer power through his talents, his achievements. He was the son of a victorious general, which certainly facilitated his task. His father was that Xanthippe who emerged victor at the Battle of Mycale.[32] Pericles himself began his career with a command in the army. Then he devoted himself to politics. He spoke perfectly, which was indispensable for one who dreamed of commanding the Athenians. Aristophanes says in *The Acharnians* that Pericles 'spoke with thunder and lightning'. Whence his nickname 'the Olympian'. Physically he was very handsome, which would not hurt him, but he had a defect in his form: he had a head that was too big, 'disproportionate', said Plutarch, to the rest of his body. So the sculptors have represented him with a helmet on his head. The image that Kroilas[33] has given of him is not less worthy of admiration and made to inspire respect. Pericles, who spoke loudly when it was a question of making his policy triumph, distinguished himself at rest by the majesty of his features, the calm and the naturalness of his attitudes. The instructions received at the paternal house had no doubt prepared him for the role that he played. He had undergone the personal influence of the scientist philosopher Anaxagoras of Clazomene. A friend of the arts, he was associated with Phidias.[34] When he became a great builder, he assigned to him the great works whose relics still fill us with enthusiasm.

---

32 The Battle of Mycale (ca. 479 B.C.) was one of the two battles that ended the Persian invasions of Greece.

33 Kresilas (fifth century B.C.) was a Greek sculptor famous for his statue of Pericles with a Corinthian helmet.

34 Phidias was a fifth century B.C. sculptor and architect whose statue of Zeus at Olympia was one of the Seven Wonders of the Ancient World.

An aristocrat in his instincts but concerned about the public welfare, Pericles depended on the people, sometimes to counter the conservatives. And the people of Athens, whom their historians and poets have blamed so much for their fickleness, maintained Pericles in power for forty years. Out of these forty years there were fifteen of absolute power which Pericles profited from to make Athens the most noble city that has ever adorned the surface of the earth. He detested Sparta and would have liked to destroy it forever. The magnificent speech that he made on the first dead soldiers of the Peloponnesian War explains this animosity and justifies it. Pericles was for freedom against slavery, for beauty against ugliness, for civilisation of peace against a barbarism of war, for Attic humanism against Spartan chauvinism and coercion. The adorable canvas that he depicts of Athenian life under his government gives an image of a society where men accomplish joyfully that which they did elsewhere, and still do today, in torment. Historians obsessed with military glory inclined always not to give full justice to Pericles. Bossuet[35] ignores him and it is Alexander who, in his eyes, embodies the heroic period of Greek civilisation. In fact, the Greece of Alexander already reeks of decadence and it is indeed Pericles, the καλός κἀγαθός Athenian par excellence, whom it is fitting to place on a pedestal. He loved virtue like Socrates, he was a valiant soldier like Themistocles, fair like Aristide, eloquent like Demosthenes. Never did a great nation give itself, with a surer instinct, a better qualified leader.

Then what always happens happened. This nation that Pericles had loved so much and that he had served so well finally turned against him. This man, of well-established honourableness, found himself accused of having squandered the public treasury and even of having neglected his duty in favour of himself and in favour of his friends. Phidias, the great Phidias, was thrown in prison for complicity with the leader of the state and if Pericles was not himself dead of the plague, nobody knows how he would have finished his career.

---

35 Jacques-Bénigne Bossuet (1627–1704) was a distinguished theologian, orator and court preacher to Louis XIV.

A pitiable fate prevented him from emptying to the dregs the cup of bitterness that the people always finally pour into those who dominate them. At least when he died he had not yet committed any serious fault of a sort that would have tarnished his renown. He gave evidence up to the last day of his will and character. That is a thing that democracies rarely pardon.

Glorious in his public role, he was not happy in his private life. His children accused him of parsimoniousness and perhaps reproached him from the bottom of their heart for not having profited from his omnipotence in increasing his wealth and that of his family. Insensitive to these reproaches, he remained faithful to the rule that he had posited in his funeral oration for the victims of the Peloponnesian War: 'Elegant without affectation, philosophers without softness', he had said of the Athenians, 'we sometimes make use of wealth but never boasting of its favours. We do not allow dishonour to fall upon the poverty that one professes but upon the indolence that does not attempt to free itself from itself.' Personally, Pericles had not been happier in his household than in his family. He finally separated from his legal wife because she liked the pleasures of expense too much. It was then that he began a liaison with the famous Aspasia of Miletus, whom he did not marry because the law forbade an Athenian of good family to marry a foreigner, but whom he linked intimately to his life. Aspasia was certainly not a model of virtue; she was especially not a model of those elevated virtues that Christianity later demanded of women, but this courtesan, who had acted as a go-between, was remarkably educated, remarkably artistic and one would be wrong in judging from our own perspective the fine and good ménage that she established with Pericles. She contributed to the greatness, the splendour, the good reputation of Athens. Accused in her turn of all sorts of misconduct during the tempest that was unleashed on Pericles, she was defended by the latter in a touching defence speech which shows to what degree this man, austere and strict in the exercice of his magistracy, had also a tender and generous heart. He tolerated the worst experiences without complaining. He considered it his duty not to let the sadness with which his domestic troubles in particular filled him appear in the least, but he reached a point one day when he could no longer master Nature. Plutarch shows him losing first several children without collapsing but, when Paralus, the only son that remained to him, followed the others into the grave, Pericles broke down in spite of all the efforts he made to harden his heart. He still had the courage to place on the corpse of his last child a crown of flowers, but afterwards 'he poured out for the first time in his life a torrent of tears' and this feature, so simply human, renders him greater and more dear.

Apart from this outburst, never did a man 'know himself better' and master himself better. Nobody showed himself more indifferent to insults. We know the story recounted by Plutarch of that young debauchee who, meeting Pericles at the agora, began to insult him and accompanied him, vociferating, up to his house. Impassible and as if he heard nothing, Pericles continued on his way. When he reached his house, he did something better. As night had fallen, he ordered one of his servants to take a torch and to lead the ill-bred man whose insults he had just swept aside back to his dwelling.

Far from it (one need hardly remark) that all these 'illustrious' Athenians whose life Plutarch narrated were at the moral height of a Pericles. The consciousness of good and evil was obviously less developed among the Athenians than among the modern Christians worthy of this name. One could be popular and not belong at all, or only very little, to the elite of the handsome and good. Alcibiades, for example, of whom it was said that the Athenians of his time saw themselves in him as in a mirror, was καλός but was hardly ἀγαθός, and not at all καλοκαγαθός.

His brilliant personality offered, nevertheless, a powerful psychological interest in the fact, especially that it shows to what extent the Athenians, who were hardly superstitious, had this superstition of corporeal beauty. An impeccable physique spontaneously created a favourable preference to the benefit of the one whom the gods had advantaged in this way: 'You think', wrote Plato, 'that you need no one and that your merits are so great, beginning with the body and ending with the soul, that there is no man in the world that you could not excel. For you think first that you are very handsome and very great. Then you are of the most noble family of this city.'[36] The same account in Plutarch.[37] He specifies that Alcibiades owed 'to the fine proportions of his body' the prestige that he enjoyed in the agora. No doubt his liberalities towards the people and his gift of speech contributed to seducing his electors but 'the beauty of his body', as Plutarch says, certainly did more than everything else. Dear Athenians, an artistic people and somewhat frivolous, too inclined to judge people on their appearance! One does not see the elector of today voting for the candidate with the most seductive appearance!

It was far from the truth that the beauty of the body, in the case of Alcibiades, went hand in hand with a beauty of the mind. Alcibiades was, in his private life, a very bad subject. He got drunk and then forgot himself to the point of frequenting the homes of women of bad reputation. And when his legitimate wife complained and threatened him with divorce, he beat her like Sganarelle.[38] He did not have that mastery over himself that made Pericles such a superior man. His flexibility belonged rather to Odysseus or Ulysses, that other very typical personage whom one would hesitate to offer as a model. Alcibiades alleged that 'by remaining faithful to his nature he might have wounded those with whom he was made to live'. So he made himself everything to everybody, 'delicate in Ionia, drunk in Thrace, ostentatious with the Persian satrap Tisaphernes'. Alcibiades was a politician with the manners of an aesthete but nothing more. Plato sees in him a young man well gifted but perverted by a bad education. And in fact bad masters abounded in Athens since the age of Pericles.

---

36 Socrates to Alcibiades in the dialogue attributed to Plato called *Alcibiades I*.
37 Plutarch, *Parallel Lives*, 'Alcibiades'.
38 The protagonist of Molière's play *Sganarelle, ou le Cocu imaginaire* ('Sganarelle, or the imaginary cuckold'), performed in 1660.

Aristophanes vilified Socrates and the Sophists too much. Not everything in their teaching was blameworthy. Would the current of ideas that they created be comparable to the movement inspired by the French Encyclopedists of the eighteenth century or by the German 'doctors' of the 'Age of Enlightenment'? Socrates and the Sophists aimed at replacing a religion in which one no longer believed with some scientific principles in which the elite could have believed. After all, it was not such a great crime, but their lessons, badly understood, often caused more evil than good. Perhaps Alcibiades would have been 'better' if he had made an effort to understand his good masters better. The play called *The Banqueters*,[39] of which there remain, besides, only fragments, presents two young men personifying the rival schools. One of them is called The Modest (ὁ σόφρων) and the other The Debauchee (ὁ καταπύγων). The Debauchee mocks Homer, exalts the new philosophy and raises Alcibiades to the heavens. Obvious sign of a very bad attitude.

Athens was, besides, to suffer still more corrupt politicians. The demagogues and their government destroyed, or almost, all that remained of the *kalokagathia* of the great centuries. There prevailed, in the classical period, among the Athenians of good standing, a code of decorum which resembled ours in many points. One is surprised to find conclusive evidence of it among the classics. One did not speak in a loud voice or with one's mouth full. To converse in an aside during a banquet was already a sign of a detestable education. When the aristo-democracy of Pericles turned into a democracy, or even demagogy, these rules fell into disuse. Plutarch is gently distressed in the portrait that he devotes to Cleon where he opposes him to Nicias: 'Cleon threw himself', he writes, 'into an intolerable pride. He crushed the state with misfortunes whose effects he felt more than any other person

---

39 Δαιταλεῖς ('The Banqueters') was Aristophanes' first play, performed in 427 B.C.

and caused all his dignity to be lost at the tribunal. He is seen to be the first to shout while haranguing the people, throwing off his cloak, slapping his thigh, speaking while running and giving the politicians that example of *laissez-aller*, that disdain of decorum that had to induce before long a general confusion.' The dice had been cast then and the *kalokagathia*, an eminently aristocratic phenomenon, the privilege of an elite, was condemned. A character in Euripides asked: 'How could the people incapable of right reason lead the city on the right path?' Thucydides replies to this question in an infinitely ingenious page where he opposes precisely Cleon[40] to Pericles. He puts these words into the mouth of Alcibiades: 'Reasonable men know well what democracy is worth. Nothing new to be said about an acknowledged extravagance.' The experience of more than twenty centuries leaves the problem still pending, still current.

All things considered, only the relations between the two sexes (and the private life of Pericles proves it) betray in the classical period at Athens a morality inferior to ours. Woman, in this so brilliant age of humanity, was still partially a slave. She could hardly go out alone, she was not tolerated in the agora; her role consisted in governing the house, in distributing work to the slaves, in weaving wool, in weighing food, in bringing up the children. Only the courtesans were authorised to educate themselves, to be interested in the sciences and fine arts and even to maintain salons of fine minds. One will meet in Plato Laïs, the most expensive *hetaira* of Corinth. Perhaps Athens appreciated in this age housewives as estimable as Penelope, but the philosophers did not visit her. They would have had no pleasure in doing so and these Athenian women, regular wives, perfect mothers, would not, alas, have found anything natural in entertaining these learned personages. Christianity placed woman on the same footing as man, at least theoretically. And that alone is enough to demonstrate its superiority to paganism. One should take care, when all is said

---

40 Cleon (fifth c. B.C.) was an Athenian general during the Peloponnesian War who opposed Pericles' rule and strategy.

and done, not to contrast the two moralities too crudely. One knows the very judicious little poem of Victor Hugo on Virgil, precursor of Christ:[41]

> In Virgil, sometimes, a god very close to being an angel,
> The verse bears at its height a strange glow.

One distinguishes also in more than one Greek author the same glows, prelude to the same dawn. What a strange contrast in the *Philoctetes* of Sophocles, between the character of Ulysses, or more precisely Odysseus, this archetype of a certain Greek mentality, and the character of Neoptolemus! In fact, the scruples felt by the latter and the analysis of which forms the pivot of the entire drama, are they not of a Christian nature? There is already — I declare it without irony and without paradox — something Protestant in Neoptolemus. Handsome he doubtless was but he is good much more, good, pious, shy, and even tormented in his conscience, like a character of a Scandinavian drama or an English novel of the Victorian era.

Odysseus demands of Neoptolemus that he lie to Philoctetes and deceive him in order to steal his magic bow and arrows: 'Come to me for a small part of this day and I shall deliver you later to the purest religion.' Neoptolemus revolts against his seducer: 'I do not know how to do anything through cowardly artifice', he confesses. 'My mission is to help you, but I fear the term traitor. I prefer to fail with honour than to succeed with shame.' So much naïvety makes Odysseus happy: 'Experience', he declares, 'has made me understand that, among mortals, it is language that is superior and not at all physical force.' In turn, such cynicism fills Neoptolemus with horror: 'You do not think then that it is shameful to lie?' — 'No', replies Odysseus, 'if salvation depends on lies'. — 'With what effrontery do you speak such words?' asks Neoptolemus. And Odysseus replies: 'When there is some benefit to be obtained there is no benefit in hesitating.'

---

41 *Les voix intérieures*, XVIII.

The tempter, however, ends by getting his way. And that is sad. Neptolemus deceives Philoctetes and betrays him, but no sooner has he accomplished this crime than despair overwhelms him. Philoctetes, his victim, confirms it with a certain satisfaction: 'The pain of this young man erupts on his features. He repents of his mistakes.' Hercules, the *deus ex machina*, fortunately comes to end the conflict and remove from Neoptolemus his scruples and remorse. He orders Philoctetes and Neoptolemus to whip each other to Troy where the possession of magical arms will grant them victory: 'Go then like two lions that search together for their prey.'

Who would risk denying the modern emphasis of this play and of the conflict of duties that it dramatises? The Greeks foresaw everything, guessed everything, and already experienced everything, or almost everything. We have developed, increased, deepened, but we have not really invented many things. The sentiments that endow humanity with the most honour are found in an embryonic state among the Hellenes of the classical period.

Decadence had begun with Pericles. The authors who were contemporaries of this great leader accuse the young people of deserting the gymnasium for gaming houses. The young lunatics will increasingly neglect those athletic exercices that maintained that sovereign balance between the body and the soul from which was born the nobility and the greatness of the Athenian civilisation. The Macedonian victories would turn the Greek genius towards the East, to its misfortune. Hellenic civilisations, which would still be beautiful, would develop in the cities of Egypt and Asia but they would diminish the *kalokagathia* of the classical centuries. This decline is not without its brilliance but it is nonetheless a decline. Aristophanes, in *The Clouds*, already complains of the different and inferior significance that is attributed to the term Atticism. The Roman conquest would precipitate the decadence. It would be facilitated by the taste for luxury that would continuously increase and by 'that war between the poor and the rich' in which Fustel de Coulanges sees the principal agent of the

Hellenic decomposition. Athens was the only Greek city, he writes, 'where this conflict between the rich and the poor did not assume an atrocious character'. The kings who, after a period of troubles, would restore authority and reintroduce order into affairs were not, besides, worthier than that turbulent and harmful *demos* that Aristophanes called 'the beast' to which he attributed 'the stench of a seal and the backside of a camel'. Praxagora, the revolutionary woman presented by this author in *The Assembly Women*, already prefigured Communism because there is nothing new under the sun. Drunk with destruction, intoxicated by her own words, she evoked the golden age of the future, 'where there would no longer be', she said, 'either rich or poor and all goods would be shared'. Such a language sounded the death knell of this elite of beautiful and good men of whom Athens had, to the honour of Western humanity, been the eternally glorious fatherland.

II

THE ROMAN CITIZEN

THÉOPHILE GAUTIER,[1] a charming aesthete, sang about 'the bust that survives the city'. He placed art and poetry far above politics. And no doubt he was right, but art and poetry can flourish only in a land organised by a good politics. The illustrious cities that were able to create citizens worthy of them, make them live in peace and honour bearing a name respected abroad, deserve also the grateful memory of men. Among the cities of this sort whose name has been preserved by history, ancient Rome shines in the first rank. It had its emulators: the Spain of Charles V, the France of Louis XIV, the England of Queen Victoria. Germany, in its turn, aspires to play a role, but no power has ever equalled in the strength of its arms and the radiance of its civilisation the Rome of the Punic Wars and the caesars. No doubt, the artistic prestige of Rome did not rise to the same degree. Rome never possessed a temple or palace that can rival the Parthenon. Rome is beautiful in its extent, majesty, the multiplicity of its ancient monuments. It lacks the divine harmony, the grace, the measuredness, the purity of style of which the relics of ancient Greece still bear evidence. But what nobility in the Roman greatness and, no matter what the delicate may say of it, what durable influence has the admirably regulated strength of the Eternal City not exerted, and

---

[1] Théophile Gautier (1811–1872) was a French poet, novelist and playwright.

does it not still exert, on the Western world! After the passing of two thousand years, Rome remains an essential palladium of our civilisation. In some circles it is accused of having given a bad example by its triumph based on violence. Littré[2] has claimed that 'Caesar founded only a decadence ended by a catastrophe'. And, closer to us, the Englishman Wells[3] reproaches Rome for having been only an 'empire without a soul' and that had no other role, at the beginning of the barbarian age, than to cause to gleam once again over the world 'the red eyes of the ancestral ape'.[4] We do not dream of denying that there was something cruel in the genius of ancient Rome but, in order to judge Roman imperialism equitably, we should bear in mind that it was implemented before the divine message of Jesus Christ which, if it did not transform the world, at least profoundly modified its moral ideal. The Roman citizen could not be what the citizen of a modern state is today. Such as he was, he deserves admiration and respect. And if the Western world should collapse, the memory of the *civis romanus* will continue even then to honour him.

*

The Roman citizen was originally a man given to working in the fields who took to arms when his territory of Latium or the city of Rome, seat of the royalty, was threatened. The population comprised patricians and plebeians, the latter settling for the most part in the cities, scorned by the patricians and deprived of the rights reserved to authentic citizens. The unity of the Roman city was based on religion, but the population itself was very divided. Originally there was no

---

2   Émile Littré (1801-1881) was a French lexicographer who compiled the *Dictionnaire de la langue française* (1863-72) and wrote several studies on the Positivist philosophy of Auguste Comte.

3   H. G. Wells (1866-1946) was an English novelist famous for his science-fiction novels. He also wrote a very critical account of Rome in his *Outline of History* (Chs. 27-29), published in 1920.

4   H. G. Wells, op. cit., Ch. 27, Sec. 5.

equality between the citizens themselves, that is, the patricians belonging to the Roman families members of the senate and the plebeians, considered as foreigners to the city, deprived like the slaves of all civil and political rights. This rigorous distinction between the classes was quite in keeping with the Roman monarchy of the original period that is both historic and legendary. The monarchy was absolute. The power of the king was a little limited only by the senatorial assembly that was composed of only patricians. But, already under the kings, the plebeians raised their heads and claimed rights. Tarquinius the Elder, Servius Tullius, had to raise some plebeian families that were particularly restless to the patricianate. The ranks of the military too were opened to the plebeians. Armed, they had the right to speak up. And when the royalty fell in 510 B.C., they were all ready to increase their activity in the Republic.

The story of Lucretia is perhaps legendary. It is no less significative of the social phenomenon that was going to take place. A son of Tarquinius the Superb, Sextus Tarquinius, having violated Lucretia, a woman of great beauty and more virtue, her cousin, Lucius Junius Brutus, placed himself at the head of the plebeians and drove the king away. The republic was proclaimed. It was to last five hundred years and it was under this regime that Rome lived its most glorious years.

These exploits, near or distant, in Italy itself or in the countries beyond the seas, did not prevent, besides, civil strifes. The authority of the king was succeeded by that of two consuls nominated for a year and always chosen from among the patricians. And only the patricians dared to appear in the senate. The plebs reacted violently against this ostracism of the 'masses' by the high class. A struggle of patricians and plebeians was begun which lasted until the First Punic War and concluded, as previously, with the victory of the plebeians. Twice they conducted a general strike to advance their affairs, with complete success. Everybody knows the desperate resolution that they undertook in 493, on the morrow of a war in which they had shed their blood for the republic and risked not being recompensed. When the patricians refused to implement certain reforms demanded by the plebeians, the latter emigrated *en masse* to the Mons Sacer with the aim of creating a second Rome there, a Rome of small people with large hearts and just ambitions. Afraid, the patricians sent them Menenius Agrippa, who recounted to them the fable of the limbs and the stomach. Edified cheaply, the plebeians got back into line. And it was after this surprise event that the tribunes of the plebs were created.

At the end of the fifth century, the differences between patricians and plebeians had been greatly reduced. And if the struggles continued, they gradually lost their sharpness. People from one class married into the other, which did not favour civil peace. The Romans had too many cares not to understand the erosive and destructive role of internecine struggles. They never pushed social hatreds to the point that the Greeks did, to the great harm of the Hellenic collectivities. The Roman citizen was, from the beginning, a realistic and practical individual. The constitution of Rome itself attests to these precious characteristics. It did not emerge complete, like the Greek constitution, from the brain of an inspired legislator. It bore the mark of a great number of distinguished men who, all of them, contributed their building-stone. It was essentially the work of experience. And that is why this grandiose but composite monument was resistant to tests and lasted so many centuries.

The plebeians had thus become citizens but complete equality did not yet prevail. The citizens were divided into several categories. There were the *cives optimo jure* possessing all rights, the *cives sine sufragio* enjoying civil rights except political rights, finally the freedmen, the *libertini*, who enjoyed the title of citizens but whose rights were very limited.

The Roman citizens were recognised by their name. The description of a Roman name was a very complicated matter. Related to this there were unchangeable rules that were piously observed and that allowed one to see immediately whom one was dealing with. Another mark of the citizen consisted in the wearing of the toga. It was of white wool bordered with purple for the senators and certain magistrates. It was, at least in the earliest times of Rome, something of a uniform because the citizen himself had the airs of a soldier. When the messengers of the Senate came to find Cincinnatus, a fierce patrician and an assiduous agriculturist, to offer him the dictatorship, they found him working his field, at Trastevere. Cincinnatus was doubtless dressed, as people were at all times, for working on the land. Thus, the messengers of the Senate invited him to put on the toga in order to listen in dignified clothes to the appeal that was going to be addressed to him. Cincinnatus, having had this clothing brought to him by his wife, dressed himself in it, listened and accepted. Sixteen days later, he had defeated the enemy and returned to his plough. A city that produced such citizens evidently deserved its fortune. Virgil calls the Romans the toga-wearing people (*gens togata*) and this term, in his idiom, signified a homage. Horace, in the same way, writes of a handful of legionaries who deserted that they proved themselves forgetful of the toga (*togae obliti*). It is commonplace to affirm that clothes do not make the man. Nothing is less accurate. This proverb, in any case, takes little account of the military sense so strong among the Romans of the classical period.

There is today an entire school of humanitarian and pacifist sociologists who are eager to demonstrate that the military spirit is incompatible with simple virtue. The entire history of Rome, especially in its beginnings, is there to give them the lie. A mixture of rural life and camp life was the austere crucible in which the Roman soul was formed. Romulus and Remus, wild children of the wolf, had declared that commerce and the arts were not worthy of those truly free men on whom he counted to make the greatness of the *urbs*.[5] On the other hand, agricultural work conferred on the one who exercised it an undeniable nobility. A Roman citizen, no matter how poor he was, was honoured if he lived on the land, cultivated his estate, raised a

---

5   City.

numerous family, gave the example of a life that was rugged, regular and subject to the laws. There was an unfavourable prejudice with regard to the city dweller. Pliny[6] says expressly that the cowards whom one wished to vilify and the freedmen whom one refused to respect were classified among the urban tribes. The rural patricians did not want to have such company.

These worker-soldiers must have offered — *mutatis mutandis*[7] — rather marked points of resemblance to that class of people that are called squires today and who always had a taste for arms. It is among their ranks that conservative politics still finds here and there its supreme support. It was the same in the past. The rural life teaches stability, offers the taste for continuity and tradition. These warriors, these shepherds, these farm-labourers of the ancient Roman aristocracy were also of an extreme piety. The historians of the ancient Romans are unanimous in observing that their house was a sort of temple. All their actions were derived from a rite. And over all these gods ruled that of the City itself. So that there were in Rome 'more gods than citizens'. These gods, besides, did not have the gaiety, the lightness, the picturesque immorality of the Greek gods. And they provided less pernicious models. Roman virtue was well matched with the public religion of which these divinities formed the object. The most illustrious Romans were characterised by a solid piety. The famous Camillus,[8] who was dictator five times, was at the same time a priest and a soldier, practising equally scrupulously the religion of the gods, the cult of the City, and that of a morality that was one of the most rigid. Camillus having laid siege, according to the legend, before

---

6   Pliny the Elder (24–79 A.D.) was a natural philosopher and author of the encylopedic *Naturalis historia*.

7   With the respective differences taken into consideration.

8   Marcus Furius Camillus (fifth–fourth century B.C.) was a patrician statesman who was called 'the second founder of Rome'.

Faleries,[9] a schoolmaster of this town wanted to render him a pleasant service by bringing to his camp, without announcement, the sons of a rich family confided to his care. Far from being grateful to this traitor for his exploit, Camillus had virgins given to these young men. And they whipped the cunning pedagogue, who was ignorant of the large heart of the great Romans, back to Faleries.

The kings had given the example of that disinterest, that austerity, that activity that had in view only the good of the state and its good reputation. We have had the opportunity to observe that the Athenian of the time of Pericles was less individualistic than he was thought to be for a long time. At Rome, individualism never prevailed. The submission to the civic ideal began there from the top. The entire history of the first legendary kings gives evidence of that. One should read in Amyot,[10] whose naïve language reflects so well the spirit of those early times, the story of Numa Pompilius[11] and his renunciations that were so in accord with the incipient ideal: 'Now Numa Pompilius was a native of one of the best cities that the Sabines had, which was called Cures, which the Romans with their Sabine associates called Quirites. He therefore, being naturally inclined to dedicate himself to all virtues, refined himself further through the study of disciplined men and the exercice of patience and philosophy. So that he not only purified his soul of vices and passions that are esteemed by all to be reproachable but removed also from it the violence and covetousness to forcibly rob those who were at that time lauded among the barbarians, esteeming that true strength was to master and contain in oneself all cupidities through rational judgement. Following which opinion he banned in one stroke from his house all superfluity and luxuries, serving anyone,

---

9 Falerii was the capital city of the Falerii tribe allied with the Etruscans, whom Camillus fought against between 406 B.C. and 396 B.C.

10 Jacques Amyot (1513–1593) was a French writer and translator of several Greek classics.

11 Numa Pompilius (eighth century B.C.) was the second king of Rome, after Romulus.

both foreigners and those in his country, who wanted him to act as an upright judge and wise councillor, and using his leisure not to enjoy pleasures or amass wealth but to serve the gods and contemplate their nature and their power as much as the human understanding can understand of these through reason, of which he acquired such a fine name and such a great reputation that Tatius, who was king at Rome with Romulus, having only one daughter named Tatia, made him his son-in-law. But, as regards this marriage, he did not benefit so much from it that he wished to go and live in Rome with her father, and remained in his house, in the land of the Sabines, to serve it and take care of his old father with his wife Tatia, who preferred to live gently at rest near her husband, who was a private man, than to go to Rome, where she could have lived in triumph and honour on account of her father. She died, as they say, thirteen years after she had been married, And since her death, Numa, leaving his life in the city, liked living in the country and going for walks all alone in the woods and through the meadows sacred to the gods and leading a solitary life in places free of the company of men.'

Tatia was among the first to give the example of that perfect conjugal life which constituted the glory of the Romans. The women of Greek antiquity have not left a flawless reputation. The *hetaira*, who was a creation of Athens and Corinth, is a seductive type but morally subject to caution. The type par excellence of the Roman woman is the matron, sometimes surly but how respectable! They are abundant in the era, these Roman women, fierce wives, irreproachable housewives. On two occasions, violation inflicted on an honourable woman changed the destiny of Rome. We have recalled the heroic end of Lucretia who, for having been violated by the son of the king, committed suicide and, in her fall, dragged down the monarchy. And there is Virginia[12] whom her father, a fearless and irreproachable soldier,

---

12 Virginia (fifth century B.C.) was the subject of a story in Titus Livy's history *Ab urbe condita*.

stabbed to death because she had been dishonoured by a magistrate. Upon which the decemvirs were driven out of Rome.

One has to have no taste for what is great, one has to be insensitive to that heroic ideal that seeks to realise what is most generous and most disinterested in man, to contest the beauty of these great types of Roman citizens. Even today a well-bred heart beats at the exploits of Horatius Cocles,[13] and Mucius Scaevola.[14] And what quiet courage in Regulus[15] who, fallen into the hands of the Carthaginians and sent to Rome with proposals of shameful peace, dissuaded the Senate from accepting them and returned to Africa, where the enemy had him executed with atrocious tortures! What simple respectability in Manius Curius Dentatus[16] whom the enemies of Rome, desirous of corrupting him, found preparing the kohlrabi of which he was going to make his frugal dinner and who speedily dismissed the tempters! Some families, almost always patrician, provided the majority of these large-hearted citizens. The Fabii, the Quintii provided several to the Roman state during the first century of the Republic. There was, at that time, a rule scrupulously observed that was later lost: public service should never enrich those who devoted themselves to it. A great man should remain poor. Poverty only added to his merit. That was the custom. It was, I repeat, respected for a long time. Was the continuation of the Roman greatness related to the preservation of these customs, this collection of rites and norms that formed the *mos*

---

13 Publius Horatius Cocles (sixth century B.C.) was a Roman military officer who fought against the Etruscan king Lars Porsena of Clusium.

14 Gaius Mucius 'Scaevola' was another Roman who fought against the Etruscan king Lars Porsena.

15 Marcus Atilius Regulus (third century B.C.) was a Roman statesman who served as Consul of the Roman Republic.

16 Manius Curius Dentatus (third century B.C.) was a plebeian consul of the Roman Republic. The story of Dentatus' frugality is reported by the author Valerius Maximus (first century A.D.).

majorum?[17] Conservatism was all-powerful in Rome. It was accompanied by puerilities. We see the Salians, the priests of Mars,[18] singing in honour of this god in the Eternal City, and up to the first century A.D., hymns that they had ceased to understand. A minor aspect of a venerable sentiment.

The patricians held to their rank and renounced their privileges only reluctantly but how they paid for them personally! In war, the most affluent wished to fight in the front rank. Returning to Carthage after the disaster of Cannae,[19] Mago,[20] loaded with booty, spread on the ground at the feet of the notables several bushels of golden rings. And he took care to explain to them that only the members of the equestrian order had the right to wear these jewels. The best of the nation had thus died en masse! This battle of Cannae, so disastrous for Rome, provided, besides, the occasion for some grandiose events. Like the English of today or yesterday, with whom they share some similar characteristics, the Romans showed themselves often more worthy of admiration in adversity than in victory. It was Varro[21] who was the cause of the mistake of Cannae, but the Senate, considering that this general had sinned only through ignorance, went as a body to meet him and received him cordially at the gates to the city. They could not thank him for having brought back a victory, but at least they wished to render thanks to him for having shown that he did not give up hope in the Republic. What modern prince, what assembly

---

17 *Mos majorum* (the custom of the elders) was the unwritten social code of the ancient Romans.

18 The Salii were patrician youths who served as priests of Mars in a religious ritual introduced by Numa Pompilius.

19 The Battle of Cannae (in southern Italy) was a key battle of the Second Punic War fought in 216 B.C. in which Hannibal's forces defeated the Roman army under Varro.

20 Mago I (sixth century B.C.) was a king of Carthage.

21 Gaius Terentius Varro was a plebeian consul defeated by Hannibal at the Battle of Cannae.

would be capable of such serenity in misfortune? Today, one boxes the ears of a general on his first failure while the overexcited public is astonished that one does not chop off his head.

Virtue, for the Roman of the heroic era, was essentially — according to the etymology — virility. It did not exclude strength; it did not shun energy. It embraced self-control, patience in misfortune and the spirit of sacrifice for the public good pushed to its extreme limits. Lucilius[22] defined it as follows: 'Virtue, Albinus, consists in estimating the things amidst which we live correctly. For a man virtue consists in knowing all the true values. Virtue consists in appreciating that which is upright, useful and honourable, in distinguishing what is bad from what is good, in rejecting what is vain, vile and slanderous.' Christianity differs much, to be sure, from this pagan and Roman ideal but have we not retained a large part of it, and have we not seen the best of us mingle this Roman ideal with the other for the salvation of humanity? How natural and easy it is then to understand the attraction exercised by Rome on a poet like the 'great' Corneille! Heroic exaltation is the atmosphere of the Cornelian dramas and it is the soul of Rome itself in its most admirable moments, in the hours when it was realised with the greatest felicity. Of course, the Emperor Augustus such as Corneille depicts him does not resemble at all the one depicted by Suetonius, but the hero of *Cinna* is indeed Augustus as he would have liked to be, as he should have been, the crowned citizen, the most citizen of all the citizens of the city.

Cinna[23] is the apotheosis of the monarchy. And *Horace*[24] is the apotheosis of Rome, an abstraction made out of all monarchies and

---

22   Gaius Lucilius (second century B.C.) was a Roman author whose extant works are mostly social and political satires.

23   Pierre Corneille's play *Cinna ou la Clémence d'Auguste*, published in 1643, concerns Cinna's plot to assassinate Caesar Augustus though it is also a veiled eulogy of Louis XIV's tactful control of the nobility.

24   *Horace* was first performed in 1640 and deals with the battle between the Horatii and the Curiatii during the reign of the third king of Rome, Tullus

all republics. Horace, learning that he must fight against the Curiatii forgets at once the tragic distress that this duty will plunge him into and exclaims:

> No matter against whom my country employs me,
> I accept blindly this glory with joy,
> That of receiving such commands
> Must choke in us all other feelings.
> One who, about to serve it, considers something else
> In order to do what he has to do is a coward.
> This holy and sacred right breaks all other bonds.
> Rome has chosen my arm, I do not investigate anything.
> With a fervour as complete and sincere
> As that with which I married the sister I shall fight the brother,
> And to finally cut short this superfluous speech,
> Alba has named you, I know you no longer.[25]

I agree that there is something wild and fierce in the devotion to a fatherland pushed to such a point. It is for this that Mr. Wells would shout about the red eyes of the ancestral ape, but it is because Rome provoked among its children such enthusiasms that it was so great and, I dare to add, so glorious.

That said, I admit that the Romans had buried into their patriotism all the idealism of which they were capable and that they showed themselves, besides, crude, sometimes gross and down to earth as the true landsmen that they were. Insofar as they cultivated the mind they acted through immediate interest in view of a specific goal. The Greeks worked at the advancement of the sciences through love of science, πρός φιλομάτεσιν. The Romans practised it only for the profit that they could derive from it. Thus their contribution to human knowledge has been one of the most negligible. Their positive mind conducted them immediately to history, legislation, eloquence. They disdained art for art's sake, this fine fallacy. The Latin word for

---

Hostilius (seventh century B.C.).

25 *Horace*, Act II, Sc. 3.

poetry is a Greek word, *poesis*. Also, Rome produced true poets only the moment when the gentle Greek venom, infiltrating into the Latin mind, gave the latter a new turn which alarmed the austere guardians of the tradition. Until then the Romans showed themselves, as Pliny says, 'extremely eager for of all useful things and all the virtues.' And Cicero, in his treatise *De Res Publica*, further defined the duty of the good citizen with respect to the fine arts as the impregnation of oneself with that which might increase one's civic spirit (*civitati usui esse*). The Romans of the time of Cicero did not pride themselves on aestheticism, but it would be foolish to reprimand them for it. Did they not collect imperishable laurels in other domains?

*

The creation par excellence of the Roman genius, supported by its citizen-soldiers, is the imperialism of Rome. It delivered to the small town created by Romulus, which became by virtue of its conquests the most powerful metropolis of the ancient world, an empire embracing the entire Mediterranean basin and beyond. Athens, strong in its superiority and its power, had outlined in the fifth century an imperialistic effort, but it did not succeed. The disaster of Sicily sounded the death knell of its ambitions. Athens retreated even before it unified Hellenism. Rome, at the end of the third century B.C., took up this idea and made it triumph. Rome had just reduced Carthage, its implacable enemy, to nothing. The fight had been tenacious. It was a question of knowing who, Semitic Carthage[26] or Aryan Rome, was going to win in the West. The civilisation of Carthage was maritime, mercantile and corrupt. That of Rome was land-based and still healthy. If Carthage had triumphed, the West would have assumed a quite different form, probably less respectable. Therefore one should be grateful to Rome for having won in this combat. Let us therefore stop reproaching it for a spirit of conquest that began with a benefit!

---

26 The Phoenicians of Carthage were Canaanites from the Levant who spoke a Semitic language.

Montesquieu was among the most zealous in blaming in the Romans their passion for command, subjugating and usurping. There have been other historians closer to us in this direction. Thanks to its conquering mania, Rome, they say, nipped in the bud civilisations that were full of promise. My opinion is that the Roman civilisation was certainly more valuable than those that it defeated.

Rome, at the end of the third century, had settled the Carthaginian affair and solved, besides, internally, the big conflict of the patricians and the plebeians. It had conquered and almost assimilated all the peoples of the Italian peninsula. By the force of its example, the masculine attractiveness of its laws and a certain generosity in the granting of civic rights, it had turned all these populations into a 'human material', as the Germans, inclined to the most audacious enterprises, say. The Punic Wars had given to these peoples the taste for combat. They were admirably trained, eager to conquer those riches that they had already glimpsed on their distant expeditions and that they naturally envied, because the not very fertile soil of the peninsula nourished its inhabitants increasingly badly. The historians hostile to the Roman name note that this army, launched by enterprising generals into the conquest of the world and who sometimes went beyond the orders of the Senate, were no longer those of the earliest times of the Republic. It was already no longer formed of peasant soldiers, of citizen soldiers. It comprised mercenaries and battle-hardened men. This remark is only partially accurate. It applies to Carthage, which employed only mercenaries. The authentic citizens of Carthage remained traders while the mercenaries fought at a distance for their benefit, but the army of imperialistic Rome was quite different. It was motley of course, all its elements were not of the highest quality but, before making soldiers of these men, Rome had made them citizens. They did not fight solely for profit but also for the greatness of the fatherland.

Later, Rome employed, like Carthage, mercenaries, but its finest conquests were nonetheless accomplished by authentic Romans.

Like a spring that extends, the Roman power crushed, blow by blow, at the beginning of the second century B.C. and, as if trying its hand, Philip V at Cynoscephalae,[27] Antiochus III the Great at Magnesia[28] and Perseus at Pydna.[29] And it was later, in the irresistible thrust, of a steady and continuous rhythm, this action perhaps less methodical and concerted than one believed, but wonderfully connected, that delivered to the Romans — after Carthage — Spain, Gaul, Greece, Asia Minor, Syria and Egypt.

Virgil proclaimed in some famous verses of the *Aeneid* that the role of Rome in the world consisted in asserting its power over foreign peoples for their good. Rome apparently spared the conquered and conquered the proud. This is the viewpoint of a good patriotic poet but the truth is slightly different and Camille Jullian[30] has confirmed it bitterly as regards Rome and the Gauls. Rome generally ended by reconciling with the conquered peoples and assimilating them wisely, but they did not begin in this way. The generals were not less eager for booty than their soldiers. They competed with each other in the fervour of their pillage. How many treasures were featured in the triumphs of the victorious generals proceeding to the Capitol! It appeared that the conquered princes appeared in person in these processions, but the admiration of the dazzled populace was related especially to the evidence, very substantial, so to speak, of the victory: shining jewels, gold and silver ingots. It happened also that Rome left the defeated sovereign on his throne. He was then at the mercy of the victor. Thus he paid himself off carefully with the enormous tribute

---

27 The Battle of Cynoscephalae was fought in Thessaly in 197 B.C. between the Romans and the Macedonians under Philip V.

28 The Battle of Magnesia was fought in 190 B.C. between the Romans and the Seleucid army of Antiochus III the Great.

29 The Battle of Pydna was fought in 168 B.C. between the Romans and King Perseus of Macedon.

30 Camille Julian (1859–1933) was a French historian who wrote a major history of Gaul, *Histoire de la Gaule*, 8 vols., 1907–28.

that was imposed on him by the city that was queen of the world. The defeated existed only to pay, and they paid.

These contributions directly enriched the victorious generals and, indirectly, all the Roman citizens. In 167 B.C., the people of Rome were freed for some time from all manner of taxes. The war contributions paid by Macedonia were sufficient for the maintenance of the state. One understands that such a result was of a nature to reconcile the Romans of all classes to imperialism.

Rome bled to the bone the provinces that fell under its law but did not touch their gods. The fanaticism of the Spanish *conquistadores* grabbing the treasures of their victims at the same time as they built Christian churches would have appeared stupid to the Romans. They left their new subjects their customs and limited themselves to giving them laws so superior, so much more just than those under which they had lived up to that time that the prestige of the *urbs* was imposed on these subjugated peoples. The benefits of the Roman administration compensated in the eyes of the conquered the cruelties of the conquest. To such an extent that we see foreign kings, full of admiration, bequeathing on their deathbed their kingdom to the Republic of Rome.

It sometimes happened that the Senate made mistakes in the choice of its agents. It could send to the provinces pro-consuls who were extremely greedy but, informed of their extortions, it recalled them and, worse, punished them severely if their rapacity had been immoderate. Rome is, of all the human societies of antiquity, the one that possessed the most devoted functionaries, the most competent and, one may add, the most honest. One was not a Roman citizen for nothing. A long tradition of honour reminded successive generations of the duty towards the state. The historians are not all of this opinion. But I think this is quite defensible.

For the rest, it is necessary that the Roman imperialism was characterised by something of those conquests that rendered Nineveh and Babylon powerful for a while. The superiority of Rome was related to the spirit of justice of the Roman citizen. Rome did not make war in the name of a bloody god that it claimed to be the instrument of and that it was eager to impose on the conquered. Rome warred and conquered in the name of the moral superiority of the Roman citizen over peoples that did not belong yet to Rome. Rome had a lay ideal, that of justice. When it conquered, it dreamed of imposing justice through its strength and power. This is exactly the programme that Julius Caesar, so detested today by an entire school of historians, developed in 49 B.C. in front of his mutineering soldiers at Placentia.[31] The ancient world had never until then resonated with such words. Before the Romans, the Hebrews of the desert too had sworn to an ideal cult of justice but they did not separate this aspiration from their national religion. If one should be fair, it was to gain the favours of all-powerful Yahweh. Were not the Romans the first to love justice for its own sake? The two great bequests of the civic spirit of the Romans to human civilisation are, on the one hand, the imperial organisation and, on the other, the mastery of the codification of law.

It is Romulus, the legendary king, who is supposed to have given the Romans their first laws. He founded them generally on the principle that was to create, through the majesty of the Roman citizen, the majesty of Rome: the absolute authority of the father over his children. Two gods presided over the Roman house: the god Lares, symbol of the dead ancestors, and the *pater familias*, a god not less formidable, a god in flesh and bones, to whose authority everything had to cede. A father could beat, sell as slaves and even put to death his children without justice interfering in it. A father of a family could kill his wife for the least fault. Outside the paternal house, the adult son of a Roman citizen enjoyed all civic rights. In the paternal house, he was only a part of the furniture, and, even less, a piece of livestock.

---

31 Piacenza. See Dio Cassius, *Roman History*, Bk. XLI, where Caesar first delivers a lengthy speech to the soldiers of his ninth legion on the need to be loyal to the commander and not greedy in conquest and then punishes the mutineering soldiers by decimating a part of this legion.

The royal legislators who succeeded Romulus and are called in the legend Numa Pompilius, Servius Tullius, scrupulously respected this primary basis of the Roman family law. And when, in historic times, the patricians harassed by the plebeians had to publish their laws, the Twelve Tables[32] confirmed the antique precept. An austere monument, but how typical of the Roman spirit of the glorious times! And how well this Latin language, heavy, cold, abstract, but solid as bronze or iron, naturally translates the will of a legislator full of wisdom! How difficult it is to see Greek, with its exquisite graces, serving the same goal! Besides, the Romans refused to the Greeks this feeling for the law that they were proud of as an exclusive privilege. How, they asked, could a people that did not honour their word have created a durable work in legislature and jurisprudence! With what a tone Cicero, in his treatise *De Oratore*, puts in their place the Lycurguses, the Dracons, the Solons in order to better exalt the Romans! 'All may tremble', he declares, 'I shall give you my opinion. The small book of the Twelve Tables, the source and origin of our laws, seems to me in itself, both by the weight of its authority and the richness of its usefulness, superior to the libraries of all the philosophers ... With what love should we not be inflamed for a fatherland that, the only one on earth, is the seat of virtue, of power and of majesty! We should study first of all its spirit, its traditions, its discipline both because it is the fatherland, our common mother, and because we are persuaded that it has brought to the constitution of justice the same wisdom that it reveals in the formation of its immense empire.'

Rome in fact needed a law to administer its empire and then juristic studies accorded with the taste of the Romans for logic and practicality. A preordained harmony destined them to play this role of universal legislators that they acquitted, besides, so well. It was under the reign of Justinian that the Roman jurisprudence was collected after

---

32 The Law of the Twelve Tables was the set of laws promulgated in 449 B.C. as the legislative foundation of the Roman Republic.

a long delay in three works.³³ There resulted from this a renewal of its popularity that has been perpetuated to our days. Nothing contributed more to Latinising Europe than the Roman law. The Germanic world too was influenced and affected by it. Thus one is not surprised at the outcry of which the Hitlerian Germany gives a spectacle that aims at reducing, destroying, replacing the Roman law, declared to be unusable and outdated, with principles drawn solely from the Germanic tradition. Such an eclipse, it seems, could only be temporary. Europe, all of Europe and not only Western Europe, has absorbed the Roman law to such a degree that the latter will perish doubtless only with Western civilisation itself. Indeed, with the sequence of events now leading to it…

*

The imperialism did not proceed without dangers to the tradition. The conquest of Gaul opened to the Romans new and troubling horizons. This influx of wealth that was poured into Rome concealed a trap. Those works of art, those poetical works, those philosophical treatises that were often based on sophistries had their charm, but did they not cause more harm than good to the Roman soul? A man of plebeian and rustic origin, that Marcus Porcius Cato, called the Censor,³⁴ whom the Romans of the decadent period glorified as an ideal citizen of the past, perceived the danger from a distance. And if Rome did not listen to him at all, it was not his fault at all. He placed his entire crude, austere and surly heart at the service of what he considered to be a mission. Born in a family of agriculturists, originating in Sabine, he was the last peasant soldier and almost the last citizen soldier of

---

33 Justinian I (482–565) was the Byzantine emperor who revised the existing Roman law in a series of legal texts called *Codex Justinianeus*, the *Digesta* or *Pandectae*, the *Institutiones*, and the *Novellae*.

34 Marcus Portius Cato, the Elder, or the Censor (234–149 B.C.) was a Roman senator and historian. He was the great-grandfather of Cato the Younger, the contemporary of Julius Caesar.

a Rome that had begun to forget, at will as it were, the virtues that had rendered it strong and respectable. The Hellenes, who began to infiltrate Rome during his life, were in his eyes frightful braggarts. The Greek doctors in whom the high society of the Eternal City placed its total confidence and whom they compensated generously were, according to him,[35] only charlatans. He detested besides refined society, the gilded youth, the beautiful women. Women did not even have to be beautiful for him to fear them. He hated them on principle and he was heard murmuring: 'If there were no women in the world, we would still be in communication with the gods.' He boasted of having embraced his woman only one stormy day when, afraid, she had thrown herself into his arms. We know his hatred of Carthage, this Carthage which he did not stop repeating had to be destroyed. What he detested in Carthage was the enemy of Rome but, even more, the city of luxury and pleasure. He spoke of it as Mr. von Moltke[36] spoke of Paris in 1870. Cato had, besides, paid with his person in the fight against Hannibal and proudly displayed a breast covered with scars. Mommsen[37] celebrates in Cato a Don Quixote, and Gaston Boissier[38] has compared him to the Misanthrope,[39] but in fact he did not have either the idealism of the former nor the delicacy and moral greatness of the latter. Thrifty and rich, he was even more miserly. And his fortune derived for the most part from his talent in cutting corners to the detriment of his family and his servants. This plebeian detested

---

35 See Plutarch, *Cato the Elder*, 23.

36 Helmuth Karl, Graf von Moltke (1800–1891) was a Prussian field marshal who led the Prussian armies in the Franco-Prussian War of 1870–71.

37 Theodor Mommsen (1817–1903) was a German classicist and historian whose major work was the three-volume *Römische Geschichte* (1854–56, 'Roman History').

38 Gaston Boissier (1823–1908) was a French classical scholar and historian who published several important studies of classical Roman civilisation.

39 The Misanthrope, Alceste, is the protagonist of Molière's comedy *Le Misanthrope* (1666).

the aristocrats but he treated his slaves like dogs. In his book *De re rustica*, he recommends to the good farmer, with perfect cynicism, that he save money with regard to everything that is no longer useful: 'the old bulls, the exhausted cattle, the old skins, the old carts, the old irons, the old slaves and even the sick slaves.' He subjected the slaves, so long as they were in rather good health, to a regime that was certainly not made to keep them in good shape. The beverage that he supplied them was formed of vinegar and seawater. It is clear that at this rate he increased his wealth. Augmenting one's fortune was, besides, if one believes him, the mark of an honest man: 'The one who in dying leaves more than he received from his father', he wrote, 'seems almost divine'. A mediocre and dull writer, he showed that he was a good general in Spain. He subjugated the country but through a war conducted mercilessly. Harsh towards himself, Cato showed himself harsher towards others. However, one could not deny that this 'redhead with blue-green eyes' had some merits. Thus he refused to buy the popular votes, which, already then, were for sale, and when his friends sought, in his interest, to make him listen to reason on this subject: 'Is it a pornographic business', he asked, 'that you conduct with a young debauchee or the government of the world that you demand of the Roman people?' He formed for himself a noble and lofty idea of Rome. He saw it with pride conquering the universe but he would have wished that, in doing so, it preserved its rustic customs, its provincial simplicity. This was in fact impossible and he finally understood it. It is recounted that, on the eve of his death, he disregarded the principles that he had shown himself to be passionate about, but this is perhaps only a calumny and one prefers in any case to think of Cato conserving up to his suicide his intransigence and even his intolerance. When he disappeared, Rome already extended its dominion over a large part of the civilised world. He felt regarding it, however, only a steadily decreasing joy. With his pessimist's clairvoyance he had discovered the worm installed in the fruit.

Cato in his extremes is the caricature rather than the ideal type of the Roman citizen of the early Republic. In comparison with this portrait it would be necessary to exhibit that of the Roman citizen of the new model, that of the Roman citizen of the imperialistic age. Would not the character of Scipio Africanus[40] express quite correctly the new epoch? Cato detested him, Cato did not stop reproaching him and even, as Titus Livy says, barking *(allatrare)* against him. He disapproved of the ostentation of this paladin, his extravagances, his lofty airs, his contempt of the plebs. Scipio Africanus and Cato the Censor were day and night.

Scipio, however, did not render any less brilliant services to the Roman Republic of the new model. When he asked to be sent to Spain to conduct a risky and difficult war there, Rome was threatened by dangers of all sorts. He himself was only twenty-four years old and the quite recent memory of the defeat of Cannes still gripped people's hearts. What was this stripling going to do in the face of such a great task? However, he worked miracles in Spain. He reduced Carthagena in a trice. At once the local leaders fell at his feet. The rumour spread in the Iberian peninsula that a young god had assumed the leadership of the Roman legions and that resisting him was attempting the impossible. Strengthened by his success, he asked later to fight against Hannibal and won in Sicily victories that forced the Carthaginians to leave Italy. Scipio's glory grew and his personal wealth, by a fortunate coincidence of circumstances, also grew as if by magic. Adroit as well as energetic, he was able to endow his brow, which was already girdled with so many laurels, with a poetic legend. At that time the ambitious were inspired by Alexander, just as they took Napoleon as a model in the last century. Scipio astutely had a rumour spread that he had been conceived by a god, who took the form of a gigantic serpent to approach his mother. When he stayed in Rome between two campaigns,

---

40 Publius Scipio Africanus (236–183 B.C.) was a Roman general and consul best known for his defeat of the Carthaginian army under Hannibal at the Battle of Zama in 202 B.C.

or two victories, Scipio liked to go to the Capitol and remain there a long time in the shade. In any case, he took extreme care to maintain the belief of the public in his divine origin.

This great leader was evidently of a very different calibre than Cato the Censor and it is understandable that the latter could neither like nor even understand him. Between the First Punic War and the Second, the economic conditions of Roman life had also been transformed. Deep down the old Puritans were not completely wrong when they denounced the bad influence exerted on the Italian simplicity by that Carthage that was combated mercilessly. A clique of military suppliers had been created who, enriched, wanted to profit by their wealth. Customs were corrupted, or at least lost their purity. The absolute authority of the father of the family weakened and women were emancipated. Some of them even had statues erected to them, which almost killed Cato the Censor suffocated by indignation. All disciplines were relaxed at the same time, through necessity, one should understand, rather than through the malice of degenerate Romans. These wars that were conducted at a distance demanded audacity, a great spirit of initiative and enormous resources, whereas a raw discipline characterised in itself the ancient Roman society, that of the peasant soldier. Cato the Censor was worried by the appearance of these new values, the fatal character of which he was unaware of. Crafty and sly, he was not very intelligent, otherwise he would have understood (for there were already points of comparison) that all great states pass through the same phases and that one should resign oneself to the inevitable. How much did the old Prussians, the Prussians before 1870, also feel, at first, uprooted in the Reich created by Bismarck following the Treaty of Frankfurt!

The Republican era in decline is still rich in fine military acts, but the spectacle offered in the background is certainly less attractive. The 'bourgeois' republic is effaced, the proletariat grows and rises. The 'capitalists' abuse capitalism. Excessive fortunes are created. An enormous difference between the wealth of some and the wealth of others becomes the rule. The natives are irritated and one tries to calm them and dazzle them with hideous spectacles. It was towards 260 B.C. that the gladiatorial combats became common in Rome. They contributed to the general immorality by accustoming people to deriving pleasure in the shedding of blood. A horrible parody of those fights on the battlefields where the Roman soldier tested his strength, at least with equal arms, against an adversary as brave as he! Rome always had had the taste for strength. Under the dying Republic it did not adore money less. There resulted therefrom a degradation of the citizen that has been severely judged by certain authors: '*Non mos, non jus*',[41] declares Tacitus bluntly.

It is at that time that Caesar came to restore the state in his manner and regenerate somewhat the fallen citizen. The new conditions of Rome and the Roman state did not permit a simple return to the past. There were, in the middle of the Punic Wars, around 300,000 Roman citizens. Towards 100 B.C. there were around 900,000. A very small number of them, 50,000 at most, resided in Rome and the surroundings, where they exercised their electoral rights. The majority still sold their votes. The state could thus not be restored from within. Supported by his victories, Caesar regenerated it from the height of his supremacy and his prestige, but the citizen, according to the new formula, was since that time, and typically, a soldier to whom agricultural work remained profoundly strange. Caesar saved the state but by militarising it. The Roman tradition was, besides, not at all hostile to the army, as we have shown.

The Etruscan kings of the legendary times were much more soldiers than legislators. Republican Rome preserved a bad memory of royalty. A shrewd politician as well as a good captain, Caesar soon found without too much difficulty the new formula, democratic and monarchic: perpetual dictatorship. It had the advantage of not modifying too deeply the customs of the Romans, who were always

---

[41] 'Neither morality nor law', Tacitus, *Annals*, Bk. III, Ch. 28.

accustomed to dictatorships, even though temporary. The oriental customs that spread from the fact of the victories that had been gained in distant places had attenuated the instinctive repugnance of the Romans for tyranny. The autocracy of the oriental *basileis*[42] no longer provoked, under Caesar, the horror that it would have inspired in the 'pure' of the past. With a remarkable feel for what was possible and what was not, Julius Caesar, even while restoring the monarchy, avoided rendering it hereditary. It would be elective; the *dominatus*[43] would be transmitted by acclamation. And the prince would govern and reign strengthened by the support that the army gave him, the only thing that remained solid in the final years of the Republic.

Between the Republic and the Empire, Caesar plays the role of a hyphen or a hinge. Thanks to him, Rome would enjoy for two or three centuries conquests, victories, material prosperity. Much has been discussed about the services rendered by Caesar to his fatherland. Imbued with the ideas of his time, Montesquieu[44] seems almost to think that it would have been better if Rome had died a natural death then. Caesar's soldiers, if one believes him, 'did not have any civic virtues any longer'. And what indeed was a Rome without those citizens of the old style who had created its glory? One is less mordant today about this. And it is Mr. Jérôme Carcopino[45] who writes with full authority: 'Caesar's subjects were citizens imbued with the value of the human personality.' One can bring forward many facts in favour of this thesis. I recalled above that Caesar wanted the Roman

---

42 Kings.

43 Rule.

44 Charles-Louis de Secondat, Baron de Montesquieu (1689–1755) was a French historian and philosopher whose major historical work was the *Considérations sur les causes de la grandeur des Romains et de leur décadence* (1734, 'Considerations on the Causes of the Greatness of the Romans and Their Decadence').

45 Jérôme Carcopino (1881–1970) was a French historian who wrote several works on ancient Rome.

Empire to cause justice to prevail. According to Dion Cassius,[46] he said to his soldiers: 'We should think of justice above all. With it the force of arms can conceive all manner of hopes. Without it nothing is firm.' What a generous style! Did it awaken an echo in the hearts of his rough and avid soldiers? One would hope so. Besides, Caesar gave them less noble speeches on occasion. Here is a proof of it: one knows the meaning of the Latin term *quirite*. The *quirite* was the citizen considered as an individual; it was also the distinction between the civil and the military. This name, which was flattering, lost its shine as the citizen of the early times squandered its aura. Under Caesar, this term had become almost an insult to such an extent that the Emperor used it one day to bring some soldiers back to duty who threatened to desert if they were not granted additional wages.[47] Caesar rose to the tribunal and announced that he agreed to the claimed recompense but added: 'And now, *quirites*,[48] I dismiss you.' *Quirites*! It was as if a lightning had struck these roughnecks. They felt positively insulted and one sees, from the characteristics of this type, the metamorphosis that the Roman state had fallen prey to. They were going full sail to military despotism. Brutus, a chimerical spirit in the manner of Cato the Elder,[49] was able to cherish the dream of a total return to the Republic. His virtuous crime did not serve anything. The die had been cast. Another Rome, another Roman citizen had appeared on the scene.

*

Caesar's century had been ardent and fecund in politics and in intellectual matters. The reign of Octavius, who assumed the title of Emperor from the age of 38 and received from the Senate the sacred name of Augustus, was distinguished by a greater stability. Everywhere people

---

46 See Dio Cassius, *Roman History*, Bk. XLI.

47 This revolt took place in 47 B.C. (see Dio Cassius, op. cit., Bk. XLII).

48 Citizens, that is, not soldiers.

49 See p. xii above.

aspired to peace, and the Emperor Augustus forced himself to realise the desire of his people. More even than Caesar he tried to reconnect with a past whose greatness he was obsessed by. If Rome had gained in power it had lost in morality, in virtue. If it was not possible, on the other hand, to return to the customs of the early Republic, who prevented one from being inspired by it?

Augustus had been in his youth a great debauchee. Borne to the leadership of the state, he changed his conduct and intended that those around him improve following his example. He affected wearing only very simple togas henceforth, tailored and stitched in his palace. He demanded of the women and girls of his house that they tend the home and weave wool. He punished severely a child whom he held dear, Julia, whose conduct was notorious. Religious scepticism had made immense progress, or immense ravages, in the last years of the Republic. Augustus restored the cult of the gods to honour. In doing which he limited himself, besides, to adoring himself because he was one of them; but all these monarchic and theocratic novelties were realised in the name of a return to the ancient rules, and Augustus deployed so much skill that he was able at least to deceive others. Tacitus praises him for having partially realised the return to the Republic: *quaedam imago reipublicae.*[50]

His testament discovered at Ankara gives a correct idea of his reign. The emperor boasts of having, of his own accord, confided the government to the Senate and the Roman people. He declares however 'that he surpassed everybody in authority', which did not prevent him, he continues, from being only the first of the citizens: *princeps civium*. In fact, he retained all the sovereign rights but he returned to his programme of letting people believe that, under his rule, he had shared dominion with the people. That, though, would have been a sad master. The Roman Empire was great through its military power but the Roman people were degenerating and falling every day one

---

50 Tacitus, *Annals*, Bk. XIII, Ch. 28: '*Manebat nihilo minus quaedam imago rei publicae*' ('There remained nevertheless some shadow of the republic').

step lower. Augustus, who preached virtue to them, gladly did everything to stupefy them. He complacently enumerates in his Ankara testament the naumachias,[51] the combats with wild animals, the gladiatorial combats with which he regaled them. What an education! And how could this regime of *'panis et circences'*[52] not have prevented any real return to moral health?

But the facade, under this prince, was of austerity and piety. The nostalgic appeals to the past of Rome, so apparent in the works of the best authors, fitted in with the political ambiance and corresponded to the will of the prince.

The poets of the court celebrated at that time, each one more than the other, the ideal citizen of the past, *temporis acti*,[53] and painted of this ancestor a portrait doubtless more beautiful than true. There were no poets in the time of Cincinnatus and Mucius Scaevola. Thus the Roman citizen of the heroic age was bathed in an atmosphere of legend. He was great, no doubt, but the literature under Augustus made him greater yet.

What, anyway, is Aeneas in the immortal poem of Virgil but Emperor Augustus or, at least, Emperor Augustus with the features with which he wished to be represented? He makes war reluctantly, he concludes peace joyfully. He is liberal, good, pious, sensitive, virtuous: 'Learn from me, my child', he says, 'virtue and true work. Others will teach you to be happy.' The *Aeneid*, in its numerous episodes, is nothing but the prefiguration of the unique destiny reserved to Rome, *'Tu regere imperio populos Romane, memento.'*[54] There is in this very

---

51 A naumachia was a staged naval battle that served as a spectator sport in ancient Rome.

52 Bread and circuses.

53 Of past times (from Horace, *Ars poetica*, 173: *'laudator temporis acti se puero'* ('one who praises the past when he was a boy').

54 The words of the shade of Anchises, Aeneas' dead father, to Aeneas in Virgil, *Aeneid*, Bk. VI, 851: 'You, O Roman, remember to govern the nations with your power!'

seductive work a magnificent sentiment of the Roman majesty and a patriotism which could inspire youth even today. Virgil does not limit himself, in fact, to glorifying Emperor Augustus. What an ardent love of the Italian land and of all the good and beautiful that it has produced in the well-known verses: 'Hail, mother fecund in harvests, blessed land, mother fecund in men!' (*Salve, magna parens frugam*).[55] The civic sentiment does not infuse less the *Georgics*, consecrated in principle to farming, that great business of the first Roman citizens. The famous description of the life of bees, in Book IV, is fully mixed with political allusions and nothing is more ingenious, more amusing than the effort of the poet to identify these bees with real *quirites*! An implacable censor could even find fault with all this communism celebrated by the author: 'Alone among all animals bees raise their children in common. Only they inhabit a city and common dwelling places (*consortia tecta urbis habent*) and live governed by imposing laws. Only they have a fatherland and fixed homes and, foreseeing the winter that is going to come, they give themselves up in the summer to work and place in common the wealth that they have amassed. Some of them watch over the survival of the state; their task regulated in this manner, they will gather pollen in the countryside. The others, retained within the house, place the first foundations of their hives … Others raise the young infants, the hope of the nation … There are others on whom has been allotted by fate the guarding of the gates and, taking turns at the watch, they observe the rain and the clouds in the sky.' Finally, and this is what these good citizens do best, they reproduce without experiencing love. It is quite surprising to see Virgil, who sang its praises so well in the *Aeneid*, making it a virtue for his little *quirities* to do without it, but the text is formal: 'One thing that is wonderful among the bees is that they perpetuate themselves without uniting, without getting enervated by the languishing pleasures of Venus, without

---

55 From Virgil, *Georgics*, II, 173: '*Salve magna parens frugum, saturnia tellus, magna virum*' ('Hail, Saturnian land, great mother of crops and men').

giving birth with difficulty ... They choose in this way a new king and replenish their kingdom with little citizens.'

Horace has celebrated no less eloquently this moral and material renaissance desired by Augustus and achieved by him, but perhaps he was less sincere than Virgil in his civic flights. In any case, he gives evidence of a broad eclecticism when he simultaneously takes pride in being 'one of Epicurus' group of pigs' and in fulminating against the young Romans who are guilty of taking too much delight in the voluptuous dances of Ionia. Alas, the Romans of the past were much worthier: 'Male children of rustic soldiers, they had learnt to till the land with heavy hoes and, docile, in view of their mother who was respected, they loaded onto their shoulders the wood cut in the forests when the sun, lengthening the shadows of the mountains, freed the tired bulls from their yoke and its disappearance finally brought in the hour of rest. How destructive time alters things! Our fathers were less worthy than their elders, we are less worthy than our fathers and we will leave behind sons who are more depraved still.'

Faithful to the formula in fashion, Horace sings in praise of Romulus, founder of the '*urbs* in a style in which the Hellenic grace shines through in spite of everything. Romulus, the first citizen of Rome, also becomes under his pen the ideal citizen: 'The man just and firm in his designs never staggers in virtue; nothing shakes him, neither the furors of a people who order him to do evil nor the menacing look of the despot, neither Auster, the turbulent king of the stormy seas nor the thundering hand of Jupiter. If the broken world were to crumble, its ruins will strike him without moving him.' But let us turn a few pages and we find the famous *Dialogue of Horace and Lydia* that Musset translated[56] and that, delicious as it is, is not very edifying. One finds in Horace traces of dilettantism, to say no more. He genuflected before the sublime but preferred for his personal account more pleasant regions. And no doubt he would not have exchanged his comforts

---

56 Alfred Musset (1810-1857) published a translation of Horace's Ode, Bk. III, 9, along with an imitation of it, in his *Poesies nouvelles* (1850).

as a Roman of the Empire for the turnips and broth of the leaders of the nascent Republic.

And the work of Titus Livy, the greatest historian of the age, is another typical work. I have said that the practical genius of the Romans moved easily in this sort of study. Titus Livy brought to it little critical attitude but much nationalist spirit. He aimed, as he himself admitted, at tracing the descending curve of the Roman ideal and genius in the course of the centuries. It was thus not at all a scientific goal that he proposed to himself, as in the case of Polybius, but a moral goal. With the great support of good examples he would urge the Roman people to elevate themselves. And perhaps Titus Livy contributed something, in fact, to the formation of the elite which, in the wake of the Caesars, under the Flavians and the Antoninians, offered the spectacle of those virile qualities that the historian had celebrated as the privilege of the citizen of the past. Which would tend to prove that one never loses one's time in teaching good things. Blessed be the apostles! A delayed harvest can, if the grain does not die, make the one who was its producer tremble into his tomb. They say that the destiny of a people is like a river that does not return to its source. And that is true, but an enterprise of re-education conducted with talent and perseverance can, if not prevent decadence, at least delay it.

Furthermore, the Roman citizens of the time of the Empire, as degenerate and depraved as they seemed in the literature of the time, participated in the great good fortune of savouring peace, this famous *pax romana*, the more welcome in that it followed one of the most atrocious of civil wars. Already in 40 A.D., Virgil announces it in his fourth eclogue: 'A long series of renascent centuries will appear.' And the poet Horace, the intrepid drinker of Falernian wine, writes, on the morrow of Actium, the famous ode: 'Now, my friends, we must drink, we must tread the ground with a free foot.' More sober but hardly less poetic, Pliny the Elder dedicates to the glory of the *pax romana* this magnificent image: 'May this divine benefit last forever which seems to have given to the world the Romans, like a second sun, in order to enlighten it!'[57] Just like the first, this second sun had certain tasks. Nero was a monster, Domitian and Commodus were not worth very much. The historian Gibbon has nevertheless formulated this sentence: 'If a man were called to fix the period in the history of the world, during which the condition of the human race was most happy and prosperous, he would, without hesitation, name that which elapsed from the death of Domitian to the accession of Commodus.'[58]

So the Roman citizen enjoyed within the extent of the organised Empire a prestige that was never to reach such a degree again.

Already in the sad times of the civil war, these words, 'I am a Roman citizen', generated all sorts of respect. What an advantage Cicero took, in his petition against Verres regarding the insulting torture inflicted by the insolent proconsul on Gavius:[59] 'Judges, a Roman citizen was beaten with a stick in the middle of the forum of Messina. No moan emerged from his mouth and in the midst of so much pain and so many intense blows one heard only this sentence: 'I am a Roman citizen'. He thought he would brush aside the torments and disarm his torturers just with these words, but no! While he repeatedly claimed this sacred and august title, a cross, yes a cross, was prepared for this unfortunate man ... To dare to bind to a cross a man who said he was a Roman citizen!'

Gavius had claimed his Romanness in vain, he had to suffer the insulting torture, but it was enough for the apostle St. Paul a century later to adduce his quality as a Roman citizen to avoid a punishment by whipping. A sad evidence of the influence that this title of nobility exerted throughout the ancient world. For having preached the new faith in Jerusalem, St. Paul had aroused the hatred of those Jews who,

---

57 Pliny the Elder, *Naturalis Historia*, Bk. XXVII, Ch. 1.
58 Edward Gibbon, *Decline and Fall of the Roman Empire*, Vol. I, Ch. 3, 'The Constitution in the Age of the Antonines'.
59 From the speeches made by Cicero in 70 B.C. during the corruption trial of Gaius Verres, former governor of Sicily (see Cicero, *In Verrem, Actio Secunda*, Bk. V, Ch. 64).

in the preceding century, had secured the crucifixion of the Christ on account of a similar misdeed. Stirred, the Jews surrounded the apostle and threatened him. A tribune had the delinquent led to the fortress and, as a prelude to his trial, ordered that he be flagellated, but St. Paul did not allow himself to be intimated. Speaking to the centurion who had to direct the operation and had already had him bound, he asked, 'Do you have the right to flagellate a man who is a Roman citizen and who has not been regularly sentenced?' Troubled by such a precise question, the centurion had the tribune informed of what had happened. And the tribune rushed over: 'Are you really a Roman citizen?' 'Yes, I am', replied the apostle. 'It is a right', observed the tribune, 'that I bought at great cost.' 'And I', replied St. Paul, 'I have had it since my birth.'

The tribune did not extend the interrogation much further. He had the apostle freed, gushed with excuses and said that ignorance was his justification.

Thus the quality of a Roman citizen, invoked by the apostle, allowed him to pursue a propaganda, justified certainly, and by which the world has greatly benefited, but of which one should recognise that it undermined in its foundation the grand edifice of the Roman state. Christianity was the religious regeneration coming from the East that, up to that time, had been far from giving Rome lessons in good conduct, but it was also the introduction into Rome of certain principles, certain values which would promptly kill the Empire. The Roman gods were the gods of the city and Christianity struck at the heart of this doctrine of the state, the basis of Roman politics.

For the Roman citizen, fully devoted to the earthly fatherland, Christianity substituted the faithful Christian, placing the heavenly fatherland above the other. With the coming of Christianity, religion also ceased, as Mr. Franz Cumont[60] writes, to be a public duty, 'and

---

60 Franz Cumont (1868–1947) was a Belgian archaeologist and historian famous for his documentation of Mithraism and his study of *Les religions orientales dans le paganisme romain* (1906, 'Eastern Religions in Roman Paganism').

became a personal obligation'. The ancient world which was in total decadence was going to die of the enthusiasm with which the poor, the unfortunate and all the good souls favoured this novelty. A novelty that, besides, has been tested, since it continues to inspire in the believers after two thousand years their most generous movements and those impulses that still distinguish the human being from the brute.

But let us not ignore, for all that, the role played at the dawn of history by Rome and its immortal child: the Roman citizen.

III
THE RENAISSANCE MAN

THE EUROPEAN, and especially the Italian, of the Renaissance projects onto the civilised world, at the dawn of the modern age, an image worthy of the greatest admiration. At that time man really raised himself above himself. And that ideal type of superman dear to the philosopher Nietzsche, it is no doubt in the Italian *quattrocento* and the *cinquecento*[1] that it was bound to become — and even, occasionally, became — a living reality. There is, however, something excessive and therefore unjust in the enthusiasm shown to the Renaissance by some of its historians and in their zeal to depreciate the previous era. The Middle Ages, the 'mediaeval' institutions, the barbarism and the darkness of the Middle Ages! With what contempt certain adorers of the Renaissance think they must write or pronounce these words! If one were to believe them, the Renaissance was a revelation, an apocalypse, a miracle of the same sort as the 'Greek miracle', that other erroneous formula that scientific history has given the lie to. Since the death of the ancient world, Europe is supposed to have lived in darkness and suddenly the sun of renascent antiquity illuminated it, rewarmed and fertilised it. Désiré Nisard[2] saw in the Renaissance 'a magnificent scene or recognition between the sons and

---

1 *Quattrocento*=fifteenth century; *cinquecento*=sixteenth century.
2 Jean-Maris Désiré Nisard (1806–1988) was a French literary critic.

their fathers, between the past and the future'. In fact, the occurrence of the Renaissance did not have this dramatic character. The transition from one era to the following, from one civilisation to another, was made not suddenly, not in a burst, but almost harmoniously and almost unobtrusively. We know that time does not respect what one does without it. When the Renaissance shone and triumphed, it had patiently and piously conquered its claims to such a glory.

The Renaissance still represents, in the blossoming of the human species, an era beautiful and fecund in a different way than the Middle Ages. The Roman Empire had realised through force the moral unity of the world, which was conquered by its arms. Heir to the Roman Empire, Christianity tried to unify its heritage both through restraint and through persuasion. The successors of St. Peter were thus the successors of the Caesars. The notion of Christianity had been substituted for that of *imperium*. For having instituted order in the chaos provoked by the invasions, the mediaeval clergy has a right to the grateful recognition of men. The Church contributed to the restoration of the feeling of hierarchy. It supported feudalism in its regulatory and pacificatory aspect. The Middle Ages are Christian, almost uniformly Christian. One sees then what one was never to see again: all the civilised or Christian (which was the same) peoples obeying laws almost identical. Literature and philosophy are strangely similar, at that time, from one nation to another. Humanity is gregarious, society is corporative. Those who occupy the foreground, the leaders of that time, are less individuals than categories or classes of individuals. And all served the same God. Catholicism held in Europe the place that the Olympic Games held in Greece. And the councils were comparable to the Amphyctionic assemblies.[3] The peoples thought they would find world peace and the individuals their individual peace in the sharing

---

3   The Amphyctionic League was a religious body composed of twelve tribes of the region of Thermopylae. The League had considerable social and political power in addition to its guardianship of sacred shrines, such as the Temple of Apollo at Delphi.

of the spiritual and temporal power in the form then existing: the double reign of the Emperor and of the Pope, these two halves of God.

The masterpiece of the Middle Ages is chivalry. And chivalry is indeed the work of the clergy, in any case, of the Christian religion. To make of those Goths, Visigoths and Ostrogoths, who had invaded, conquered and colonised the West, human beings, to inculcate in them the feeling of honour, that superhuman power was necessary that emanates from the Gospel. No doubt there remain some traces of barbarism in chivalry, but what greatness and what nobility in the figure of a Roland and in the historic personage of Godefroy de Bouillon![4] How many such gleams among those 'darknesses of the Middle Ages'!

The fine arts, it is true, had fallen somewhat into childishness. The notion of the beautiful, or of absolute beauty, had disappeared or been obscured. The clergy, which should have encouraged the respect for the past, gave a less than good example. Boccaccio has drawn a severe picture of the disorder in which the Benedictines of Mt. Cassin left their library. Manuscripts were cut up, miniatures were stolen. With irreplaceable parchments they made psalters that were sold at a little profit. Ah, certainly it was time that the Renaissance came to save what remained of these treasures!

Also, the Renaissance was incubated (and I repeat this) within the flanks of the mediaeval chaos before the Italian *quattrocento*. Already, much before 1000 A.D., the court of Charlemagne had been the theatre of a renaissance of antiquity, of course partial and very limited. Dante, who lived and composed in the High Middle Ages, heralds in many aspects the *quattrocento*. In France, the crude works of the Hundred Years' War delayed the arrival of a more civilised era and left to Italy the privilege of such an initiation. One nevertheless discovers, from the fourteenth century and especially in the fifteenth, precursory symptoms. One sees at that time the popes leaving their share to the

---

4   Godefroy de Bouillon (1060–1100) was one of the leaders of the First Crusade who was made ruler of the Kingdom of Jerusalem in 1099.

kings of France and to aim instead at a temporal supremacy over Italy. Around the same time arises Joan of Arc, daughter of the people who instructed the fine and genteel lords. Louis XI, a real king though he was, then raises the bourgeois spirit against the feudal spirit. And, in the literature of the French Middle Ages, what a reaction against the purely mediaeval spirit and what bursts of a new spirit! The authors of fables mocked priests and monks all the time but in general they respected the doctrine itself. One sees, however, from the thirteenth century, the author of *Aucassin et Nicolette*[5] breaking with this troubling custom. Threatened with Hell because he wishes to make Nicolette his mistress, Aucassin openly declares himself a free thinker. He prefers Hell to Paradise because he thinks he is sure to find there 'good clerks, handsome knights and beautiful courteous ladies who have two or three friends besides their husband.' This is already, in the French High Middle Ages, the spirit of Boccaccio and of certain Florentine or Roman humanists. No, the Renaissance was not a spontaneous movement provoked by a handful of writers, thinkers, artists who were suddenly emancipated. It does not for that reason merit less a place of honour in the calendar of the great and fine days of Western man. Since the Athens of Pericles one had never seen anything so perfect on earth as Florence or Rome, one could almost say, as the whole of Italy of the *Rinascimento*.

*

Another thing: one has for too long limited the word 'Renaissance' too narrowly to the resurrection of antiquity alone. The first people who used this word gave it a broader meaning. The Renaissance was for them not only the renaissance of a mostly forgotten Greek civilisation and Roman civilisation but also the renaissance of the individual, his redevelopment, his renewal. The human being was reborn and not only through contact with Roman literature that was better

---

5   *Aucassin et Nicolette* is an anonymous *chantefable*, or sung story, from the thirteenth century.

understood and Greek literature, until then ignored and suddenly discovered, but thanks to other concomitant and parallel phenomena, the formation of nationalities, the inventions that were favourable to material progress and to spiritual progress, the discoveries of the explorers who broadened the field of human activity. The men of the Renaissance stopped, at the same time, believing that Europe alone formed the entire universe and that the earth alone counted in infinite space. The Middle Ages had been an era of faith, a theological era. With the Renaissance the scientific spirit experiences a triumphal reentry. The Greek and Latin authors who were ignorant of the reign of theology, had necessarily to find favour among an elite in love with empiricism and filled with defiance of dogmas. All these sentiments were too natural among the Italians for them to plunge again into the Latin manuscripts, they limited themselves, in short, to renewing the national tradition. They had always felt very keenly the relationship that connected them to their ancestors through language and mentality. Italy was not fully covered with ruins for nothing. One could be unaware of the greatness and the splendour, one could use its lime for building, these glorious vestiges did not for all that form less of an ambiance that did not fail to influence the works of literature and the artists.

One of the most robust geniuses that the Renaissance formed at its apogee, Michelangelo, formulated the ideal of this epoch in a magnificent manner: 'My eyes', he wrote, 'avid for beauty, my soul avid for its salvation, have no other power of climbing to heaven than by contemplating beautiful forms.' The ideal of the Renaissance, what was most generous and almost unique in it, is a religious faith in the beauty of the world, in the value of life, in the capacity given to each individual to impose his law upon Nature.

What a difference between this philosophy and that of the preceding centuries! And what a poor figure scholasticism cuts before this formidable flight of the human genius! Not that scholasticism was without merits. The thinkers of the *Rinascimento* disdained them too much, looked down on them from too high. One is never just towards that which one replaces. Scholasticism had, in its time, marked a stage on the path of spiritual progress. It attested to, if not the triumph of reason, at least to the exuberance of reasoning taking pleasure in giving free rein to itself. Scholasticism, no matter what people may have said, absolutely did not exclude the critical spirit. It contributed its share to science. And today one considers as inaccurate the famous formula that reduces this philosophy to the humble station of a servant to theology, *ancilla theologiae*. Scholasticism had already drawn from the springs of Latin and even Greek wisdom. Plato and Aristotle had provided their stone to this monument. What is the quarrel of the realists and the nominalists, this capital issue of scholasticism, if not, in a still rough form, the eternal contest of Idealism and Empiricism? In an age when the conservation of the faith was of utmost necessity for the maintenance of Western civilisation, which was still quite threatened, scholasticism offered this great advantage of effecting a successful synthesis of science and religion, but it goes without saying that this science, which it prided itself on, was quite relative. The authors of the Renaissance derived joy in demolishing it. What sarcasms did the physics of scholasticism not provide them, deriving everything from these four elements: earth, water, air and fire! But one can laugh today, in just repartee, at certain hypotheses issued by the greatest scholars of the Renaissance. The generations that follow will laugh forever, if they have the heart to laugh, at the scientific theories of those who preceded them. On the other hand, if one sets oneself a little higher, one observes that scholasticism marked a perceptible progress and that the discoveries and inventions of the Renaissance later allowed other more important progresses.

Scholasticism was, in a way, a sedentary philosophy which was practised in cells and cloisters closed to the opinions coming from the public. The philosophy of the Renaissance is a philosophy of the open air, as that of Plato had been in the past, and it is from this that its superiority is derived. The Renaissance rehabilitated at the same time the individual and Nature, which the Middle Ages, too scrupulously theological, monastic and clerical, had exaggeratedly depreciated. The Italian poets of the Renaissance sing the delights of rustic life and the charms of the countryside in an age when French poets and chroniclers still despise the land and its works and ridicule the peasants. We see at the very beginning of the *quattrocento* Pier Paolo Vergerio di Padua[6] maintain that the education of the body should go hand in hand with that of the mind. One should, he says, honour once again the gymnastics dear to the Greeks, one should teach young people wrestling, racing, archery and horse-riding. It is already the pedagogy that the two great moralists of the French Renaissance, Montaigne and Rabelais, were to encourage: 'It is not a soul, not a body that one trains', wrote Montaigne, 'one should not separate them into two and, as Plato says, one should not exercise one without the other but conduct them equally like a couple of horses harnessed to the same yoke.'

Rabelais went further in exhortations of this sort and we see him citing Pythagoras just as Montaigne invoked Plato. His animosity towards monastic education is expressed in his creation of an Abbey of Thélème[7] where the only rule is: 'Do what you wish'. Scholasticism is very clearly aimed at in the passage where he shows the Sophists, still too valued in his age, making Gargantua read his map so clearly that 'he could say it by heart backwards'. With what result? He tells us further by showing us the unfortunate object of this instruction as 'mad, stupid, a dreamer and an idler'. That's the effect of such an absurd discipline.

*

---

6   Pier Paolo Vergerio the Elder (1369–1444) was an Italian humanist educator whose work *De ingenuis moribus et liberalibus studiis* (1402–03, 'Of Honest Manners and Liberal Studies') was very influential in the Renaissance.

7   In Rabelais' *Gargantua et Pantagruel* (1532–1564), the Abbey of Thélème is an anti-monastery for those who wish to live as they will.

The historians of the Renaissance are agreed in seeing in Leon Battista Alberti[8] one of the most typical personages of the movement in its beginnings. Jacob Burckhardt,[9] who is still an authority, has qualified him as a 'universal giant'. Universal is precise, giant is excessive. The giant of the Renaissance would be Leonardo da Vinci, who would astonish the world fifty years later, or it would be Michelangelo. Leon Battista Alberti is an initial sketch of these supermen, but he is already, certainly, a very great man. He did not belong to the true nobility, he was of simple patrician origin, born in a family of merchants. In that too he is typical. One sees, towards the end of the Middle Ages, first in Italy, then in the rest of Europe, the barriers that separate the classes bending, the castes getting mixed, equality achieving progress. The Albertis had been very rich but the generation before Leon Battista had experienced great reversals. Leon Battista himself had been born in exile in Venice, but when an edict issued in 1428 allowed him to return to Florence, he hastened to benefit from it. Within the Florentine ambiance, admirably appropriate to his talents and his tastes, he felt perfectly at ease. Equally and harmoniously given to the works of the mind and to the exercices of the body, he rode, practised fencing and relaxed writing books. He expressed himself with the same ease and elegance in Latin and in Italian. Although he remained a bachelor, he published a book on the family, where the ideal of the Renaissance, or the balance of the body and the mind, is encouraged with a force of persuasion that will not be surpassed. The German historian Voigt[10] highlights in the precepts of Alberti 'strong traces of the Hellenic

---

8   Leon Battista Alberti (1404–1472) was an Italian humanist author and architect.

9   Jacob Burckhardt (1818–1897) was a Swiss art historian whose most famous works are *Die Kultur der Renaissance in Italien* (1860, 'The Culture of the Renaissance in Italy') and *Die Geschichte der Renaissance in Italien* (1867, 'The History of the Renaissance in Italy').

10 Georg Voigt (1827–1891) was, like Burckhardt, a historian of the Italian Renaissance and his most famous work is *Die Wiederbelebung des classischen Alterthums oder das erste Jahrhundert des Humanismus* (1859, 'The Revival of Classical Antiquity or the First Century of Humanism').

kalokagathia'. And that is precise. Leon Battista Alberti, to be frank, does not advance very far in the many furrows that he digs but how would this mathematician who was also a jurist, this moralist who was also a painter, a sculptor, an orator and a physician, have been able to treat deeply all the subjects that he took on? He was a genius but diffuse. It is perhaps in architecture that he created his most striking work: the Rucellai Palace in Florence. A believer and Catholic, he undertook the defence of Christianity against the strong minds that were beginning to smash it, but his true religion was beauty. He was seen crying emotionally before the adorable sites that form in Florence a girdle worthy of it. Magnanimous and generous, he left to the public the earnings that he derived from his inventions. Of a slightly imaginative temperament, sometimes cheerful and sometimes taciturn, he embodied the 'artistic temperament' such as the modern times know it. He liked glory, like all the great men of the Renaissance, who were also very proud men. He extolled energy, which is not a less certain index of the new era that humanity had just entered. He had taken as his motto: 'What man wants he can do'. And, as for himself, he could do almost everything that he wanted.

*

The Renaissance produced a particular type: the humanist. Humanism is the special turn of mind produced among the Italians, at the dawn of the modern age, through the contact with Latin and Greek letters. Humanism was, like the Renaissance itself, a liberating movement. It was a question of escaping the despotism of the theologians and, for that, people allowed themselves be dominated, dazzled, almost enslaved by the writings of the ancients, extracted in the dust of the libraries. Florence was the nursery *par excellence* of the humanists. A powerful dynasty of leading merchants, the Medici, set the model there for the love of letters and the arts, but the humanists did not delay either in finding their path to Rome, where prospects that were no less alluring were presented. And one sees the strange phenomenon of the pontifical court opening all its great doors to these unbelieving humanists, Florentines and others, who boasted of their unbelief. The papacy was from this time in decline. Outside Italy, even in Italy, the spiritual primacy of the successors of St. Peter was contested. Thanks to the support lent by some of them to the humanists, the Vatican regained some prestige. And what Christian dogma no longer gave it the renown of men of letters attached to the pontifical court rendered to it, at least temporarily, but to the detriment of Christianity itself, and this cannot be doubted. One could say with reason that humanism played the role of a serpent within the bosom of the papacy. A day came, besides, when the Popes, after having offered ample sacrifices to fashion, took a step backwards. The death of Leo X and the sack of Rome[11] had to sound the death knell of the humanist adventure at the pontifical court.

With what despair has a Paolo Giovio[12] affirmed and cursed this decadence: 'The elegant orator', he observes, 'no longer finds the admiration that in the past welcomed his speeches. The occasional talks and the sermons fell low.' When humanism flourished in the shadow of the popes, what beauty, by contrast, in the funeral orations that were pronounced by men trained by the best masters! Now (it is still Paolo Giovio who speaks) the funeral discourses are too often pronounced by 'monkeys dressed in mourning clothes who dishonour the Christian pulpit.' One is justified in wondering if the humanists themselves had not begun by compromising religious eloquence. Assuredly, they spoke well and wrote in a pure style. Their harangues, composed on the model of Cicero and Quintilian, respected the rules. They were stuffed with quotes, borrowed, besides, from profane authors. They sinned in their heaviness and pedantism. And they were made on every occasion, thus out of context. The least bishop, the least

---

11 Rome was captured by Charles V, Holy Roman Emperor, on 6 May 1527, and this was followed by a looting of the city by foreign and Italian mercenaries.

12 Paolo Giovio (1483–1552) was an Italian historian noted for his records of contemporary history and biographies.

ambassador was received at the Vatican with torrents unleashed with an eloquence that was brilliantly worldly. The humanists attached to the pontifical court prided themselves on treating all subjects, on fashioning an oratorial style on no matter what, on no matter whom. Now secular experience shows us that there is nothing more demoralising than a mania of rhetoric cultivated, systematised and industrialised to this point. Gian Francesco Poggio Bracciolini,[13] generally known by the name of the Pogge, was, along with Filelfo and Valla, a perfect model of Italian humanism in its best period. And one is grateful to these scholars for the love that they showed for the poetry of antiquity. The Pogge did much, besides, to save what remained of the ruins of Rome. One day he exploded in rage at the sight of manure displayed on the Capitol and this rage was a fine thing, but his *Facetiae*,[14] simply obscene, throw, on the other hand, a disappointing light on the talk among the employees of the Roman Curia when their work was done. They lacked, to say the least, style and dignity.

All things considered, this Francesco Poggio Bracciolini, called the Pogge, was a great man of letters, but also a great boor. And perhaps he earned the masterly pair of slaps that the Greek Georgios Trapezuntios,[15] whom he had publicly insulted, applied to him during a Homeric dispute. When the humanists were accused of treading on the toes of Christian morality, they responded by celebrating the Stoic morality, which was, according to them, superior. They boasted also of having created and restored, following the rules fixed by the Athenians, the morality or the religion of the code of honour, but it happened that they defied the new morality with the impudence with which they defied Christianity in the high seat of St. Peter. This same

---

13 Gian Francesco Poggio Bracciolini (1380–1459) was an Italian humanist who was responsible for the discovery of several important works of Latin antiquity.

14 *Facetiae* was a collection of obscene jokes published by Bracciolini in 1470.

15 Georgios Trapezuntios (1395–1484) was a Greek scholar and philosopher who came to Italy from the Byzantine Empire just before the Fall of Constantinople and discovered and translated several classical Greek works.

Pogge, who had received priesthood even though he did not wish to exercise it, led for a long time a private life that was little edifying. He began by fathering three bastards whom, without the least scruple, he made soldiers, which was an elegant way of sending them to their death. Then, having fallen in love with a certain Lucia, he had by her twelve boys and two girls. In fact, at 55, he finally married and, proud of becoming legal, he announced his decision to Cardinal Consalvi, who was interested in him, in a letter full of the cynicism typical of the age: 'God granted me his grace when I erred outside the right path. Now that I have re-entered it he will bestow on me his benefits with a more liberal hand.' Poggio, really, did not have any doubts. Or rather, he must have doubted everything to bring God into the scene in such a scandalous situation. The Renaissance was a prodigious era, a torrential outburst but also, sometimes, a volcano of sparkling mud. And one would not paint this era in the right light if one were silent about all the mediocrity that it retained in some of its most brilliant sons.

Humanism, however, had begun very well with Petrarch and the rapid decadence of his school must not prevent one from rendering a just homage to its founder. Even though he was born at the dawn of the fourteenth century, to be precise in 1304, Petrarch had through his genius gone ahead of his time and even his immediate successors. He was, properly speaking, the first modern man. Precursors are rarely favoured in this way. A sombre anguish before the infinity of deciphered enigmas generally constitutes the price paid by innovators and reformers. Petrarch did not escape this fate, and his Latin dialogue *De secreto conflictu curarum mearum*,[16] attests to the entire extent of his distress. The force of the Middle Ages restrains him, the radiance of the prefigured Renaissance attracts him. Courageously he rejects the past and throws himself into the future, but at the cost of all sorts of torments. Ah! How far he is from the indifference and euphoria

---

16 *The Secret Conflict of my Cares* is a trilogy of dialogues written by Petrarch between 1347 to 1353 about free will and faith, inspired by the works of St. Augustine.

the spectacle of which the humanists were to later offer! He himself traced his mental state; he showed in what proportion there entered in it the love of love (his Platonic feeling for Laura de Noves[17] caused him more pain than joy), a natural melancholy that he calls *acedia*[18], which hardly any longer resembles the Christian contrition of the sinner in the Middle Ages, and finally this need of glory by which he is devoured and whence arises this excess of the self which was to be the distinctive mark of all these powerful initiators of the Renaissance.

Reading Petrarch, one is struck by the already perfect form that this humanism takes in him, which his successors restricted themselves to exploiting and to sometimes compromising. At first, Petrarch chooses well his ancient models: Cicero for his style, Virgil for his poetry, Seneca for his morality. Among the Greeks, he disdains Aristotle and places Plato on a pedestal, causing in this way, as the first, a breach in the edifice of scholasticism that will not be repaired. In his historical writings he does not appear as more than a vulgar compiler in the manner of the chroniclers of the Middle Ages. He draws only from pure sources. He already practises textual criticism. His style is natural but personal; it is not the conventional language of historiographers, his forerunners and his contemporaries. Even though he wrote in Latin and he counted on his Latin works to gain immortality, he reveals a very lively awareness of the Italianness of everything that he represents. His is the glory of having been the first nationalist author. While Dante was still only a Florentine, he is already Italian. It is in this spirit that he reconnects with the Latin tradition and serves his cause by showing all that there is of humanism, consequently, all that is useful for the moderns in the ancient authors. A poet of a sensitive soul, he is moved gently, like Leon Battista Alberti, by the beauty of the external world. He clears the path for the alpinists by climbing,

---

17 Laura de Noves (1310–1348) was the wife of Count Hugues de Sade and may have been the original of the 'Laura' whom Petrarch constantly refers to as the object of his Platonic love.

18 Listlessness, indifference.

as the first, Mt. Ventoux on 21 April 1336. A genius and ambitious, he collects the laurels that he wanted. In a ceremony renewed from antiquity, which filled his old heart with a gentle intoxication, he was crowned poet at the Capitol in 1341. An august ceremony that marks a date in the history of civilisation when one can rightly celebrate the birth of the *Rinascimento*. An enemy of superstition, he delivers rough blows to astrology, that science of the stars that was at that time honoured, and to which the sovereign intelligence of a Goethe was, we may note in passing, to render homage again centuries later, but, in the face of the humanists, his disciples and his emulators, Petrarch remained faithful to Christianity: 'Why', he asked, 'would I not, as a Catholic, share in a hope that I encounter among the pagans?' Let us guard in our memory the image of Petrarch, prince of the humanists and the first among them. And let us lament that his posterity did not resemble him more closely.

*

The enthusiasm of the men of the Renaissance for pagan civilisations and the zeal with which they sought to have the customs of antiquity revived was to be inexorably translated into a weakening of the Christian religion. Perhaps the historians who claim to be free thinkers have exaggerated the impiety of the *Rinascimento*. But this impiety is not less striking for all that. Already Boccaccio affirmed it, rejoiced in it, and justified the progress of irreligion with this sophistry: 'It was a completely different affair when the primitive Church still had to defend itself against the pagans, but today, thanks to Jesus Christ, the true religion is strong and powerful, paganism is destroyed, the Church

victorious. One can therefore study paganism without danger and revive it.' Boccaccio spoke of it with ease. And if there had been only Epicureans like him to maintain the Christian faith, it would have been threatened very strongly. Narrators, poets, dramatic authors competed in scepticism and sometimes atheism pure and simple.

Luigi Pulci,[19] the famous author of *Morgante Maggiore*,[20] speaks in these terms of the soul and the place that it occupies: 'It is fully in the body like a candied grape in a very hot white bread or grilled food in a split bread. And one who thinks anything else has his head backwards.' All the Florentines, all the Italians of the Renaissance, did not profess ideas so basic. There were simple citizens and honest humanists 'who were tormented by the infinite' in spite of themselves. There were others who, even while pretending to believe in nothing during their fine years, began, with the approach of old age, to fear eternal damnation and take some precautions, but the general tendency at that time was indeed the forgetting of Christianity in favour of a return to the gods of Olympus. Without any malice, and utterly naturally, Paul Jove called the cardinals *senatores* and the carnival *lupercalia*.[21] Another humanist, Jovianus Pontanus,[22] called a saint *divus*[23] and confused the genii of paganism with the Christian angels. Popes imprudently favoured this confusion and the clergy followed their example. When Sicione[24] suffered the rigours of a siege, the canon Tizio dug up a formula of Macrobius[25] and, after having celebrated a mass, cast against the enemies an anathema of a rigorously classical style With the exception that, instead of saying '*Tellus mater teque Jupiter obtestor*',[26] he pronounced '*Tellus, teque Christe deus obtestor*'.

---

19   Luigi Pulci (1432–1484) was a Florentine poet and diplomat.

20   A parodistic epic poem about a giant converted to Christianity by Orlando (Roland).

21   A purificatory festival celebrated every February in ancient Rome and dedicated to Lupercus, a god of wild animals, including the wolf that suckled Romulus and Remus.

22   Giovanni Pontano (1426–1523) was a humanist poet and essayist.

23   A divine being.

24   Sikyon was a Greek city in the northern Peloponnesus.

25   Macrobius (fifth century A.D.) was a Roman author noted for his Neoplatonic *Commentarii* on Cicero's *Somnium Scipionis* ('Dream of Scipio') and *Saturnalia*, a study of ancient Roman religion.

26   From Macrobius, *Saturnalia,* Bk. III, Ch. 9.

Parallel to this disastrous current which threatened to sweep away the entire Christian civilisation, to the irreparable disadvantage of humanity, one distinguishes, however, if one should pore over these great Italian centuries with love, a spiritual and Christian current. Less apparent than the other, it successfully combated the harmful influence. And, all things considered, one can affirm that it did not contribute less to the greatness of this 'Renaissance man', whose complex physiognomy, variable through the years and places, I seek to determine.

I do not think that the monk Savonarola,[27] who intervened energetically in Florence when the scandal went beyond the limits, rendered eminent service to the cause that he defended. He opposes to detestable excesses ridiculous excesses. Can one agree with him when he writes that the sole merit of Plato and Aristotle consisted in enunciating arguments that could be used in the war against heretics? Besides, he added, Plato and Aristotle 'are certaingly trembling in Hell.' He condemned science, philosophy, the fine arts, everything that had been the soul of the Renaissance and everything that had enchanted his contemporaries. In this way he went against his century too much to be able to dominate it for a long time. His success was ephemeral. But one meets, beside Savonarola, great minds, less intransigent, who, while remaining within the general line of the *Rinascimento*, deplored the 'transvaluation of moral values' that he accomplished in a brutal manner and that he pushed too logically to its extreme. These well-advised innovators forced themselves to reconcile, harmonise the ancient spirit and the spirit of the day. The influence of Plato was, in this respect, singularly beneficent. And we know of the cult that was dedicated to him by the most visible humanists of the Renaissance. Whatever there is of spirituality in the whole of the literary production of this epoch derives generally from Plato. The Platonic Academy

---

27 Girolamo Savonarola (1452–1498) was a Dominican friar active in Florence who decried the secular Renaissance and sought to reform the Church in a rather proto-Protestant manner.

of Florence[28] was founded in order to study him and understand him as a group. It had set to itself as its programme the reinvigoration of Christianity by Platonising it. A man of the Church, Bessarion,[29] distinguished himself through his zeal. A Platonist, this Greek philosopher did much to Christianise this Greek philosopher. Did he not merit more praise in this than plunging him into Hell, as Savonarola did?

No, the Renaissance was not this unilateral triumph of materialism, atheism and Epicureanism that has been too severely condemned by certain historians who are concerned to justify the Reformation in the name of 'Roman ignominies'. I recalled the errors of the clergy and even of the popes, but the clergy were not more unanimous than the guild of literary figures and artists in the adoration of antiquity in its aspect most opposed to mediaeval asceticism. How many priests, how many monks, protested, following the example of the Dominican Giovanni Domenici,[30] against this too exclusively pagan nourishment with which the educators overwhelmed the youth! Giovanni Domenici reproached the masters, the parents for speaking to the children about Jupiter and Venus 'before instructing them on Jesus Christ and the Holy Spirit'. How many similar testimonies one can cite! It was not at all dead, the little blue flower of Christianity, which was too often trampled underfoot and disdained. It was to undergo new blossomings.

Among those who continued to cultivate it, it is appropriate to cite two Platonists, who are typical and have remained more readable than Bessarion: Marsilio Ficino and Pico della Mirandola. Marsilio Ficino

---

28 The Florentine Academy was sponsored by Cosimo de' Medici (1389–1464) and led by the Neoplatonist Marsilio Ficino (1433–1499).

29 Bessarion (1403–1472) was a Greek humanist and Catholic cardinal bishop who contributed to the revival of ancient learning in the Renaissance.

30 Giovanni Domenici (1355–1419) was a Dominican cardinal who wrote a work on classical studies called *Lucula Noctis* and a pedagogical work, *Regola del governo di cura familiare* ('Rule of Governing Family Care').

wrote a commentary on Lucretius when, in his forty-fourth year, he fell seriously ill. It was in vain that he tried to comfort himself with the pagan philosophers. He did not recover his peace and his health until his return to the faith. Then he threw his commentary on Lucretius into the fire and plunged with all his heart into pious studies.

The case of Pico della Mirandola[31] is less dramatic and less an 'idealised image', but what a testimony in favour of the Renaissance all the activity of this brilliant humanist is! The Italian *quattrocento* produced nothing that does it more honour. Pico della Mirandola first studied, at Bologna, all the languages and all the philosophies with that enthusiasm, with that lack of method, with that sublime dilettantism that is, as it were, a mark of the Renaissance. His erudition was prodigious but did not intoxicate him and did not mislead him at all. Equally versed in Christian theology and in ancient philosophies, he also dreamed of reconciling them. He adored Plato like the best of his contemporaries and strove to discover subtle concordances between Platonism and the Mosaic teachings. Like Petrarch, he combated superstitions, especially astrology. He combated astrology in the name of Christian morality because astrology allowed one to attribute the misdeeds of the individual to the influence of the stars. A scrupulous moralist, Pico della Mirandola defended free will with all his strength taking extreme care of the dignity of the human being. Besides, he made this dignity the object of a magnificent discourse, which is very significant in the Renaissance. Also mediaeval theology belittled the progeny of Adam and Eve, the fallen and cursed creatures. Even while remaining a Catholic, Pico della Mirandola renders to man the place that he really occupies in the universe, at least in the visible universe, namely, the first. Let us cite as an example the page where God, having created Adam in his image, is shown giving freedom to man: 'I have placed you', declares the Almighty to his creature, 'in the centre of the

---

31 Giovanni Pico della Mirandola (1463–1492) was a Renaissance philosopher who wrote several important treatises on Greek and biblical learning. He was also a founder of Christian Kabbalism.

world in order that you may easily cast your glance around you and better see what it contains. By making you a creature that is neither heavenly nor terrestrial nor mortal nor immortal, I wished to give you the power to form yourself and conquer yourself. You can descend to the level of the beast and you can raise yourself to becoming a divine being. When they come into the world, the animals have everything that they need to have. You alone can grow up and develop yourself as you wish, you have in you the seeds of life in all its forms.'

Would not the inestimable benefit of the Renaissance and its precious heritage be the rehabilitation of the body of man and his heart? At this task nobody has worked with more knowledge and with a better conscience than the good humanist Pico della Mirandola. After having loved pleasure very much, perhaps a little too much, he was, like Marsilio Ficino, touched by grace and became quite Christian in fact, after having been that up to then only in hope. When he died, reports one of his biographers, 'he had conserved only that which was strictly necessary in exquisite foods and dishes.' At least one is glad for his sake to learn that he was not absolutely deprived of these.

*

Let us consider now the reverse of the coin: the immorality, the cynicism and even the crimes of certain great personages of the Italian Renaissance. The magnificent literary and artistic flowering of which the peninsula gave evidence during two centuries did not at all result in a general peace that was solidly based but went with a phenomenon that is not unique in history, with a frightful anarchy.

Feudalism was wrecked and the modern society had not yet been formed. There was hardly any other law in force any more than the law of the strongest. In politics as in the fine arts it was the triumph of individualism. Greatness of body and greatness of spirit belonged to the one who knew how to conquer them. The Renaissance is the age par excellence of the *condottieri*,[32] who are often only brigands

---

32 Mercenary captains in the wars of the Middle Ages.

who had reached the highest posts in the state through hard work. The exploits of these tyrants, too willingly divested of all scruples, had nothing edifying about them, but this is indeed the spectacle that Italy of the *quattrocento* offered throughout the peninsula. Machiavelli has enunciated the status of these governments in his famous work. One could observe in defence of the Italy of the Renaissance that this Cesare Borgia who had served as a model to Machiavelli was more Spanish than Italian, but Sigismondo Malatesta[33] — not to mention others — was an authentic Italian and was not worth more morally. The chroniclers of the age used admirable euphemisms to designate these criminals who attained power by way of crimes. The same terms served, besides, for adventurers using the sword and those using the pen, the paintbrush and the chisel: *uomo singolare, uomo unico*.[34] At the supreme degree of success, this wonderful person was the *uomo universale*[35] and people celebrated his *virtù*. It is fitting to note the particular sense in which the Renaissance took this very elastic word. *Virtù* was not at all (oh, no) virtue in the sense in which we understand it; it is a collection of virile qualities, energy, courage, the primacy of the self, the arbitrariness of the unrestrained personality. Stendhal in his *Promenades dans Rome*,[36] Nietzsche in his *Jenseits von Gut und Böse*,[37] have rehabilitated this morality of the adventurers of the Renaissance. It allowed us to foresee that which German National Socialism promotes and Mr. Alfred Rosenberg glorifies in his *Mythus*

---

33 Sigismondo Malatesta (1417–1468) was a nobleman and *condottiero* who became lord of Rimini at the age of fifteen. Amidst his many military adventures he was excommunicated in 1460 for various sins by Pope Pius II and uniquely 'canonised into Hell'.

34 A singular man, a unique man.

35 A universal man.

36 Marie-Henri Beyle ('Stendhal') (1783–1842) published a diary of his Italian journeys in 1829.

37 *Beyond Good and Evil* (1886).

des zwanzigsten Jahrhunderts.[38] However, it has nothing very seductive in a typical person such as Sigismondo Malatesta. The son of Pandolfo Malatesta, Sigismondo lived from 1417 to 1468 and, if he astonished Rimini by his courage and his magnificence, he scandalised this city more by his amorality. At thirteen, he caused a bloody riot, which did not prevent him, besides, from showing already an enlightened taste for the sciences and the arts. He discovered Leon Battista Alberti and overwhelmed Leonardo da Vinci with his beneficence. Fully imbued with the spirit of antiquity, he professed a devotion to Scipio Africanus, whom he revered like an ancestor. He was full of contrasts, without loyalty or law towards his enemies but full of respect for artists and full of comprehension of masterpieces. Infatuated with the beautiful Isotta, he married his mistress in a Christian church. He committed other more shameful mistakes. Rejected by a very beautiful German woman, the legitimate spouse of the lord of Bornona, he attacked her armed, killed her, and enjoyed an ignoble pleasure over her corpse. He even tried to do the same with his own son, but the latter met him with a stab of his dagger and the affair apparently did not continue. This same rogue was, for the rest, capable of sending poems full of tenderness and sweetness to any beautiful woman whom he wished to conquer.

One can say, if not to excuse Malatesta, at least to explain Machiavelli, champion of the *condottieri*, that they limited themselves, in short, to extracting from the existing state of affairs a philosophy in harmony with the facts. A great prince must, according to Machiavelli, possess the following five qualities: compassion, fidelity, humanity, piety and sincerity, but could one expect so many merits of a powerful man? Machiavelli thought that one should not demand the impossible. So he limited himself to asking that the prince give the appearance of possessing all these virtues. Everybody knows the chapter where Machiavelli asks of the shepherd of the people that he

---

38 *Myth of the Twentieth Century* (1930).

guard at once the lion and the fox, or else everything would go wrong. And, certainly, this absence of true principles or even this display of perverse principles attests to a society singularly devoted to the will of violent men and their bad passions.

Machiavelli's prince was only a fictive personage, one does not dare to say an ideal figure. A man who was not, like Malatesta, a political tyrant but a very great artist has marvellously translated in his life and perfectly expressed in his memoirs the strange customs tolerated by the Italian Renaissance: I mean Benvenuto Cellini. Was he greater as an artist or as a miscreant? His works, disseminated throughout Europe, continue to please the eye but the narrative of his authentic life, reported in his *Vita*, continues to disarm the reader with a rare display of ignominies. Cellini was an assassin and not just an occasional assassin, that is to say, a passionate man who commits a murder once by accident under the influence of rage but a customary assassin, a dangerous recidivist, as one would say today, a bandit who premeditated his crimes. His most excusable murder is perhaps that through which he avenged his brother. Cellini struck the murderer with a stab of the dagger 'between the neck bone and the nape.' The blade, directed by an expert hand, penetrated so far that it could not be extracted. Cellini had acted on this occasion from a familial feeling. He could not allege this excuse the day he killed his old enemy Pompeo. This was also a very memorable *fatto di sangue*:[39] 'My hand', he recounted, 'was armed with a little dagger that was well sharpened, then I crossed, in a bound, the line of assassins and I seized my swindler by the neck with so much speed and sang-froid that none of those who surrounded him could help him.' Cellini struck his victim twice on the face. On the second blow, Pompeo fell dead. Two blows of a stiletto on the face! Cellini does not for all that maintain less that he did not have the intention to kill, 'but', he explains, 'one does not measure one's blows.' If Pompeo died, it was thus his fault. On another

---

39 Bloody deed.

occasion, in France, Benvenuto Cellini measured his molestation more carefully and contented himself — how wisely! — with a semi-vengeance. With the aid of long and solid dagger ('I have always had', he observes, 'a taste for fine weapons') he pierced 'a wicked rogue who took him to court in his legs and arms' so well that he rendered him impotent for life. Thus it was a great error to provoke Benvenuto Cellini, such a great artist, a man of so much *virtù*! (Cellini constantly uses this word.) It was the heavens, nothing more and nothing less, that had directed the arm armed with the fine dagger on that day. As proof the sentence with which the illustrious goldsmith terminates his history of assassinations: 'Giving thanks to God for that, as for all things, I hoped to live some time without being disturbed.'

Cellini also believes in God and it is this that distinguishes him from the impious ones, so numerous among the people of this age. When Cellini proceeds to the casting of his famous Perseus, he kneels, invokes the heavens when the melting of the metal proceeds: 'Oh my God,' he murmurs, 'my God who was resurrected from the dead by the Almighty to mount gloriously to heaven!'

When the operation is completed and successful, he kneels again, 'thanking God with all the effusion of his heart.' Pride, which is such a sharp sentiment among the great men of the Renaissance, this exaltation of the liberated personality which distinguished Petrarch already, took in Benvenuto Cellini immoderate, criminal proportions. He believes in God, but treats him on a footing of equality, or near equality. There is no doubt that to a genius of his stature everything is permitted. Did he not, besides, find a pope[40] for himself who abounded in this sentiment and encouraged him in his casual manner? When Benvenuto committed another crime, the Holy Father showed a strong irritation against him. He was even about to reprimand the guilty man severely when Benvenuto, skilled in managing effects, showed him suddenly the magnificent sculpture at which he was at that moment

---

40 Pope Paul III (1468–1549).

working. The pope, dazzled, did not have the courage to blame such a great artist. Turning to the accusers of the brilliant goldsmith, he told them: 'Know that men who are unique in their profession should not be subjected to the law and Benvenuto is one of these men.' A singular age when a masterwork causes everything to be pardoned by the head of the Church.

The Middle Ages held the great artists in mediocre esteem. The admirable monuments that they erected are mostly anonymous. Moving from one extreme to another, as it often happens, the Renaissance exalted and adored the original and powerful artist. And Cellini thinks that that goes without saying. It even seems to him quite natural that God overwhelms him with exceptional honours in spite of his crimes: 'I do not wish to be silent', he writes, 'about the most marvellous thing that ever happened to a mortal. I have to report it to prove that God has deemed me worthy of receiving his secrets. Since that vision of which I spoke, there remained over my head — a miracle — a halo that all those to whom I wished to show it perfectly clearly saw.' One has accused Cellini, like Machiavelli, of being reckless, but this recklessness is part of the consciousness of the new man, the modern man, who emerged from the astonishing mixture of gold and mud of which the Italian *Rinascimento* is formed.

Only one is wrong (I still insist on it) in thinking that the mud overcame the pure gold. I have shown this already through the example of Petrarch, Leon Battista Alberti, Pico della Mirandola. How much do the life and the entire moral personality of a Leonardo da Vinci too argue in favour of my thesis! In many respects, especially in the admirable balance of his body and his soul, Leonardo da Vinci recalls Leon Battista Alberti, but, born fifty years after him (1452–1519), he incarnates the Renaissance at the apex of its power, at the apogee of its empire over human beings. Leonardo was physically remarkably handsome and remarkably strong. Besides, according to Paolo Giove, he was 'of a charming temper, very brilliant, completely liberal.' A testimony confirmed by Vasari[41] himself: 'Without speaking of the beauty of his body', he wrote, 'which cannot be praised too much, he brought to each of his acts a grace more than infinite.' And Vasari, after having observed that, since his death, his glory has grown greater, concludes in these terms: 'Truly admirable and heavenly was Leonardo, son of Piero da Vinci.' A veil of mystery still surrounds his life. Among the men of his time, he appears like a sort of magus, like a prophet, who was also a scholar. Bent over his retorts and crucibles, he appears like a scientist. Wielding the paintbrush with the genius that we are familiar with, he appears like an incomparable artist. In him are combined these two inclinations of the human mind that were claimed to exclude each other: a robust curiosity and an aesthetic feeling beyond compare.

He was a great engineer and a great physicist. He dreamed of tunnelling through mountains to allow people to communicate more easily; he anticipated aviation. The taste for antiquity, which one learned at that time through the written word, was combined in him with a singular inspiration which was that obedience to Nature of which Jean-Jacques Rousseau was to make a religion — one that is suspect, besides. Leonardo was, in this respect, a prelude to Rabelais. And, because he adored Nature, he wanted to extract all its secrets from it. Scholasticism had made of science a tangle of divine mysteries; it had accurately determined the number of the celestial spheres that cover the face of God from mortals. For Leonardo, science is a mystery, no doubt, but a mystery that man can penetrate through experimentation. A hundred years before Galilei, a long time before Bacon and Descartes, Leonardo da Vinci lay the foundations of science such as we know it. Anatomy, optics, botany fascinated him. Did he believe in God? Was he a Christian, strictly Christian? This is less certain. In his religion of Nature, where God is alive and where he sought to

---

41 Giorgio Vasari (1511–1574) was an Italian architect who is renowned for his biographical work *Le vite de' più eccellenti pittori, scultori, e architettori* (1568, 'Lives of the Most Excellent Painters, Sculptors and Architects').

apprehend Him in his multiple aspects, there was a rather modern Pantheism, but he rendered to the Holy Book many significant and categorical homages. Why would he have written in this way if he had thought otherwise? During his life, one could, in Florence and Rome, permit oneself all audacities. It is therefore not through oratory precaution or anything else but that he accepted the Word of God, and we know through an irrefutable document that, when his last hour was come, he confessed his belief in Jesus Christ and died as a disciple of the Lord. The Christian morality that he practised as well as he could, to which in any case he conformed his acts as well as he could, certainly did not have anything ascetic about it. Leonardo loved beauty too much in all its forms to practise mediaeval abstinence. His entire life was a protest against the fear of the body and the contempt for beauty that were considered for a long time as supreme wisdom, but if his morality neglects too much the greatness of sacrifice, it encourages effort. And that is again that in which he was modern. The life of Leonardo da Vinci represents a sustained effort, wonderfully successful and a magnificent model. It would suffice to prove that the great men of the Renaissance perfectly respected what is respectable even while opening up new paths.

Another *uomo unico,* Michelangelo brings forward a similar testimony. To those who defend Aretino[42] by observing that he limited himself, like Cellini, to expressing the spirit of the Renaissance — which is defensible —, one may recall that Michelangelo treated Aretino as a vile reprobate. The Renaissance produced bandits but also how many courageous men who disavowed them and how many men of genius who pushed them into the shade!

*

This great Italian effervescence that changed the face of the European world extended its reformative action into yet another domain, up

---

42 Pietro Aretino (1492–1556) was a satirist and blackmailer who was a notable figure in Renaissance Italian society.

to then reserved to the whims of men: the education assigned to women. This cult of the energy of the human personality, which the Renaissance had made its religion and to a certain degree its idolatry, penetrated the convents and the gynaeceums.[43] Gates that had been too jealously locked were opened. Young girls and women were taught Latin, even Greek, and literature and all the fine arts. Married women were admitted into the associations of men; they were given a say there, to play a visible role there, to parade their beauty and their knowledge. Does not the life at Athens owe a part of its attractiveness to a certain category of Athenians? When the big cities of the Italian peninsula prided themselves on returning to the customs of antiquity, why would they have neglected this pleasant particularity that was so apt to delight the humanists young and old? It is possible that this promiscuity was not always beneficial to morals. There was in Italy, during the Renaissance, a family life as there has always been but it was not always irreproachable. The adultery of the husbands was normal, that of the wives was frequent. And only those purists were offended whose ridiculous intentions are decried by the chronicler Bandello:[44] 'What folly among men to believe that their honour and that of their whole family is attached to the desires of a woman!' Young girls were still held strictly under supervision, but wives disposed of their person very freely, to the great shock of the Nordics, who had remained more chaste and whose business called them to Rome. Women were at that time, in the countries of Northern Europe, very strictly cloistered and supervised. Later, they were to take a striking revenge. Today feminism flourishes especially in the northern countries. And it is indeed in the Latin countries that women delay the most in emancipating themselves.

The history of Italian poetry of the *quattrocento* abounds in heroines free of all prejudices, audacious and virtuous in the manner of

---

43 The women's quarters in a house, counterpart of the 'andron' or men's quarters.
44 Matteo Bandello (1480–1562) was an Italian writer of novellas (*Novelle*, 1554, 1573).

Benvenuto Cellini and Machiavelli. The *virago*[45] was a fashionable type, an admired and even respected type. The Bradamante[46] of Ariosto is a female *condottiero*, drunk with voluptuousness and combats. And one finds her prototype in the real heroines, her contemporaries. It is perhaps Caterina Sforza[47] who served as Ariosto's model. The Venetian Sanudo[48], who dealt with her, treats her as a 'very cruel virago, but of great character.' And certainly she made, as a virago, a very successful career. She had married a certain Girolamo Riario, nephew of Sixtus IV, and lived with him in a castle at Forli, but Girolamo Riario, having provoked some resentments, was attacked in his fortress and stabbed by his enemies. The latter, with a common passion, threw out of the window the entirely naked corpse of their victim with a dagger planted in his throat. Caterina Sforza, an intrepid widow, swore to avenge her husband. After having sustained a siege in the citadel, she emerged at the propitious moment with her soldiers and was fortunate enough to kill all those to whom she owed her widowhood. A second marriage was not less productive of adventures. Once again some conspirators put her husband to death before her eyes. Not less resolute than the first time, she mounted a horse, entered the quarter of her enemies and conducted a massacre there that included even children. A relative peace marked her third marriage. Her third husband, a Medici, contented himself with siring, with Caterina Sforza, the last of the great *condottieri*, Giovanni delle Bande Nere.[49] By all accounts she had overdone it, but women of this temperament and character were not at all rare during the *Rinascimento*.

---

45 A virago was a woman displaying heroic, that is, manly, qualities.
46 Bradamante is a female knight in Ludovico Ariosto's epic *Orlando Furioso* (1516).
47 Caterina Sforza (1463–1509) was the descendant of a family of noble *condottieri*.
48 Marino Sanudo (1466–1536) was a Venetian historian.
49 Giovanni delle Bande Nere (1498–1526) was a *condottiero* in the service of Pope Leo X.

Italy had given the example of the fertile return to antiquity and to Nature. It had presented to Western civilisation this proud gift: the Renaissance man. The other countries followed the movement with more or less rapidity, with more or less slavishness, correcting, retouching according to their mentality the model proposed by Italy. In France, the Renaissance blossomed only in the sixteenth century but immediately assumed a great flourish. It has been maintained that the French architecture of the Renaissance, adding to the general contours that had remained Nordic the graces of Italian ornamentation, was in short only an Indian summer of the French Middle Ages. That is the thesis of the Englishman Walter Pater,[50] I think it is very weak. In any case, the rupture with the Middle Ages is very perceptible in literature: in Ronsard, Rabelais, Montaigne. It has been said of the works of Rabelais that they were the Bible of the Renaissance. Rabelais belongs to the Renaissance through that adoration of Latin and Greek that bursts out in his style and in the turn of his thought itself. Nourished on ancient literature, he wishes that his pupil imitate him in that. He wishes also that this young man demand of the ancients lessons in conduct, good conduct. He wants him to be virtuous, not a *virtuoso* in the Italian manner but rather Stoic and, in fact, little Christian. The morality of Rabelais is already secular morality just as his religion is natural religion. The French seventeenth century was not to accept this heritage in its entirety. It would be the century of Bossuet and Pascal; it would ask of the Holy Scripture and the Church Fathers those lessons of an upright life that Rabelais asked of the ancient authors, but the sixteenth century, among the great French moralists, draws wisdom from quite different sources. In a general way, the French sixteenth century is Rationalist in the manner of those secular monks of the Abbey of Thélème whose convenient motto I recalled above and which provokes in Rabelais this remark: 'Free men, well-born, educated, communicating in honest company, have instinctually

---

50 Walter Pater (1839–1894) was an English essayist famous for his *Studies in the History of the Renaissance* (1873).

a goad that pushes them to virtuous deeds and draws them away from vice.' It is not at all certain that the abbey of Thélème was that virtuous refuge of which Rabelais speaks, but his conviction is absolute. He believes in the supremacy of Reason just as Montaigne, that other son of the Renaissance, did. Montaigne, in spite of his Scepticism and his Epicureanism, has moral aims. He also, if he went to the logical end of his doctrine, would have declared the ancient authors more suited to forming the mind of youth than religious authors. He also replaces the law of God with the law of Nature, prelude to this religion of honour dear to certain contemporary philosophers. What then is the aim of life if not 'to enjoy one's *being* loyally'? Mediaeval monasticism is not less contrary to Montaigne than to the author of *Pantagruel*. Certainly one must love virtue, but virtue in the manner of Montaigne is not of a very difficult praxis, one acquires it, according to him, 'through shaded paths that are grassed with sweet flowers.' This is again the flowery pathway of the Abbey of Thélème. The religion of the declining Middle Ages had turned very fine minds against Christianity. The morality of the men of the Renaissance, even of the best of them, bears the mark of this discredit, which is, besides, regrettable.

For the world to return to Christian ideas it was necessary that humanism reach Germany, acclimatise itself there, develop and finally bear that fruit with a rather coarse peel: the Reformation. The spirit of the Italian Renaissance was introduced into the German lands in the second half of the fifteenth century. Johann Reuchlin[51] is one of its first and most zealous promoters. He realises humanism in the best sense of the word. He really demonstrates in his works that superior human sense that the study of antiquity sheds on the chosen. The Renaissance implanted, acclimatised in Germany should have, it seems, logically entailed this fortunate consequence: the formation of a united Europe. What a different aspect the civilisation on our continent would have assumed if the Christian spirit represented by

---

51 Johann Reuchlin (1455–1522) was a German Catholic scholar who was influenced by Pico della Mirandola's Christian Kabbala.

Roman Catholicism and the spirit of Graeco-Latin antiquity revived by the Renaissance had fused into a superior humanism! The moral unity of Europe would have resulted naturally therefrom. At all times and up to the immediately contemporaneous age, the Germans have been easily inflamed by the great ideas coming from abroad. The enthusiasm of Reuchlin was followed by the enthusiasm of Ulrich von Hutten[52] and so many others! Luther himself began by being infatuated with humanism and, in the novelties that he propagated later, one perceives the persisting trace of his old friendships. When he advised the lukewarm to 'sin strongly', when he displayed his motto: 'One who does not like wine, women and song remains a fool during his life', he revealed, perhaps more than he himself knew, an inveterate attachment to the Epicurean dogmas of the miscreants on the other side of the mountains; but he found that the study of the writers of Greece and Rome soon no longer suffices the thirst for knowing everything, experiencing everything and transforming everything which devours these German humanists. So they added to the study of profane books that of the Holy Scripture. With eyes trained by humanism they read the Gospel and drew from it a new philosophy, a new faith. The discovery of the printing press, which was a Germanic phenomenon, supported their aims. Awakened by Rome, they turned against Rome. Ulrich von Hutten is not less frightened than Luther by the spectacles that the Eternal City offers! 'What you like in Rome', he writes to his friend Crotus Rubianus, 'you will no longer find in Rome.' He enters into contact with Luther but he finds him a little too soft: 'It is with sword in hand', he declares, 'that we will try to reform the world'. And in fact the Lutheran Reformation was nothing but the Renaissance phenomenon transplanted to the Germanic world and adapted to its customs. At the origin of the German Reformation there was indeed the Italian Renaissance with the new or renewed values that it had established. Ulrich von Hutten, who was to reject humanist Italy, this

---

52 Ulrich von Hutten (1488–1523) was a German knight who became a Protestant reformer.

nurse, as Rabelais would have said, 'whose milk had made it vigorous and strong', recognised implicitly the whole extent of his debt when he emitted on 25 December 1518 this *cri de cœur* that has remained famous: '*O saeculum, o literae, juvat vivere!*'[53] The *quattrocento* had spread in the world a ferment that was going to produce, through action and reaction and from cascade to cascade, further miracles. The entire modern world is a tributary of this outburst that pushed an elite of Italians, towards the end of the Middle Ages, to revive Greece and Rome gloriously and, in this invigorated atmosphere, to reanimate the human personality. O the joy of living, the joy in literature and its promises! How sweet and comforting is the shout of thanksgiving emitted by Ulrich von Hutten! After the Dark Ages, in which we tremble and whose confusion constantly offers a vague resemblance to the Middle Ages, will new generations in their turn experience a Renaissance?

---

53   In an autobiographical letter written in 1518 to the Nuremberg councillor Willibald Pirckheimer, Hutten declared, 'O this century, this learning, it is a joy to be alive!'

IV

THE FRENCH GENTLEMAN[1]

THE SIXTEENTH century had been a revolutionary century. It was a question of finishing with the Middle Ages, of striking down what remained of feudalism. In this role, the men of the Renaissance showed themselves ardent and magnificent, hot-headed and fiery to the point of criminality. They had fought with words and the pen. The best writers of this age were polemicists, the best soldiers civil war soldiers. At the dawn of the seventeenth century, the crude operation is finished and the modern age begins. It promises in France to be particularly brilliant. In the superior ranks of the French society, the elite feels a need for cooling down, regularity, order and discipline. The French have always had a charming taste for social life with the spiritual communication that it supposes. They have always delighted in cordial and cheerful conversations, in subtle and spiritual dialogues. The tradition had not been completely lost during the civil strifes; it was revived when the flames of discord were quenched. People had discussed, harangued, preached for a whole century. Conversing for the pleasure of conversing, conversing in which one competes only intellectually, triumphed once again.

The new French society, more precisely the society of Paris, differed very much from the old. Monarchy, consolidated, was about to

---

1 The French term is *honnête homme* ('honest man').

reach its apogee, as an institution, with the king who was to be called the Great King or the Sun King, but the society being formed was already — nobody disputes this any longer today — a society that was strongly influenced by the bourgeois, if it was not already a bourgeois society.

We know the phrase of Saint-Simon[2] on the century of Louis XIV: 'a long reign of the vile bourgeoisie'.[3] For a relic of feudalism, for an uprooted lord who had remained as 'old school' as possible, the monarchy of Louis XIV deserved this shocking qualification. It no longer sufficed to be well-born to make a career in the great occupations, the robed magistracy, in the army even. With the exception of the ambassadorships and the high military commands, all the offices had become accessible to all. Louvois'[4] father was a petty banker, Colbert's[5] a draper, Fléchier's[6] a grocer and Massillon's[7] a provincial notary. All these men, who were about to carry France to its pinnacle, descended, as the inconsolable Saint-Simon again said, 'from some boor from somewhere'. And as for the authors, they were of even more common origin. For a Rochefoucauld, who was a duke and for a Fénelon, who was noble, how many people, as Villon would have said, of low extraction: Molière, Corneille, Racine, Pascal, Boileau, La Bruyère! Education and knowledge began to give access to positions and open all doors.

---

2   Claude-Henri de Rouvroy, duc de Saint-Simon (1760–1825) was a French socialist political thinker.

3   See Saint-Simon, *Mémoires complets et authentiques ... sur le siècle de Louis XIV et de la régence* (1853, 'Complete and Authentic Memoirs ... on the Century of Louis XIV and the Regency').

4   François Michel, marquis de Louvois (1641–1691) was the Minister for War under Louis XIV. His father, Michel Le Tellier, was a lawyer.

5   Jean-Baptiste Colbert (1619–1683) was Minister of State under Louis XIV from 1661.

6   Esprit Fléchier (1632–1710) was Bishop of Nîmes and an eloquent preacher.

7   Jean-Baptiste Massillon (1663 –1742) was Bishop of Clermont and noted for his sermons.

Intellectual superiority, on the other hand, passed slowly from the ranks of the nobility and the clergy into those of the bourgeoisie. Already careers were opened to talent. Money, whose domination was affirmed in conjunction with the progress of the third estate, allowed the common but rich bourgeois to advance their sons. And the king, who possessed from his predecessors, if not from his own experiences, a certain defiance with regard to the nobles showed the weakness (to speak with Saint-Simon) to encourage the bourgeoisie not only in its social ambitions but also in all its aspirations.

It was then that was born this term 'gentleman', as we shall see, because it is in the image of this French seventeenth century, the richest but also the most diversified in its unity of all the centuries in the history of France. The nobleman can perhaps be a gentleman, the gentleman can be a nobleman, but there is no necessary identity between the two terms. There is no longer a need to be a nobleman to be a gentleman, a chivalrous man, an honourable man and especially a great man. Which is not to say that this bourgeoisie in rapid rise did not create some prejudices for itself and did not offer homage to notions as absolute and as arbitrary as those of the preceding centuries. Whereas in Florence a gentleman could devote himself to business without deviating, with what a haughty tone a boorish bourgeois woman represented on stage by Molière would exclaim, reflecting the current opinion: 'There cannot be anything more *merchant-like* than this procedure!'[8] The term gentleman itself, created by bourgeois authors, is sometimes employed in the sense of a noble by writers who wish to ennoble it. Furetière[9] presents in his *Roman bourgeois* a young girl wishing to enter the Church : 'Certainly', he writes, 'the applicant was beautiful and, if she had been born outside the bourgeoisie, I mean if she had been raised in high society, she could have given much love to a gentleman.' Furetière did not at all have, ah no, what one

---

8   Molière, *Les précieuses ridicules*, Act I, Sc. 4.
9   Antoine Furetière (1619–1688) was a French novelist whose *Roman bourgeois* was published in 1666.

calls today a class consciousness. He even pushes a little farther the lack of bourgeois pride. A gentleman, in the sentence that I just cited, means — it is clear — the opposite of bourgeois, thus a gentleman, but among how many authors of the same age do we find the expression 'gentleman' in a totally different sense! I have drawn up a list. Let it suffice for me to cite one example from it. Du Ryer,[10] who had a pretty comedy, *Les Vendanges de Suresne*, staged in 1635, presents on stage a person called Palmedor, a noble but without fortune, who seeks the hand of the daughter of the rich bourgeois Crisène. Doripe, the wife of Crisène, would be flattered by this union, but Crisène, who has some judgement, reveals to his wife all the inconveniences of such an alliance. Wasn't the father of Orasie quite mortified for having wished to 'join the nobility to the bourgeoisie'?:

> And since his son-in-law failed his expectations
> He has been receiving more adventures than rent.
> Gentlemen pity him today
> He is visited only by police sergeants.

'Gentlemen', is this term not taken here in a totally different sense than that given to it by Furetière? The gentlemen who pitied Orasie's father, who was imprudent enough to give his daughter to a high society libertine, can only be bourgeois. Gentlemen, on the contrary, must laugh among themselves of the bad trick played by one of their own on an ambitious merchant who wished to rise above his class. I stop my commentary here. I only wanted to straightaway point to what is fluid in the notion of a gentleman. We shall soon examine that in greater depth.

One place that has been much maligned because it was not understood well, the Hôtel de Rambouillet, has largely contributed to making of French society and the French language in the seventeenth century those masterpieces that are unique in their kind. The

---

10 Pierre du Ryer (1606–1658) was a French dramatist.

marquise of Rambouillet[11] was herself a member of an elite. Mlle. de Montpensier,[12] whose judgements are rather severe, praised her as 'a model of respectability, knowledge, wisdom, gentleness'. She was aided in her role as mistress of the house by her daughter, Julie d'Angenne, recipient of the famous garland, who married that Duke de Montausier praised by all his contemporaries as a perfect gentleman. To better appreciate the pleasant company that met at the Hôtel de Rambouillet one should recall that it was still the society under François I.[13] Of course, this king loved and patronised the fine arts but in his circle what coarseness, what corruption! How instructive, if not edifying, the anecdotes of Brantôme[14] are! A creation like the Hôtel de Rambouillet was not imaginable under the reign of the Valois.[15] The marquise brought together at her home not only the upper crust of the Court, but also of the city, the people of 'polite society' and men of letters. The last conversed with the others, more elevated in rank, on a footing of almost absolute equality, which was a great novelty. It is in this refuge, embellished by the arts, the Muses, and good manners, that the literature of the Grand Siècle[16] flourished, and not at the court of Louis XIV. The Hôtel de Rambouillet was almost as frequently attended by women as by men. Not wishing to be prudish, the female friends of Mme. de Rambouillet nevertheless did not demand less that the talk

---

11 Catherine de Vivonne, marquise de Rambouillet (1588–1665) was an aristocratic hostess who turned the Hôtel de Rambouillet into one of the most important literary salons of seventeenth century France.

12 See the *Mémoires* of Anne-Marie d'Orléans, duchesse de Montpensier (1627–1693).

13 François I (1494–1547) was King of France from 1515 to 1547.

14 Pierre de Bourdeille, Seigneur de Brantôme (1540–1614) was a biographer and author of the *Memoires ... contenans les Anecdotes de la Cour de France, sous les rois Henry II. François II. Henry III. & IV* ('Memoirs ... Containing the Anecdotes of the Court of France, under the Kings Henry II, Francis II, Henry III & IV').

15 The House of Valois ruled France from 1328 to 1589.

16 The Great Century.

maintained in their presence be chaste and decent. They exercised in this direction an influence that is reflected even in the verses of Racine and Corneille. We know that the author of *Le Cid* read his tragedies at the Hôtel de Rambouillet before presenting them on the stage. And he was not alone. The Abbé Cotin,[17] a regular at Rambouillet, also declares: 'Women of quality have polished my manners and cultivated my mind.' Boileau[18] himself needed some lessons from the marquise and her friends. A single example. He had written on the subject of Mathurin Régnier[19] and, to be sure, crudely:

> Would be fortunate if, less bold in his salty verses,
> He had never led his Muses to the [bordello]…[20]

Criticised by the 'society people', who certainly had some connections with the Hôtel de Rambouillet, he modified these somewhat free verses in the following manner:

> Would be fortunate if these discourses, feared by the chaste reader,
> Do not reek of the places frequented by the author,

language that is certainly much more genteel. There had been until then a high barrier between religious morality and the morality of high society. Under the influence of polite society in its beginnings, this distance diminished. Good company banished from the language certain expressions that had been admitted until then, even in the salons, and against which the clergy alone warred. It is in this way that the word 'immodesty' was banished in favour of the word 'obscenity', which Molière uses in his *Critique de l'École des femmes*. One may observe, besides, that through a strange revolution, the word 'obscenity'

---

17 Charles, Abbé Cotin (1604-1681) was the author of several prose and poetical works.
18 Nicolas Boileau-Despréaux (1636–1711) was a French poet and literary critic famous for his *L'Art poétique* (1674) based on Horace's *Ars poetica*.
19 Mathurin Régnier (1573–1613) was a French satirist.
20 See Boileau, *L'Art poétique*, Chant II, 173.

appears today 'stronger' than 'immodesty'. Like books, words have their fate and nothing is more pleasant, we may observe in passing, than the study of these variations.

A word that has remained closely connected to the history of the Hôtel de Rambouillet, the word 'affected',[21] supplies us another example. Originally there was no fault attached to this word immortalised by Molière. He, besides, took care to specify, through the title which he supplied to his play, that the affected women he mocks are only the ridiculous affected women, or the affected who came from an inferior milieu, a provincial milieu, and who copied unsuccessfully the Hôtel de Rambouillet. Molière himself frequented the famous hotel and was very happy there. And the ridiculous affected women would never have had their entry, big or small, at the marquise's. And when Mme. de Rambouillet disappeared and when other salons, less glorious but not less useful to manners, letters and the arts, were created, the same rules prevailed there. Among the latter, the salon of Mme. Cornuel[22] shone brilliantly and Chaulieu,[23] who composed an epitaph for her, said of her, using the expression which we are concerned with:

> One sees at her home incessantly
> The elite of the most gentlefolk.

But the fashion had been set in motion and the salons remained from that time a French institution par excellence. The democratic orthodoxy demands that we regret this. Literature as a whole was in trouble, they say, on account of their predominance. Is this quite certain? I admit that French literature, in its finest age, this classical period of the seventeenth century, has nothing popular and in an age such as ours, when the people alone count, one may see in it an inferiority.

---

21 Précieuse.

22 Anne-Marie Bigot de Cornuel (1605-1694) was the hostess of a famous literary salon in Paris.

23 Guillaume de Chaulieu (1639-1720) was a poet and protégé of the duc de Vendôme.

It is quite evident that Shakespeare in England, Schiller in Germany, speak to the hearts of the masses more strongly than the Frenchmen Racine and Corneille, whom the masses hardly appreciate, but if French literature is this exquisite, refined thing that is *sui generis*, is it not because it was the creation of gentlefolk living in a chosen society and composing for a restricted group of amateurs in their image? It is a curious thing this French literature of the seventeenth century — of which its denigrators have been able to say that it only watered down commonplaces — addressed itself to a small public, an elite public that would have been open to a more rare and nuanced psychology, but the only goal of the authors was at that time to please with ease, and almost mocking this restricted society. They never sought to edify, moralise, reform; that was the work of the clergy. In his intellectual plays, Molière is so fluid that one wonders even today what the exact significance of *Tartuffe* and of *Le Misanthrope* is. To divert pleasant people, make beautiful eyes cry, move sensitive hearts, that was the last word and the sole aim of these masterpieces that entertain us still and still draw tears from us. 'One considers in France only that which pleases, that is the great rule and, so to say, the only one', says La Fontaine in the Preface to his *Fables*. He repeats it in the Preface to *Psyché*. His principal goal was always, he admits, 'to please' and he admits that to succeed in that he considered with the greatest care 'the taste of the century'. To please gentlefolk, to divert gentlefolk — the greatest authors and the finest minds of the seventeenth century did not think that they would be humiliating themselves in recognising that as their goal. For having inspired so many fine works of a pure taste, this Parisian society of the seventeenth century must have itself had some very pleasant qualities and an influential power unlike any other.

*

It is almost impossible, I repeat, to give a unique definition of 'gentleman' that would embrace all the meanings that were attached to this term in the seventeenth century. This term that was used constantly in different periods expressing the ideal of the one who used it. It even changed meaning from one person to another. One could try the same experiment today on the expression 'a wise man'. Wisdom is not the same thing for Peter as it is for Paul. A letter from Corbinelli[24] to Bussy[25] (which Bussy was, besides, only half a gentleman) indicates already what is vague about this formula. On 27 February 1679, Corbinelli wrote these words: 'I cannot tolerate it that one says that such and such a person is a gentleman and that one person understands by this term one thing and another another thing.' Corbinelli continued to request Bussy, arbiter of good style and well versed in fine language, to define for him not only gentleman but also chivalrous man, a good man, an honourable man. A week later, on 16 March 1679, Bussy complied in these terms: 'The gentleman', he replied, 'is a cultivated man who knows how to live; the good man is related to religion; the chivalrous man is a particular quality relating to generosity and frankness; the honourable man is a man of his word and that is related to probity.' Bussy's explanations are not satisfying in all aspects. But as regards the gentleman he was right and indeed said: 'The gentleman was really, at the end of the Grand Siècle, cultivated and pleasant. He was thus the man who, in all circumstances of life, conducted himself properly and did what was appropriate, *quod decet.*'[26] Without being invited by anybody to do so, La Bruyère also tried to define the gentleman, and La Rochefoucauld likewise. The gentleman, in the *Caractères*[27] and the *Maximes*[28] is

---

24 Jean de Corbinelli (1615–1716) was the author of a *Histoire généalogique de la Maison de Gondi*.

25 Roger de Rabutin, comte de Bussy (1618–1693) was a cousin of Madame de Sévigné and the author of a *Histoire amoureuse des Gaules* ('A Love History of the Gauls').

26 That which is proper.

27 Jean de La Bruyère (1645–1696) was a French moralist. His *Caractères* (*Les Caractères ou les moeurs de ce siècle*) ('The Characters or the Customs of this Century') was published in 1688.

28 François, duc de La Rochefoucauld (1613–1680) was a French moralist. His *Maximes* (*Réflexions ou sentences et maximes morales*) was published in 1665.

sometimes the cultivated and pleasant man, sometimes the good man. It is interesting to encounter in the instructions of Louis XIV to his grandson Philippe V, who was leaving for Spain, a sentence where 'clever man' and 'gentleman' are confused in the same praise: 'Have a total belief in the duc d'Harcourt,' writes Louis XIV, 'he is a clever man and a gentleman and will give advice only related to yourself.' In this sentence of the king's, 'gentleman' is certainly taken in the traditional and literal sense of an honourable man. And here is something that does not simplify the problem or help us make our ideas precise.

The gentleman, for Balzac, is one who excels in politeness, propriety and manners. Chapelain[29] makes honourableness and virtue synonyms. Chapelain is supposed to have invented the word 'civility' or at least made it current. Balzac[30] then sponsored this word, ornamenting it with commentaries that are, besides, quite subject to caution. He claims that the Romans with their civility did much better than the Athenians with their Attic ethos. Civility is, besides, for Balzac the essential attribute of the gentleman.

At the very beginning of the seventeenth century, in 1606, Nicot[31] already defined the gentleman as Balzac was to do later: '*Bellus homo, urbanus, civilis*'.[32] This interpretation of the term 'gentleman' in the sense of cultivated man, pleasant in society, and with good manners (without considering his deep morality) is the one that will prevail increasingly as the seventeenth century proceeds. The gentleman of the

---

29 Jean Chapelain (1595–1674) was a poet and founding member of the Académie française.

30 Honoré de Balzac (1799–1850) was a French novelist and dramatist of the 'Realist' school.

31 Jean Nicot de Villemain (1530–1604) was a French diplomat who compiled one of the first French dictionaries, *Thresor de la langue françoyse tant ancienne que moderne* (1606).

32 'A handsome, urbane and civil man'.

end of this period will find in the person of Chevalier de Méré[33] his historiographer, commentator and dialectician. And the subject will seem even so attractive to Méré that he will dedicate to the gentleman a whole series of writings the knowledge of which is important for one who wishes to appreciate the French society under Louis XIV.

Méré, besides, shared at that time the perplexity and the embarrassment that are mine today. This man, so well placed to know what a gentleman is, hesitates and weighs before formulating this judgement: 'It cannot be explained', he confesses, 'in two words'. I think so too! In a dialogue in which 'the knight' and 'the marshal' speak about it, the marshal declares: 'This word almost includes everything but one who would ask me what it is I would find it difficult to answer.' Let us observe in passing this encyclopedic definition of gentility and the analogy that it offers with the interpretation that the Greek moralists made of the *kalokagathia*. Gentility is the virtue that encompasses all the others and presupposes them all and one cannot place anything above it. It is pleasant to see two great centuries communicate through the ages an ideal that is so similar. This definition, when all is said and done, does not suffice the awakened curiosity of Méré. It excites the marshal to seize his subject more closely. The marshal and the knight agree in positing in principle that 'in whatever form gentility presents itself, it is always pleasant and it is in this principally that one may recognise it', but what a circuitous way of reaching this banal conclusion! Gentility or the taste for gentility does not at all generate a taste for concision and this is, when all is said and done, very fortunate. If he had been more restrained, Méré would have taught us less about it.

Let us note already how ephemeral, how fugitive, this ideal of the gentleman was that was typical of the most brilliant period of the French seventeenth century. The gentleman of the eighteenth century

---

33 Antoine Gombaud (chevalier de Méré) (1607–1684) was a French writer who adopted the title of one of his characters called 'Chevalier de Méré'. Two of his most famous works were the essays *L'honnête homme* and *Discours de la vraie honnêteté*.

would be already something quite different. One finds a curious proof of this in the *Dictionnaire de l'Académie française*. The 1694 edition contains a definition of the gentleman which fully disappeared from the new edition published in 1718. And here is the suppressed paragraph: 'Gentleman, besides the definition touched on by the first article and which means the honourable man, the good man, includes also all the pleasant qualities that a man can have in his civil life: *He is a perfect gentleman, one must have many qualities to be a gentleman*. Sometimes one also calls a man in whom one considers only his pleasant qualities and social manners a gentleman. And in this sense gentleman means only a chivalrous man, a man who converses well, of good company'. Is there not a sad confession in the deliberate suppression of this commentary? One wonders if the 'immortals'[34] who decided on it understood all that was painful in this death sentence. Let us at least try to revive this phantom of the past, of a noble past, that nothing will bring back to life. The gentleman, this fossil, is hardly less distant from us in space and time than the Athenian καλός κἀγαθός of the fifth century B.C. The dead pass by increasingly quickly and everything that seems to you to have an elite air about it is increasingly condemned to disappear quickly.

*

One should, before sketching the silhouette of the gentleman according to Méré, at least touch upon a sentence of Faret's[35] book on the same subject: *L'Honnête Homme, ou l'art de plaire à la cour*.[36] This title and the content of the work recall closely the famous treatise of the Italian Baldassare Castiglione on the *Cortegiano*.[37] For Faret, the

---

34 The forty members of the Académie française are called *les immortels*.

35 Nicolas Faret (1596–1646) was one of the first members of the Académie française.

36 The Gentleman, or the art of pleasing at the court. This work of Faret's, inspired by Baldassare Castiglione's *Il Cortegiano* (1528), was published in 1630.

37 'The Courtier'.

gentleman and the courtier are the same. This author published the first edition of his book in 1630, thus thirteen years before Louis XIV, in an age when the term 'gentleman' had not yet assumed the meaning at once so special and so fluid that it was to assume later. Faret does not at all distinguish 'the gentleman' from 'the good man'. In his view, these two expressions 'designate the same thing', which is not at all the case for the more subtle chroniclers and moralists of the second half of the century. Faret intended in writing his treatise to orient the gentleman to the court, to become a courtier in taste and style. With his advice, Faret wished to acquire for the service of the prince efficient men recruited from outside the narrow milieu of the nobility. And this aim was in conformity with the spirit of the age. To these ambitious men, who were burning to rise in rank, Faret gave very wise counsel. His book is, in short, a 'means of rising'; one would say in the slang of today a treatise on 'careerism'. An amusing detail: Faret did not leave to the gentlemen whom he aimed at making courtiers any illusion on the future arena of their adventures. He posits, in fact, that at the court, as everybody knows, 'corruption is almost ubiquitous'. The memory of the Valois was still very alive in the period when Faret composed his work. He would certainly not have spoken in these terms of the court of Louis XIV, where, if there was gallantry, there was style and dignity. Besides, Faret demands of his gentleman, desirous of conquering the court, that he distinguish himself precisely by the purity of his conduct and the integrity of his faith. By showing himself moral in this society that is not very moral he will progress quickly. For this court of France, if it has its defects, does not lack merits. And first of all it is more sensitive than any other to personal qualities: 'One should say frankly', observes Faret, 'that our court has this advantage above all that exist in the world that a gentleman, even if he be born so low as not to dare approach the great except with the submissiveness of a slave, if it happens that he can make them recognise what he is worth, he will see them rival one another in taking pleasure in raising him to their level.' The long century of the vile bourgeoisie thus apparently began before Louis XIV. Such is the conclusion that one draws from a reading of Faret, and no doubt he would not have gone to so much trouble in favour of the bourgeois concerned to make a place for themselves at the court if he had not judged this venture relatively easy. Faret does not write of slipping into the court, of penetrating the court, but of 'throwing oneself' into the court and it does seem, from the context, that this vigorous expression betrays the crux of his thought. Faret proposes to his readers admission to the court as a conquest requiring some efforts. One requires not only intellectual qualities but also physical qualities. Faret observes that 'a good body of good stature, rather medium than too tall, rather thin than too fat', will facilitate one's ascent. It is good to know 'to play the lute and the guitar, to be versed in games of chance'. These allow one to mingle with the great. For example, the gentleman anxious to advance will do well to resist 'the speaking demon'. People speak too much always, especially at the court. It will be suitable to wear fine accoutrements. The more attention one pays to one's dress, the better it will be: 'It is one of the most useful expenses that one makes at the court.' And when the gentleman has succeeded, when he finally is a figure in the retinue of the king, let him avoid pride: 'Let him have a mind strong enough to find himself among his equals and his inferiors without giving evidence of having been surprised by these fumes.' All these counsels speak of good sense and a practical mind but they are of a generality, not to say banality, that does not teach much about the true gentleman, the one of the reign of Louis XIV, the one that Chevalier de Méré took so much trouble to define and fix.

 Who was Chevalier de Méré, whose works we are going to go through and what claims did he have to undertake the 'study of the gentleman'? His claims were numerous and diverse. Méré was the youngest of his family, a family of good ancient nobility, originating in Potou. Having come at a young age to Paris, he established solid friendships there, both in the court and in the city. He had known

Mme. de Maintenon[38] when she was still only Françoise d'Aubigné and had given her excellent counsels, it seems, to 'make a career'. In return, she dazzled him with her natural elegance and her intelligence. The critics who have occupied themselves with Méré, from Sainte-Beuve[39] to Mr. Boudhors,[40] insist on the role that she played with the historian of the gentleman as a model of all decorum. Chevalier de Méré had received a good education, but his instruction was precarious like that of the majority of the gentlemen of his age. While Balzac decided to glorify the Romans, Méré declared that he preferred the Greeks to them, which was not so absurd, but the arguments with which Méré sustained his thesis are of the weakest intelligence. He had taste and some wit though he still did not have much of these, but his knowledge was nil. As he was not rich and he had to live, he gambled for what is called material comforts. And when bad luck pursued him, he did not hesitate to correct his bad fortune through shameful means. In other words, he cheated at gambling. We know that the seventeenth and eighteenth centuries granted cheaters an indulgence that we no longer give them. At least Méré expiated these errors and some others in a repentant old age spent on Poitou territory. He entered life with immense hopes: 'At the age of seventeen', he wrote (in 1624), 'I heard people say, "Here's a young man who is a gentleman, I would like my son to be like him."' That is anonymous praise and therefore suspect, but there are better ones. Méré was particularly proud of a remark made about him by François V, duc de La Rochefoucauld, father of the author of the *Maximes*. Méré, who had the young Pascal as a friend but who had never learnt from him that the self is despicable, reports in these terms the praise of the duc de La Rouchefoucauld: 'He used to say about me that I was the most accomplished young

---

38 Françoise d'Aubigné, Madame de Maintenon (1635–1719) was the mistress of Louis XIV.

39 Charles Augustin Sainte-Beuve (1804–1869) was a French essayist and literary critic.

40 Charles-Henri Boudhors was the editor of the works of Méré.

man of France and that nobody had more wit than me.' For an adolescent, who embarked on the conquest of society with such a brilliant horoscope, Méré did not obtain what he had been promised and what he promised to himself. He consoled himself by forgetting in a quasi-devotion the praise that he had pronounced of Epicurus, the practical application that he had made of his doctrine and the excessive hopes of his youth. He died in a very edifying manner in an austere solitude but very close to God, deploring 'the vicissitudes of the world' and well preserved 'in a keen conviction of the truths of Christianity'. If he had waited for the time of his retirement and his penitence in Poitou to discourse so abundantly on the gentleman of that century, he would have sketched a quite different image of him. It is because he composed in the fullness of his ardour and under the influence of that brilliant society where he spent his leisure (Méré had a friendly relationship with the marquise de Rambouillet and the marquise de Sablé)[41] that his books as a 'social moralist' form such an authentic and pleasant testimony.

In writing on the gentleman, Faret assigned to himself a political aim, Méré a purely social. Sociable as people were in his time and in his milieu. Méré limits himself to setting down in writing his ideal of the high society man. And this is the origin of his *Discours* and as it were its entire substance. There is no doubt a strong portion of fabrication in his portrait of the gentleman, he dreamed him as much as he saw him. A good Frenchman, he makes it known that this gentleman according to his taste is a strictly French specialty and that neither the Italians, nor the Spanish nor the English possess anything similar. A precise affirmation in one sense, imprecise in others. It is perhaps a retort to the proud claims of the Italian authors who, at the beginning of the seventeenth century, still tended to treat all foreigners as barbarians. A spectator dazzled by this civilisation that enters France

---

41 Madeleine de Souvré, marquise de Sablé, (1599–1678) hosted a literary salon in Paris.

in the seventeenth century, Méré claims supremacy in good manners for his country. And his claim seems entirely justified.

Méré thinks that the French language borrowed from the Latin language the expression 'gentleman' but that it expanded its meaning. And this is indeed well perceived. The gentleman, as he conceived him, has as his first attribute that he is a man of leisure. Méré recruits his phalanx of gentlemen from 'among the idlers who do not have a profession though they are not without merits.' And the word 'idler' does not imply any fault for him. The gentleman can be rich or possess just enough to live on, but he should not work to eat, he should not be too 'bureaucratic'. Mr. Colbert was a great minister and a man of great gentility, but he was too bureaucratic, too busy to be a gentleman in the sense in which Méré understood it. The gentleman is not necessarily noble by birth, but he should have received an excellent education and should by himself improve it from day to day. He does not need to be scholarly: 'I have seen people', writes Méré, 'who knew everything that one presents (of morality and philosophy) but who were found to be bad company because they did not know how to live. And I know others who have studied only the world who are received pleasantly everywhere.' The gentleman should above all love the company of those like him. He should especially be pleasant to women. Conversations with women 'are indispensable to perfect oneself in gentility.' The French society is the only one where the close contact between men and women of quality was always the rule. It must continue! Méré's ideas reflect this courteous tradition. His treatises are in large part a recipe for the art of pleasing, in particular women. To please women, to please men, to please the public was really the obsession of the French seventeenth century in its most 'refined' period. And this is one of the reasons why Méré prefers the Athenians to the Romans. What prigs that Scipio Africanus and that Cato of Utica were! Because Socrates was more insinuating than brusque, Méré sets him far above them. Méré, besides, had a very false idea of Socrates, as of other Greeks, and it is not certain that the real Socrates would have seemed worthy to him of the laurel of 'gentleman', but Socrates wanted to please in order to seduce minds and hearts, and nothing more was required for Méré to praise him to the skies.

The gentleman should be benevolent, tolerant, welcoming. We recall the *Lettres Persanes* where Montesquieu shows Parisians being frightened in the company of an Oriental: 'Can one be Persian!' Those Parisians, so keen on their own superiority, were not of good education: 'A gentleman with a broad vision', writes Méré many years before Montesquieu, 'is so little subject to prejudices that, if an Indian of rare merit came to the court of France and he could explain himself, he would not lose any of his merits there.' The real gentleman is, in short, the exact opposite of an egoist. He does not relate things to himself but acts and thinks in relation to others. He acts on this principle that 'felicity is the final goal of things' (there were Epicurean traits, I repeat, in Méré) and that, in order to receive it, one must give it: 'One should not think so much of one's pleasure', writes the knight, 'as of that of the people whom one frequents.' One should have religion, certainly, and even virtue, but on the attitude of the gentleman towards virtue Méré formulates counsels that are peculiar only to him, in their way rather daring and that would not have been approved of, I am afraid, by Bossuet. Virtues, like the rest, according to Méré, must produce 'felicity'. What did he mean by that? Méré is quite explicit: virtues are to be sought only insofar as 'they serve our happiness'. The French seventeenth century was a century of great moralists who were also gentlemen. I doubt that they would have had ideas of virtue that the friend and adviser of Mme. de Maintenon prided himself on. One wonders if the latter must not have, especially when she gained entry into a court that was going to become devout, disapproved somewhat of the extremely light philosophy of her childhood friend. I have not found anything, besides, in the writings of the time that allow one to form a reasonable opinion about it.

There is another quality, or as Méré would say, another virtue, indispensable to the gentleman: naturalness. Méré writes in a formal style, and simplicity does not seem to have been his forte. He does not, however, insist less on all that the gentleman gains by showing a detached air, doing everything as if in play. He even employs, in order to express these ideas, the same words as other authors greater than himself treating the same subject: the gentleman, if one were to believe him, is one who is not overly excited by anything. Méré formulates his thought in this manner: 'It is to be hoped, in order to be pleasant always, that one would excel in everything that suits gentlemen without, however, being too interested in anything, I mean, without doing anything that does not present itself of its own accord and without saying anything that might prove that one wants to assert oneself.' Is the similarity with La Rochefoucauld and La Bruyère not striking?

From a distance, the seventeenth century seems a rather solemn age. One sees the Grand Siècle dominated by Louis XIV, the beribboned, feathered, bewigged monarch. And when the king in his old age fell into piety it was worse still. I wonder to what degree the image that Chevalier de Méré, this dandy, gives of his century is consistent with the reality. Contrary to Faret, he maintains that the ideal fatherland of his gentleman is not the court, it is the 'high society', and he sketches a very eulogistic picture of high society to the detriment of the court. It was necessary, in order to please high society and to be accepted by it, to conform to the code of decorum that Méré has sketched. In other words, if it was necessary to be natural, it was necessary also — let us call a spade a spade — to appear superficial and light. The most original part of Méré's treatises is that wherein he expresses sentiments about this that do not agree at all with ours.

Today we reserve all our esteem for the specialised scholars, men with a single subject and a single specialisation. The seventeenth century, an age of the society and the salon, looked down upon these people and held them at a distance. I have recalled already this generally accepted opinion on the literature of the time of Louis XIV, that it had excelled in commonplaces. This is quite accurate. In this brilliant society, which made and unmade the reputations of authors, people feared boredom. Now, it is true that people who know too many things and cannot help discoursing on them effusively induce monotony and boredom. Méré, always so polite, makes them understand this in a blunt manner. It is true that Julius Caesar, whom he accuses of being boring, was dead when he criticised him, but his criticism is for that reason only more peremptory: 'Caesar', he writes, 'liked to describe his machines of war, even informing us of the names that his soldiers gave them and we willingly let these details pass.' Speak for yourself, sir, and for the people of your century and your class. We are less disgusted and less jaded. There were, besides, even in your time, more profound minds than yours who did not share your prejudices at all. Leibnitz, whom I apologise to for citing in the same breath as you, ranked you 'among those society people who have a lot of wit and mediocre knowledge', but you rightly pride yourself on not knowing anything about it and you were, for the rest, in very good company. I see that one of your contemporaries praised you for having stripped the sciences 'of what is dry and wild in them'. I am sure that this praise, if you knew it, pleased you very much. And how well deserved it is!

The healthiest and most trained minds of the seventeenth century feared beyond everything that which we call erudition. Scholars, they made the contempt of knowledge a profession. Already Montaigne, this wellspring of science, refused to the gentleman the right to know all about it: 'It is indeed true what one says', he wrote, 'that a gentleman is a man who is mixed.' Does he understand by this a man who is a part of all societies or a man with varied knowledge and consequently not deep? I opt for the latter sense, which the contexts seems to confirm. In any case, Montaigne's sentiment accords with that of Méré. The gentleman will be 'in the French manner, a little of everything and nothing at all'. In his masterly edition of Pascal, Mr. Brunschvicg[42] observes, besides, that Boileau also propagated this manner of viewing

---

42 Léon Brunschvicg (1869–1944) was a French philosopher who edited Pascal's *Pensées* in 1904.

things. Down with the specialists and let the poets themselves know how to do other things than rhyme verses!

> Let not verses be your eternal work
> Cultivate your friends, be of good faith.
> It is not much to be pleasant and charming in a book,
> You should also know how to converse and to live.[43]

Molière is also of the same school. Does he not put in Alceste's mouth this advice that he certainly approves of:[44]

> And do not at all leave, no matter how much they insist on it,
> This reputation that you have of a gentleman at the court
> In order to take that of a ridiculous and miserable author
> From the hands of a greedy printer!

That Boileau and Molière, both pure *littérateurs*, reason in this manner is imaginable especially if one keeps in mind the tastes of the century, but that Pascal,[45] a great scholar, a matchless mathematician, also attaches little importance to specialists is something that does not stop astonishing. Pascal, however, did not seek to howl with the wolves. Must we think that the prejudices of Méré regarding the few charms that a society stuck in a single discipline offers were so widespread that they had infused Pascal perhaps in spite of himself? Like so many others, he tried to define the gentleman in his *Pensées*. He hardly speaks of it any differently than Méré. It is not, according to Pascal, pronouncing the eulogy of a man 'to say of him when he enters that he is very skilled, for example, in poetry'. Pascal shares the contempt of Méré for specialists of all sorts, even if they be poets. He does not like to hear it said of such and such a person that he is a good mathematician or an eloquent preacher but indeed 'that he is a gentleman'. And

---

43   *L'Art poétique*, Chant IV.
44   Alceste is the eponymous misanthrope of Molière's play *Le Misanthrope* (1666).
45   Blaise Pascal (1623–1662) was a French mathematician, physicist and philosopher who was a Jansenist.

he adds: 'This universal quality alone pleases me.' This thought is quite naturally close to this text of Méré's: 'To be a scholar is to have read much but to say good things about everything that presents itself and to say them in a pleasant manner is the farthest that the mind can go and is the masterwork of intelligence.' This identity of views regarding the gentleman that is so striking in Pascal and Méré is explained partially by the paradoxical friendship that tied these two authors in their youth. They were to part later, but Pascal, on his entry into society, frequented, as we know, one of the lightest societies and Méré was one of his companions in pleasure. This friendship was prolonged even beyond what would have been natural, and it would not be impossible at all that Méré appeared importantly in the form of the *Provinciales*.[46] This fact is reported throughout by Father Rapin[47] in his memoirs and I know that this is a source subject to caution. However, I transcribe this anecdote. It relates so directly to my subject that I could not but report it, or at least point it out. Pascal, having begun to edit his *Lettres provinciales*, informed Méré about it, whose reputation as a 'good professional mind' made him an approved judge in this sort of thing: 'You have not yet grasped it, my friend,' Méré is said to have told Pascal, after having read his first *Lettres provinciales*, 'as long as you speak only with the grace that fills your letter you will interest only monks and scholars in your disputes. If you wish to draw the attention of gentlemen, you must entertain them.' Persuaded by this speech, Pascal apparently reformulated his work, which became what we know of it. Is Father Rapin's anecdote authentic? One could say in this case that the *Provinciales* are the finest work of Méré, and

---

46 Pascal's *Lettres provinciales* (*Les Provinciales, ou les lettres escrites ... a un provincial*) are a series of letters composed by the author in defence of the Jansenist Antoine Arnauld against the Jesuits.

47 René Rapin (1621–1687) was a French Jesuit whose most noted works are the posthumous *Histoire du jansenisme* and *Mémoires sur l'église, la société, la cour, la ville et le jansénisme* ('Memoirs on the Church, Society, the Court, the City and Jansenism').

significantly. I use this term only to the degree that it helps me to define the gentleman of the seventeenth century, an original combination, seductive too, of innate good taste, acquired refinement, unconscious aestheticism, triumphant reason and unshakeable good sense, but we do not know it yet in all its aspects. Méré shows it to us, I repeat, in its uniquely social, too uniquely social setting. In the whole picture, in the true and the perfect gentleman of the French seventeenth century, there is a moral greatness and loftiness that Méré was not concerned with and that his works hardly give a hint of.

*

He discoursed so long on this subject, and with such a visible pleasure, that one must take his writings — which are very light, but to which he attached great importance — very seriously. Méré ended, rightly, after having examined in all its aspects the problem of 'gentility', by citing some examples of particularly gentle men, in the sense in which he understood it. He did not very felicitously give a body to his ideal and that is why I attach only a relative importance to his 'doctrine'. When he sees in François V de La Rochefoucauld, father of the author of the *Maximes*, the perfect model of the 'great lords, the gentlemen', one is inclined to — if one cannot but — recall the friendship that this person showed to Méré when he was still a young man and the confidence that he professed in his future. The praise that Méré offers to him quite resembles a *quid pro quo,* but when Méré sees in a certain Saint-Surin another paragon of gentility, one less easily agrees, if one takes the trouble to instruct oneself on the subject. This Saint-Surin, whose full name was Henri de la Mothe-Fouquet, Baron of Tonnay-Boutonne and Saint-Surin,[48] was only very relatively, in all respects, gentle. A Protestant, he betrayed the people of his religion without gaining thereby the esteem of the Catholics. He had, writes Mr. Boudhors, a mania for double-dealing and delighted in deceiving everybody with

---

48 Saint-Saurin (1590–1632) was a Huguenot diplomat whom Méré called 'le plus honneste homme de son temps' ('the most honest man of his time').

everybody to such a point that, after having lost all respect in France, he had to seek his death in Holland. His fine manners were not more generally accepted than the rest. Méré himself cites the objection that Mme. Cornuel makes to him; 'I see', she replied to his praises, 'that you mean this Saint-Surin who was such a poseur.' It is very likely that a pretentious gentleman was a false gentleman. Did naturalness not figure in the list of principal qualities given by Méré? Méré does not seem to have been more fortunate in his models of gentlewomen. He considers as the best a certain marquise d'Anguitard, née Anne Arnould de Saint-Simon,[49] whom he counts among the greatest ladies of all time. Now, this marquise d'Anguitard is not less suspect than the other idols of the knight. She was convicted of having publicly accused a very rich nobleman called Gibaud of seducing her daughter and that in the hope of having her married to the wealthy man who had supposedly caused her harm. The Machiavellian plan forged by the marquise d'Anguitard failed. It is also not very fine and one cannot help thinking that Méré chose the object of his admiration quite badly.

A perfect society man, but to the exclusion of all truly superior merit, was Méré. One is not surprised therefore to see that, in his portrait of the gentleman, he ignores two things that are, however, essential: religion and reason. The seventeenth century had the merit and the privilege of dealing directly with both. People placed so much emphasis on reason that it was possible to maintain that it played an excessive role in the literature of the time that was harmful to true poetry. And, on the other hand, nobody or almost nobody doubted in this age what was called the truths of the Christian religion. The distractions of the senses produced deviants as they have always done, but these deviants did not become atheists and old age brought them back almost always contrite and repentant to the foot of the altars. This is the story of all the gentlemen whose obscure or glorious names fill the seventeenth century. It is the spirit itself of this immortal

---

49 Anne Arnould de Saint-Simon was the Protestant wife of Jean Poussard, seigneur d'Anguitard.

literature, of which the sceptic Sainte-Beuve observed that it expresses with a unique force and fervour 'humanity seen in and through Jesus Christ.' Racine, in his petulant youth, did not stop adoring guilty pleasures. He had even paid a heavy tribute to sin, but with what speed he returns, still young, to Christianity and the Church and what care he took to make his son an irreproachable Christian! I reproduce at random, really at random, this passage typical of one of his letters to his son: 'Remember that one cannot be a gentleman without paying all one's debts first to God and then to men and there is only religion that teaches us the methods and helps us to satisfy both men and God.' Méré naturally demands — it goes without saying — that his gentleman practice religion, that he bring to it even a certain ostentation, but it was for society, it was for the gallery. There was nothing of the anguish of his friend Pascal in the rituals to which the gentleman in Méré's style yielded. The real concerns with which the life of the knight was filled were not of a very Christian sort. And one could say that Bossuet refutes precisely Méré and his temporal gospel of decorum in the numerous places where he fulminates against the society people: 'As the society people', says Bossuet, 'always dissipated, do not know the efficacy of this peaceful and inner action which occupies the soul in itself, they do not think that they act if they are not agitated, or move if they do not make some noise.' Méré thought he had to write that 'gentility [in the sense in which he understands it] is not useless in salvation, it contributes to it very much.' Bossuet, in what can be called his Philippics[50] against the society people, takes exactly the opposite view of this opinion: 'The society people', he would say of Méré and those who resemble him, 'lie to God and lie to themselves in claiming to conduct side by side a life of pleasure and true piety. These two things exclude each other absolutely.' Bossuet does not stop denouncing the vanity of the dissipations that fill the life of Chevalier de Méré and his kind: 'Is it', he asks bluntly, 'worth the trouble to

---

50 The *Philippics* are the series of speeches made by Cicero against Mark Anthony.

damn oneself?' If all the intellectuals of the seventeenth century do not share the sombre fervour of Bossuet, they still show themselves greatly influenced by it, all of them. There is certainly in the authentic gentleman of the seventeenth century more religion, I would gladly say more piety, than the pleasant verbiage of our gallant knight would make one suppose.

There is also more reason, more healthy and true reason. How reasonable was the gentleman of the time of Molière and La Fontaine, de la Bruyère and even this Corneille, whose sublime should not fool one! The coryphaei[51] of the Revolution divinised reason and adored it under the features of a character of the Comédie française that one paraded on the streets pleasantly unclothed, but the gentlemen of seventeenth century merely bore the image of reason in their hearts, honoured it through their acts, and served it through their writings when their vocation was to write.

The Middle Ages had encouraged asceticism and mysticism. The sixteenth century had broken with these traditions brutally, glorified and discovered the individual and Nature, celebrated energy, even disordered. The French seventeenth century harmonised these two extremes. Between the purely pious ideal of the Middle Ages and the sometimes impious naturalism of the Renaissance it re-established a balance. Hierarchy, order, measure, good taste, such could be the watchwords of the seventeenth century, but reason seemed finer to it than all the rest. The *Discours de la Méthode*[52] is an apology for reason conceived as the only instrument in which man can have confidence to penetrate the mystery of the creation. That indeed was the thought of Descartes. And as for Malebranche,[53] he went so far as to discover in reason the image of God itself. Reason! Perhaps this great century loved it too much. At least some fine minds reproached it for this.

---

51 Leaders, originally of the chorus in ancient Greek dramas.

52 Descartes' philosophical treatise published in 1637.

53 Nicolas Malebranche (1638–1715) was a French rationalist philosopher.

And really, when Malherbe[54] takes pride for having the death of his two children for a reason he exaggerates somewhat: 'And twice reason made me resolve well that I should no longer remember it', but, on the other hand, what a greatness almost reaching the sublime in good sense, common sense, in reason to this degree: 'Therefore love reason', Boileau would say. And one is not at all surprised to find this advice in him, but Corneille, I repeat, the heroic Corneille, also claims to place reason above everything or at least reconcile it with the moral heights in which he was wont to hover. Romanticism, such as flourished among the Spanish, for example, which Corneille relished greatly, hardly finds a place in his best works and one encounters in the *Place Royale*[55] these significant verses:

> We should never nourish love that does not yield to us,
> I hate it if it forces me and I wish
> That all my vows depend on my will.

Emperor Augustus would exclaim in a burst of exaltation: 'I am the master of myself as of the universe'. And Molière, always a little down to earth, makes one of his characters say: 'Perfect reason shuns all extremes — and wishes that one be wise with sobriety.' The masterpiece of Mme. de Lafayette,[56] *La Princesse de Clèves*, is fully infused with the same doctrine, the ideal of the true gentlemen of the age. The Princess of Clèves is almost a saint by virtue of being a gentlewoman. All her words, her acts betray what one should indeed call that 'ideal of reason', the last word in wisdom. And her husband, who was not less a gentleman than she was a gentlewoman, indeed pronounces one of those sentences that reveal the profound aspirations of an age when he declares to her after having discovered her love for another: 'I wish to confide only in you. In the mood in which you are, by allowing you

---

54   François de Malherbe (1555–1628) was a French poet of the Classicist school.
55   *La Place royale* was a comedy written by Corneille in 1634.
56   Marie-Madeleine, comtesse de La Fayette (1634–1693) was a novelist whose most famous work is *La Princesse de Clèves* (1678).

your liberty, I set stricter restrictions than I could have imposed on you.' There is something magnificent, I affirm at the risk of repeating myself, in this poise and in the moral health that it attests to. And such words are so much more significant in that they are addressed to a woman, a creature supposedly fickle and about whom one risks sometimes deceiving oneself by giving her too much credit, at least according to the sentiments of the dramatic authors and novelists. One believes generally that this novel, of which the protagonists are Mr. de Nemours and the Princess of Clèves, reflects a real story that may have had as its principal characters Mme. de Lafayette and the duc de la Rochefoucauld. One cannot in any case imagine a worthier meeting of fine people and fine souls. Nothing is more 'classical' than the conception of life in general, and of love in particular, that emerges from *La Princesse de Clèves*. And in this pure ideal what moral superiority to the sensational and subversive novelties that Romanticism was to set in fashion two centuries later!

*

Yes, it is in the great writers of the Grand Siècle, in their works and even in their life, so singularly consistent if one examines them closely, that I derive the notion that seems to me the most correct of a gentleman and of gentlefolk. Corneille had nothing of the gentleman in the strictly society sense that Chevalier de Méré gives to this term. But does he not have anything of the gentleman in the larger and higher sense that is also associated with this term in the seventeenth century? If he lacked a little tact in relation to his contemporaries, he had probity, generosity and heart to offer. Modest, he left his laurels, according to Racine, 'at the doors of the Académie' and above all he 'did not pride himself on anything', following the advice preached by all those who depicted a gentleman. He himself held the ideal of the gentleman in high esteem and avowedly aimed at making his characters speak 'as gentlemen and not as actors'. Writers did not constitute in the seventeenth century that state within the state that they founded later and that they have striven to maintain since that time. There is no claim to being a 'high priest' among the best authors of the great age, but a praiseworthy concern to live as gentlemen among gentlemen. Saint-Simon no doubt thinks of offering a lively eulogy to Racine and saying the best that he could when he observes: 'Nothing of a poet in his trade and all of a gentleman.' Saint-Simon was to write one day of the same Jean Racine: 'Everything in him, finally, was typical of the good man', which signified certainly something still more elevated.

Molière, who produced in his dramatic works such an advanced depiction of the customs of his time, dealt many times with what I shall call the subject of the gentleman. The play that could pass as his masterpiece, the *Misanthrope*, shows the gentleman of the seventeenth century in his two aspects taken to the extreme: the society man or courtier and the good man. If one reads the *Misanthrope* immediately after the works of Méré, one cannot but be struck by the resemblance of Philinte[57] to the society ideal formulated by the knight. Along with Philinte, Méré would have applauded the poor sonnet of Oronte. According to Méré, a man of good company had to observe such a conduct, but I am inclined to think that Molière personally reserved all his sympathy for the blunt and veracious Alceste. The model for Alceste is the duc de Montausier, who married Julie d'Angennes, daughter of the marquise de Rambouillet. Montausier considered himself so flattered by the character that Molière had sketched of him that he embraced him, as we know, at the première of the show to thank him. It has been maintained that Molière targeted Jansenism in the depiction that he presented of the rigorism of Alceste. This is not certain, but the tenderness of the dramaturge and his respect for this austere and sour character seem evident to me. From the moral point of view, Molière placed Alceste above Philinte and perhaps there is in fact, as has also been maintained, something of his

---

57 Philinte is a character in Molière's *Le Misanthrope* who has a tendency to forgive the faults of his acquaintances.

personal experiences with la Béjart[58] in the quarrel that sets Alceste and Célimène against each other on the boards. A playwright, and a playwright in an age when the theatrical people were held in low esteem, Molière strongly resented the mixed dealings to which his trade obliged him, but how superior he was to his milieu and how much of a gentleman and even an honourable man he showed himself in his conflict with la Béjart! Speaking to Chapelle of this conjugal misadventure, which wounded his heart in a deadly way, he did not hide his despair from him and added: 'I made then a resolution to live with her as a gentleman who has a flirtatious wife and is persuaded, no matter what one might say about it, that his reputation does not depend on the bad conduct of his wife.' Does such a declaration not reveal very remarkable and very honourable scruples? Louis XIV, who judged characters very well, was greatly justified in treating Molière as a gentleman. We know that he murmured to him while serving him a wing of his chicken at dinner: 'Here I am busy making Molière eat, whom my officials do not consider to be good enough company for them.' How many Philintes, how many gentlemen of second rank in the king's entourage, and how infuriated he must have been by them! It is besides a trait that honours the monarch that he remained sensitive, in the midst of the flatteries of which he was the object, to the self-respect that Molière and Alceste possessed in common.

La Fontaine belongs to another category. He is a good chap, but one would hesitate to call him straightaway a gentleman. For that one would, in any case, wait for the grand repentance that his old age marked. Was this repentance proper? Assuredly, if one bears in mind the ideal that was that of the age and to which the elite conformed. La Fontaine had written in the full possession of his genius tales full of knowledge, but full also of the licentiousness of the Middle Ages, that of the fables and the *Cent nouvelles nouvelles*.[59] La Fontaine had

---

58 Armande Béjart (1640–1700) was a famous actress and the wife of Molière.
59 A collection of tales supposedly narrated at the fifteenth century court of Philippe le Bon, Duke of Burgundy, and compiled by Antoine de la Sale.

himself led a rather unregulated life. He engaged in his youth in casual love affairs, and even with servants, spending more than his earnings, but the good man was indeed the good man of the century in that he did not include any perversity in his errors. He admitted how wrong he was in comparison to him and that he would have done better to lead another life. How should he have lived? He proclaims it in some charming verses that express so well the rule of this gentleman that he was apparently not that I cannot resist the pleasure of recording them:

> For I have not lived, I followed two tyrants:
> A vain reputation and love have shared my years.
> What is living, Iris? You can teach us that,
> Your reply is ready, I seem to hear it already:
> It is enjoying true wealth in tranquillity,
> Making use of one's time and one's leisure,
> Paying the honours due to the Supreme Being,
> Renouncing Phyllis in favour of one's self.[60]

Clearly La Fontaine had practised a wisdom or a folly that still has the air of the antiquity which had nourished him and of the Renaissance from which Europe was emerging. Naturalism, paganism perhaps, had inspired his life and partially his writings. There is nothing austere, nothing ascetic, nothing Jansenist in the *Fables* any more than in the *Contes*, but the good man was not less a gentleman in his way, after all, and it is really showing much pedantry and rigorism to accuse and criticise his mentality as well as his morality. I admit that in a century when, in spite of the customs of the court, the morals of individuals were generally good, La Fontaine did not precisely offer the best example, but this charming man was of a weak character. And with what sincerity, what spirit he forced himself when he grew old to obtain his redemption!

Méré, who held the duc de La Rochefoucauld, father of the author of the *Maximes*, in such high esteem, seems to have appreciated the

---

60 'Discours en vers', 1684.

author himself less. I would be surprised if the latter did not share this lukewarm attitude. It happens constantly that the author of the *Maximes* discourses on the gentleman in the spirit of the century, since this expression was of such general usage and corresponded so much to the prevalent aspirations, but the noble duke evidently places his ideal much higher than the frivolous knight does. And when he writes for example: 'It is to be really a gentleman to want to be exposed always to the view of gentlemen', one sees Méré shaking his head in disapproval. La Rochefoucauld, a moralist, besides hovers in spheres much higher than those where the spruce author of the *Dialogues* flutters. La Rochefoucauld does not distinguish between the two meanings that were given to the expression in the seventeenth century: the meaning of a man of good company, of a well-bred man, and the meaning of a good and virtuous man. We know that Mme. de Lafayette, who burned with desire for the noble duke, lent several traits of his character to the duc de Nemours. It was not possible to give a more elevated, a grander image of the author of the *Mémoires*. His pessimism is, besides, inspired by the purest quintessence of Christiainity. And one discovers, on looking closer at it, a touching Christian humility in those remarks of Le Rochefoucauld that are apparently most inspired by the code of society. His self-portrait is in this regard a precious piece that proclaims with eloquence the superiority of these great souls of the Grand Siècle: 'What is still bad in me is that I have sometimes a scrupulous sensitivity and a too severe critical attitude ... I normally maintain my opinion with too much fervour and when one defends an unjust side against me, sometimes by becoming passionate about reason I myself become not very reasonable. I have virtuous sentiments, fine inclinations and such a strong desire to be a complete gentleman that my friends could not offer me a greater pleasure than to warn me sincerely of my defects.' La Rochefoucauld was obsessed by this fear and this scruple to such a point that he returns to it in another fragment: 'There is one sort of politeness that is necessary in the dealings of the gentlemen; it makes them listen to raillery and prevents them from being shocked and shocking others by certain excessively dry and harsh ways of speaking that are often thoughtlessly expressed when one maintains one's opinion fervently.' One should juxtapose this to the purely society precepts of Méré, who recommends to the gentleman as he conceives him to not have any (or almost any) opinion at all and to howl with the wolves, or with the sheep, according to the consensus of the place where he finds himself.

Of course, there are gentlemen and gentlemen, as a certain character of Molière's maintains that there are faggots and faggots. La Rochefoucauld's gentleman is — to his honour — affected by the oversensitive and difficult temper of the great lord who has a very virtuous and honourable mind.

An attentive reading, with note-taking, of the *Caractères* of La Bruyère leads me to the same conclusion as a reading of La Rochefoucauld. When La Bruyère talks of the gentleman (and he speaks constantly about him), he has in mind at once the man of good company, according to Méré, and the virtuous and upright man. If the matter had great importance or if it really needed to be demonstrated, I would multiply the quotations here. Some examples will suffice. La Bruyère certainly takes the word 'gentle' in the sense of virtuous in this thought that everybody knows: 'A gentleman is paid for the application that he has for his task, by the pleasure that he takes in doing it and is not interested in the praises, the esteem and the recognition that he sometimes lacks.' La Bruyère was of a character hardly less ill-tempered than La Rochefoucauld's. The latter embodies aristocratic moroseness, the former bourgeois moroseness but both were bilious, severe and harsh censors. Even while respecting, as was proper, what Pascal, more detached, calls the greatnesses of the flesh, La Bruyère treated without restraint the characters of his time who seemed to him unworthy of respect. And in his chapter on 'Judgements',[61] he lashes out at the gentleman with so much intensity that his remarks turn into

---

61 La Bruyère, *Les Caractères,* Ch. XII.

satire, almost diatribe. It is the gentleman whose gentility is only a façade, it is the society gentleman whom he thrashes in this page that is very worthy of the moralist who, comparing the elite and the people, finally exclaims: 'I wish to be the people'. La Bruyère distinguishes very arbitrarily two principal types: the clever man and the good man. And the gentleman holds, for him, the middle place between them or at least should be at an equal distance from both. La Bruyère took pleasure in denigrating his century. It was an element of his panache. He indulges in it fully in this passage: 'The distance between the gentleman and the clever man is weakened by the day and is on the point of disappearing. The clever man is one who hides his passions, who is aware of his interests, who sacrifices much to these, who has been able to acquire some wealth or conserve it. The gentleman is one who is not a highway robber and does not kill anybody, whose vices, in short, are not scandalous. We know well that a good man is an honest man, but it is pleasant to imagine that every honest man is not a good man.' Is this really 'so pleasant' to imagine? We catch in the act here that *delectatio morosa*[62] into which La Bruyère, the moralist, so often falls. His job of living in the company of a 'lord' forced him to live in society. And he did not like society people at all. There is, in the very cruel page that I just transcribed, a bad-tempered prejudice that is opposed precisely to the favourable prejudice of Méré. And these contradictions help us in any case to form an exact and complete idea of the gentleman, a crucial character under the reign of the Sun King.

As for the gentlewoman par excellence of this very radiant age, would it not be, more even than Mme de Lafayette, Mme. de Sévigné,[63] less stiff and less affected than the author of the *Princesse de Clèves*? We recall the exclamations that a reading of Montaigne draws from her: 'Ah! the dear man! He is such a man of good company!' How much has one tried to apply the same compliment to her!

---

62 Gloomy, dark pleasure.

63 Marie de Rabutin-Chantal, marquise de Sévigné, (1626–1696) is renowned for the letters written to her daughter from 1671 onwards.

Her good graces, her 'gentility' were so imposing that that wretched Saint-Simon could not avoid speaking of her, on her death, in cordial terms. He deigns to agree that she knew 'an extreme lot about everything without ever wishing to seem to know anything.' That is exactly the mark of a gentleman and a gentleman according to Méré, La Rochefoucauld and La Bruyère. Ah, no, Mme. de Sévigné 'did not show off about anything'. Virtuous without prudery, spiritual without striving to be that, naturally agreeable and of a goodness to which society women no longer strove, what an exquisite creature! Her taste was excellent and what good humour! What cheerfulness! Mme. de Sévigné is the smile of the Grand Siècle. And the model of the gentlewoman is the gentleman in his most general and enchanting aspect.

*

The French seventeenth century had been an organic age par excellence. The institutions, the beliefs, the customs themselves of the elite acted in complete accord. Nothing grated, but the chance accidents of this sort hardly last. From the end of the seventeenth century, one sees the state staggering in spite of the stiffening of which Louis XIV, aging and devout, gives an example. Then the Regency demolishes at will, as it were, everything that constituted the greatness of the preceding age. And the following reigns further accentuated the decadence. Reason had been, in the seventeenth century, conservative and constructive. Rationalism and Empiricism rise to the assault of institutions. A subversive philosophy fundamentally undermines an antiquated order of things. Was not the idea of progress predominant in the seventeenth century? In the eighteenth century, it acquires the force of a dogma. It contributes to the fall of ancient disciplines. Going beyond the preceding century, the eighteenth century reconnects with the spirit of the Renaissance. Méré placed much discretion in his portrait of the gentleman in his aspect of an individual given to pleasure. The love of pleasure, the cult of voluptuousness, seemed henceforth to be that which was most natural and permissible. Nothing astonishing if these new sentiments influenced the ideal of the gentleman as he was conceived up to then and modified it deeply. The gentleman of the new age has been described by Voltaire in the 'Mondain'.[64] The portrait is pleasant, like everything from Voltaire, but how can one not be struck by the moral inferiority of the character he sketches in comparison to the ideal held by the best minds of the preceding period? There is, besides, in Voltaire's 'Mondain', a clearly aggressive intention with regard to the moralists of the past:

> Anyone who wants may regret the old times,
> I offer homage to wise Nature
> Which has, for my sake, caused to be born in this age...
> I love luxury and even softness
> All the pleasures, arts of all sorts
> Cleanliness, taste, ornaments
> Every gentleman has such sentiments.
> It is very gratifying to my very impure heart
> To see abundant creation,
> Mother of the arts and felicitous works,
> Bring us from its fecund source
> Both new needs and new pleasures.

This is not at all the language of Nicole and Bossuet (not to speak of Pascal), it is no longer even (not by far) that of La Rochefoucauld or La Bruyère. And when Rousseau, later, intends to react against all this lightness, when for this ideal of the gentleman, in which there is always mixed a background of dissipation, he substitutes the cult of the virtuous sensitive man, neither this virtue nor this sensitivity will efface the memory of the former times. The virtuous man in Rousseau's manner will applaud the crimes of the Terror, the sensitive man, sensitive in the manner of Mirabeau, will trample underfoot all sensitivity when his political passions come into play. The balance of the Grand Siècle is one of those phenomena of which world history offers only rare examples, staggered in a wonderful way.

---

64 'Le Mondain' is a philosophical poem composed by Voltaire in 1736.

The Grand Siècle was a fortunate confluence and the circle of gentlemen who were, as it were, the crowned elite of this age was another. Such masterpieces of history are rare and one cannot celebrate them too much.

We have noted the part of religion in the formation of the gentleman. It was considerable. What one would, today, call the subconscious of this human type resulted from that religious education to which all were subjected at that time. The ancient authors, the Greeks as well as the Romans, entered into another part of this formation. The Renaissance had exhumed, glorified and brought them back to life in a random manner. From the beginning of the seventeenth century, pedagogues and moralists had filtered the disparate doctrines of the classical authors and retained for the Christian religion what was best in this jumble. Would not the dual religion of duty and honour be the soul of the Grand Siècle? In the eighteenth century, that of duty sank and that of honour suffered a temporary eclipse. The minds that had remained Christian were pained by it and a curious treatise of the marquis Caraccioli,[65] *La religion de l'honnête homme*, published in Paris in 1766, provides some useful data on this evolution that we observe without being able to delay it. Voltaire and the Encyclopedists wanted to emancipate men by denying the ancient code of humanity. From this era, one cannot stress it enough, the pious minds resisted this pre-Revolution with anxiety. We see, on the morrow of the Terror and the dawn of the modern age, a new word entering into the vocabulary of the depictors of manners, the word 'conscience', while we see the notion of honour flourish once again. It is evidently a question of substituting for the religious faith that was tottering fixed rules that would allow one to live with dignity, but these variable and shaky principles did not certainly replace the commandments that inspired the conduct of the true gentleman and possessed such a solidness,

---

65 Marquis Louis-Antoine Caraccioli (1719–1803) was a French essayist and biographer who was a religious apologist.

such a rigidity. Marmont[66] has reported a conversation that he had, in person, on the nuances of gentility and honour with the great man most typical of the new age: Napoleon. This matchless warrior, who had such clear ideas on strategy, seems to have had less firm principles in morality. Speaking to Marmont of his father-in-law, the Emperor of Austria, who had just betrayed him, he said of him: 'He is not at all an honourable man because he does not keep his word and his commitments, but he is a man of conscience, a gentleman.' I do not think that in the seventeenth century, Chevalier de Méré, however full of indulgence, would have treated a sovereign who had just broken his promise as a gentleman. Napoleon thus seems to have placed honour above gentility and conscience. Perhaps it is a military sentiment. And one can believe that Alfred de Vigny,[67] who wrote these noble words about it in *Servitude et grandeur militaires*,[68] would have approved of him: 'One faith seems to me to have remained in all and to reign supreme in the armies: it is that of honour. In the name of honour a man feels something moving in him which is like a part of himself, and this stirring awakens all the forces of his pride and his primitive energy.'

Here it is the exaltation of honour as a military virtue, but other writers and moralists have also seen, in our times, in, if one may say, civil, honour the only motivation capable of imprinting on life an upright direction and of reviving in a modern way the ideal of the gentleman of three centuries ago. Prévost-Paradol[69] has very particularly written on this subject a famous page that remains, in the

---

66 Auguste Frédéric de Marmont (1774–1852) was a French general who was made Marshal of the Empire by Napoleon.

67 Alfred Victor, comte de Vigny, (1797–1863) was a French poet, playwright and novelist of the early Romantic period.

68 *Servitude et grandeur militaires* (1835) is a collection of semi-autobiographical stories examining the values of military life.

69 Lucien-Anatole Prévost-Paradol (1829–1870) was a French journalist and essayist. His work *La France nouvelle* (1868) was an affirmation of his Orléanist political views.

preoccupations that it attests to, of a striking modernness. The author of *La France nouvelle* observes, as every person of good faith must, the decline of morals founded on religion and piety. And he sees only the 'point of honour' replacing the faith that disappeared: 'This motivation', he writes, 'is honour, the last and powerful rampart of an aged society and particularly of French society. Here is the faithful image of a nation that the point of honour still sustains after religion and virtue have retreated.'

Prévost-Paradol, a morbid and desolate mind (he proved it by his death)[70] exaggerated the peril of the French society, which is not particular, besides, to France. In this state of extreme secularity, there remains of virtue a spirit of sacrifice and an unshakeable base 'of honesty', but the latter has evidently taken another form and nothing will make us forget again the gentlemen of the seventeenth century with their very distinct attributes. I have particularly sought the gentleman in literature. One could consider the gentleman in many other aspects, in all the categories of French life in this age. What great gentlemen, that is to say, what perfect types of cultivated men, men of good company and above the market of good men, are Antoine Arnault, Mathieu Molé, Lefèvre d'Ormesson, Chancellor d'Aguesseau! Chevalier de Méré would have judged them too 'bureaucratic' to fully deserve his esteem, but posterity has not shared his scruples dictated by a rather limited caste spirit. The men that I have just mentioned contributed powerfully to that reputation of a harmonious, balanced and, once again, organic age that is associated with the greatest century in the history of France and in fact something unique in the annals of Western man. There are, in a letter of Joubert's[71] written in 1809, some perfect lines on this French education of the past and the accomplished people that it formed, 'an uninterrupted succession', observes Joubert, 'of generations not scholarly but friends of knowledge and

---

70 Prévost-Paradol shot himself in Washington, D.C., where he was posted as French envoy.

71 Joseph Joubert (1754–1824) was a French essayist and moralist.

accustomed to the pleasures of the mind who multiplied in France, that country in the world where this education was best offered and perhaps best received. These characters in whom nothing excelled but everything was exquisite in its obscurity, this combination of qualities where everything was charming without anything being distinct in it, this singular moral temperance that the Swiss philosopher de Muralt[72] thought particular to our climate and that served to form what was properly called men of merit.' Joubert writes 'men of merit', but it is indeed the gentleman such as we have sketched, that he had in sight. And it is indeed, as the Swiss philosopher de Muralt observed, a flower of the French soil and its masterwork. Gentle France has not produced anything more equal to its genius and anything that does it greater honour than the gentleman of its greatest age.

---

72 Béat Louis de Muralt (1665–1749) was a Swiss writer who composed a meditation on travel entitled *Lettres sur les Anglois et les François et sur les voiages* (1725, 'Letters on the English and the French and the Voyages').

V

THE ENGLISH GENTLEMAN

ENGLAND HAS HAD noblemen in the sense that Europe continues to attach to this word. In the thirteenth, fourteenth, fifteenth and sixteenth centuries, one who was distinguished by noble blood and the virtues supposedly flowing from it, compared to the common people, was a nobleman, a gentleman. The nobleman was at that time par excellence a warrior, a man-at-arms, having a right to a coat of arms. It happened, besides, that he employed his arms against the rebels of the inferior classes, whence arose their animosity and their respect. The plebeians, rebelling under John Ball,[1] took revenge on their lords already by denying them any superiority:

> When Adam delved and Eve span
> Who was then the gentleman?[2]

In the fourteenth and fifteenth centuries, an age marked by foreign and civil wars, the nobleman, in the sense of noble blood and military customs, was on top in England as everywhere. Armed combat was at that time the virile occupation par excellence. The elder brother at war

---

1 John Ball (ca. 1338–1381) was an English priest who was influenced by the anti-Catholic notions of John Wycliffe. His participation in the Peasants' Revolt of 1381 resulted in his execution.

2 Part of a sermon delivered by John Ball in 1381.

had the upper hand over the younger son who remained in the city and was dedicated to commerce. The notion of nobility, in the sense of a superior class specialised in a military career, however, declined rather quickly in England. The constitutional development particular to this country and the changes that followed brought about its rapid decline. England has conducted bloody wars but war was never for it a national industry as it was for Prussia. And one can in fact posit, even though this thesis has been contested, that the political, social, moral evolution of Great Britain was accomplished outside the militant ideal dear to other nations.

There was not, for all that, less in the British temperament a background of violence and brutality, which persisted when the nobility, properly called, had lost its importance and was effaced by the patricianate or gentry. The Puritan current is perceptible in England even before the Reformation, but it manifested itself only occasionally. It triumphed only under the reign of Queen Victoria. The courtly air is very perceptibly similar in England and in France. One is even authorised to maintain that it was purer in France than on the big neighbouring island. The customs of the English Restoration, in reaction against the Puritan advance of the preceding age, were crude and bad, and that in the best society. Hobbes had the least flattering notion of man in general and of his contemporaries in particular. He described men as he saw them and he did not see them in very fine shape. There were probably more noblemen and more gentlemen, in the diverse meanings that the English have given to this term, at Versailles than at the court in London. The theatre of Molière is a homage rendered to the gentleman. One could not say the same of the dramatic literature in Great Britain at the same time. The well-bred Frenchman of the Grand Siècle retained a reserve of good form in his worst debaucheries. The Englishman loses all restraint when he has rejected the curb of religion and civil laws. The Frenchman is naturally sociable, the Englishman much less. Whence arises their different conduct when they yield to the influences of Nature.

But while the Frenchman was to persist in his refined, sociable, polite manners sometimes to the detriment of a very strict morality, the British were about to form an ideal which would triumph in the nineteenth century and which is, properly, that of the gentleman, understood in the English sense, an ideal that I shall try to define. This movement of purification and ascent begins just after 1688 but its salutary effects are not felt immediately. The English eighteenth century is still, as they say on the other side of the channel, quite 'immoral'. Progresses had been realised in other fields; they are little evident in the habits and customs, especially among the upper class. Montesquieu, who admired so many things among the English, hardly admired their manner of conduct: 'Money', he wrote, 'is here supremely esteemed, honour and virtue little. The Englishman must have a good dinner, a woman and comfort.' This rather low ideal seems to have been, more or less, exactly that of the Petronius of the age, I mean Lord Chesterfield,[3] whose courtesy and refined manners are celebrated. Traits that do him great honour are related about him, among others the last words, well known, that he pronounced on his deathbed. His friend Dayrolles, having made the effort to come and see him, Lord Chesterfield opened an eye to smile at him and his mouth to tell the people who watched over him: 'Give Dayrolles a chair.' The anecdote, true or not, is charming. Lord Chesterfield was not, for all that, less of a gentleman in the old style, selfish, contemptuous, deceptive and even rather perverse. The counsels that he gives to his heir, in his oft-quoted *Letters* would make the gentlemen of the age blush: 'How are your manners?' asked Lord Chesterfield of his son. 'Polish yourself, do not clean your nails in society, do not put your fingers in your nose, position your feet well and, especially,

---

3   Philip Stanhope, Earl of Chesterfield (1694–1773) was a British statesman whose literary reputation rests on the letters he wrote to his son instructing him on the manners that he should adopt in society as a gentleman. These letters were published in 1774 as *Letters to His Son on the Art of Becoming a Man of the World and a Gentleman*.

avoide the rust[4] of Cambridge'.[5] The rust of Cambridge was not only Greek, Latin and philosophy, it was also — alas! the following section of the letter proves it — the most elementary principles: 'I am assured that Mme. … is pretty as a picture and that she is nevertheless scrupulously attached to her husband though she has been married to her husband for more than a year. She does not think about this. You should polish that woman. Polish each other reciprocally.'[6] The English moralists of the nineteenth century were to judge severely, I repeat, the frivolous tone that still prevailed among the aristocrats of the eighteenth century, in Lord Chesterfield as well as in Bolingbroke[7] and Marlborough,[8] execrable rakes whom Chesterfield proposed, besides, as models to his son.

But these wickednesses were only the last flames of a fire destined to be extinguished slowly thanks to the action of the philosophers and moralists. Rousseau, exalting passion and glorifying Nature (Nature, which, he said, cannot deceive when it is, in fact, the most deceptive of guides), did not exactly announce an authentic reform of manners. And Voltaire even less. However, one sees in Great Britain,

---

4 The reference to 'the rust of Cambridge' is from another letter (101), of 11 January 1750: 'I remember that when, with all the awkwardness and rust of Cambridge about me, I was first introduced into good company, I was frightened out of my wits.'

5 Cf. Lord Chesterfield, Letter 123, 12 November 1750: 'I must add another caution, which is that upon no account whatever, you put your fingers, as too many people are apt to do, in your nose or ears. It is the most shocking, nasty, vulgar rudeness, that can be offered to company; it disgusts one, it turns one's stomach; and, for my own part, I would much rather know that a man's fingers were actually in his breech, than see them in his nose.'

6 Cf. Letter 138, 15 April 1751: 'I am assured, that Madame de Blot, although she has no great regularity of features, is, notwithstanding, excessively pretty; and that, for all that, she has as yet been scrupulously constant to her husband, though she has now been married above a year. Surely she does not reflect that woman wants polishing. I would have you polish one another reciprocally.'

7 For Lord Chesterfield's recommendations of Bolingbroke, see Letters 90, 160.

8 For Lord Chesterfield's recommendations of Marlborough, see Letters 56, 181.

in the same age, authors raising themselves up, who take their duty seriously; they call it their mission. Under the influence of religion, at that time smashed to pieces on the continent and perhaps under the influence of that law of action and reaction which makes a century given to virtue succeed a century without manners, one sees piety return in favour among the English and human and divine laws recommended once again. Men, of course, remain such as they are, but the ideal that was generally accepted, the official ideal, is transformed. And one sees being reborn those rules which will be implanted at the beginning of the nineteenth century to triumph under the reign of Victoria. Addison contributed largely to this reform; it is only right to recognise it. He had given to himself the goal of reconciling virtue with elegance:

> It was said of *Socrates*, that he brought Philosophy down from Heaven, to inhabit among Men; and I shall be ambitious to have it said of me, that I have brought Philosophy out of Closets and Libraries, Schools and Colleges, to dwell in Clubs and Assemblies ...[9]

Addison cheerfully accomplished this difficult task. He appears in the first rank of the constructors of the new ideal and we already have the outlines of the gentleman, invoked to become the model on which the British would regulate themselves in the nineteenth century, in this little masterpiece who is called 'Sir Roger de Coverley',[10] who appeared in London at the beginning of the eighteenth century in an age where it was necessary that the dominant manners be good.

Sir Roger de Coverley, baronet of Worcestershire, left the town, where one experiences only boredom, to settle in the country, in a manor that his family possessed for a long time. It is not a castle; it is only a manor but comfortable and well-furnished. And how easily and

---

9 Joseph Addison, *The Spectator*, 12 March 1711.
10 Sir Roger de Coverley was the fictional character representing a gentleman of Worcestershire who appeared in a number of essays by both Addison and Richard Steele in *The Spectator*.

regularly life flows in this place! It is not that Sir Roger de Coverley sulks about the duties that his situation in the land imposes on him. He is a magistrate, he helps the pastor at the church, he heads all sorts of charitable and philanthropic works. For, having paid court in his youth to an unworthy woman, a pretty and perfidious widow who played with his love, he renounced marriage, of which he had had a lofty idea. Now he is fifty-six years and does not think any longer about anything but keeping his retinue happy. He succeeds wonderfully in this. The entire little world of which he is the centre adores him. His character is 'human and fair'. He never speaks harshly to his servants, and his orders are received by them 'as favours and not as duties'. He personally knows the entire population of his parish, he calls all the children by their names. The poorest families are the ones that he takes greatest care of, but the entire neighbourhood has the right on Christmas day to a game of cards and a little package of black pudding. On this occasion, eight fat pigs are killed, but to enjoy the particular friendship of Sir Roger de Coverley one must attend the services and not sleep there. Sir Roger has his men wake up those who sleep during the sermon. The two great pleasures of Sir Roger de Coverley are hunting and fishing. He has killed at the hunt hundreds of foxes and hauled from the streams baskets of trout and salmon. When a fine piece of venison or a choice fish appears on the table, he likes to recount how he got them. Also, he reads little and questions about art leave him cold. He is positive, practical, down to earth, which does not prevent him from believing, like all good Englishmen, in ghosts. The manor has for a long time received visits from indiscreet ghosts. The servants were even so afraid of them that they spoke of leaving their good master. Then Sir Roger had the premises exorcised by the chaplain. This brave man slept successively in all the rooms of the manor and, chased by his prayers, the spirits fled. Sir Roger de Coverley does not like reading, but he rather likes the theatre. Only, to go to the theatre it is necessary first to go to London. And London is a big city, thus a bad place infected with brigands. When Sir Roger goes to a show in the capital, he has himself accompanied by several valets, provided with solid clubs. And with what pleasure, besides, he returns to the country and his fine house, its honest and healthy occupations, the rustic pleasures which suffice his reasonable tastes, this broad life in the open air and in bright daylight!

Sir Roger has nothing to hide. He gives an example of discipline, of respect for the laws, of piety towards God, of goodness towards men. Providence has supplied him abundantly, but he shows himself worthy of this wealth that has been allotted to him. He is a guide, a leader, a perfect gentleman. The lords who, around the same time, at Versailles, undertook a procession to the Great King would hardly have distinguished the peasants among whom he lived and would have held him in low esteem. Sir Roger de Coverley, a pure-blooded Englishman, lived in the English style and found in this life total satisfaction.

*

The gentleman is a flower, a flower that might well have achieved its final blossoming. To better appreciate this flower, we should observe the soil in which it grew.

The English nation, like all the great nations of history, is composed of very diverse races. Contrary to the theories in fashion among the Germans, which are contradicted by all the facts, mixtures are for the nations a factor not of weakness but of strength. The mixtures of which the Englishman is made up are, besides, products of isolation, on an island. The insular character of the Englishman is apparent in his history as well as in his temperament. British individualism is very accentuated, but it is an individualism *sui generis*, an individualism with a social basis. The group consciousness, the spirit of the beehive, are very strong among this people. These characteristics go hand in hand with a pronounced taste for independence. Even though it suffered four conquests, England has not, or almost not, known serfdom. In the enormous jumble of English laws, we know of none — this is Macaulay's observation — that relate to this institution, so persistent among the people of the continent. How could the Englishman not feel the effects of this? He does feel its effects. English history is the history of liberty and of English pride going hand in hand since the Middle Ages. Thus the notion of a 'chosen people' is very strong in Great Britain. Like France, England had a revolution, but in what a different spirit and for what different goals! It is not at all accidental that England arrives at self-government at the very moment that absolute power triumphs in France with Louis XIV. Self-government, self-reliance, the Englishman who is a citizen inasmuch as a subject, the Englishman, who in any case does not separate these two qualities, wishes of course to be loyal, but in the reasoned notion of his loyalism.

Kipling said of his country that it was a democracy of aristocrats, and it is indeed that. I gave the same definition of the Athens of Pericles. The law of primogeniture helps to maintain this state of affairs in England. Through the eldest sons the aristocracy acts in the House of Lords, through the younger it has its voice heard in the Commons. It plays a role in the Church and in the Army. It is not a closed caste, contrary to what is observed in some continental countries, which have been in the greatest urgency to free themselves from their aristocracy on the first propitious occasion. Open to all, the English aristocracy maintains its prestige and one can even say its popularity. Thanks to the bourgeois influx, it renews itself constantly. More than anywhere else, career in Great Britain is open to talent, to all sorts of talents. Far from begrudging superiority, the Englishman recognises it and recognises himself in it. He applauds merchants who, having become rich, climb the social ladder. He also renders homage to artistic and literary talent, but, to speak the truth, he has less interest in it than people do on the continent, especially in France. A realist, given to action rather than to thought, it is very clear that the Englishman bends lower before fortune than before intelligence. And that is one of the reasons why the Frenchmen understand the

English so little, their hierarchical world, their society that is at once unchangeable and permeable.

English society is an oligarchy where each must have the temper of his position even while cherishing the hope of improving it. At the very top, there is the governing class, those of the noblemen by birth, few in number, and of the gentlemen, more numerous. Then comes the middle class, finally the plebs. That the middle class respect the gentry is fully understandable to the people of the continent. The gentry, even if it has some rights, no longer has any harmful privileges. It recognises, on the other hand, duties and discharges them honestly, but that the plebs render homage to the superior classes and criticise these upheavals in which the revolutionaries of the rest of Europe take pleasure, that is something that goes beyond the average understanding of the person on the continent. Such, however, is the sentiment that continues in England: 'An Englishman is, from his mother's womb, an aristocrat. Whatever rank or birth, whatever fortune, trade, or profession may be his fate, he is, or wishes or hopes to be, an aristocrat.'[11] And Cobden narrated, in support of his thesis, the piquant story of a chimney sweep married to the daughter of a costermonger. This union was happy until the day when the costermonger succeeded in forcing his daughter to return home: 'But why?' the magistrate charged with the litigation asked him 'Was your daughter not happy with her chimney sweep?' — 'My son-in-law', replied the costermonger, 'is a perfect gentleman but his family is of truly very low origin.'[12] Snobbism, that is, the superstitious respect for social positions, the caste spirit raised to a system, this is also an English characteristic, which, apt among this people to reconcile opposites, goes hand in hand with individualism and the democratic conquests. Everybody being a snob, snobbism loses its venom; it becomes a conservative force, a social cement instead of being, as elsewhere, only a

---

11   Richard Cobden, *England, Ireland and America*, III.
12   See the original in Cobden, loc. cit., 'The father did not object to the character of the husband, but protested against the connection as being "so low."'

joke. On the continent, nobles and bourgeois, workers and peasants detest and fight against one another. Not in England; they support one another, but even while maintaining their distance, they are capable of acting in common for the general good. In each county one finds notable families around which the others naturally come and group themselves with the public service in view. Noblemen and gentlemen, named and classified as such by general consensus, take initiatives in the name of all. The rest of the population spontaneously obey their captains. On great occasions rank itself disappears, fortune is eclipsed and so also that solvent par excellence, political divergences. One feels united in the accepted hierarchy. And this way of thinking and acting is found everywhere, in the town as well as in the country and, in a large measure, in the parliament. The representatives of the diverse parties stare at each other stonily at the Bourbon Palace. At Westminster, one sees a Tory member chat amicably with a Labour party member without either fearing to be compromised. It can even happen that the socialist feels vaguely flattered by a public contact with a gentleman of a notoriously superior class. Also, every Labour party member, apart from some exceptions that can be counted on one's fingers, aspires, whether he admits it or not, to appear at the Court in short trousers and buckled shoes. Pushed to this point, snobbism is, I repeat, a strength. It contributes powerfully to the maintenance of the English society in that state of equilibrium that will allow it to last, in its present form, longer than the others. The novelist Meredith,[13] who has described so well the English of his time, has not failed to highlight the vitality of snobbism and its role. Essentially satirical, this author generally shows snobbism in all its puerile aspects and perhaps he sympathises with one of his characters, a German, who declares in *Harry Richmond*:[14] 'Your nobles are nothing but rich men inflated with empty traditions of insufferable, because unwarrantable, pride,

---

13 George Meredith (1828-1909) was an English novelist who was considerably popular in his time.

14 *The Adventures of Harry Richmond* was published in 1871.

and drawing substance from alliances with the merchant class.' This sentence is expressed by a German of the nineteenth century, imbued with the principles in force in his country, who has come to England with the firm intention of not rendering it justice. I may be allowed to oppose this condemnation with the familiar remark of a German officer, made prisoner during the Great War, conversing with an English colleague: 'You will always be idiots', said the German, 'and we will never be gentlemen.' Here is a remark that is truer, even though the form in which it is expressed is somewhat crude.

*

It is no doubt pretentious to try to define the gentleman when the majority of English historians and moralists declare that it is indefinable. Its role, in any case, has been so active and its prestige so vivid, the ideal that it embodies continues to be that of all of Great Britain to such a degree that there is occasion at least to try to determine the principal traits of this social type, but one should not forget that the meaning of the word has been modified as the English society itself changed, and that this transformation continues. The history of the word 'gentleman' is the history of the democratic evolution of England and a person deserved to be called gentleman under Queen Victoria who would not have been before her. However, it is under this great queen and in her image that the gentleman triumphed and he became a sort of national ideal, the perfect type of the best that the British history, soil and climate produced of the 'human plant'. Since the Reform Bill of 1832,[15] the gentleman figures as an aristocrat. What henceforth distinguishes the aristocrat and therefore the gentleman is no longer the right to bear arms and to a coat of arms but the ease of moving in good society and the membership in that particular class of 'respectable' people with the general consensus of those who constitute it.

---

15 The Reform Act of 1832 extended the franchise to small landowners, businessmen and householders with a certain income, though it did not include the working class or women in the electorate.

Above all, the gentleman should have the right apparel and no right apparel without wealth. No right apparel, in any case, without what is called 'great wealth' in France. Frugality, on this side of the channel, is a virtue. Beyond the English Channel it is much less prized. The immense colonial empire of Great Britain gives to its sons means of enrichment and expense that do not exist on the continent. Less uncomfortable, the Englishman thinks he is less bound to save. The law of primogeniture contributes to this tendency. The gentleman thus lives in a grand style and takes pride in it. And not only will he have to possess a fine dwelling provided with all conveniences, furnished with a numerous staff (the English servants are of a legendary laziness) but he will have fine clothes; he will be, as they say, well outfitted. The bad taste of the English has rightly become proverbial; the wife of the gentleman, the lady, is at most correctly dressed, but the gentleman, once again, is generally well dressed. Carlyle has set down in a famous book[16] the philosophy of clothing. Such a book is unimaginable on the continent, especially in France, where people like to proclaim that clothes do not make the man in order to appropriate the right to wear frayed clothes and sometimes threadbare.

The English gentleman, let us not forget, is the respectable man and it is to lack self-respect to dress badly.

Starting from this notion that the apparel is an essential thing and that it is perhaps the first virtue of the English gentleman, the gentleman will have a high notion of his duties as a man, of all his duties, towards God, towards his neighbour, even towards himself. We have seen the place that the sentiment of honour held in the code of the French gentleman in the classical age, but honour is a fluid and vague notion; honour varies from century to century. It was hardly dishonourable in the eighteenth century, in society, to receive money

---

16 Carlyle's novel *Sartor Resartus* (1836) is written in the form of an English review of a German work on clothes by a German philosopher called Diogenes Teufelsdröckh. It is meant to be a satire on Hegel and German Idealistic philosophy.

from one's mistress as if from one's king. The English gentleman of the nineteenth century does not recognise this frivolous code of honour which was also, besides, that of the milords of the past. He took duty as his guide and it is in the Bible — in the Bible interpreted in almost identical manner by the Church of England and the dissident sects — that he found that code by which he claims to regulate himself. And certainly there were, there still are, some gentlemen who, even while professing the Holy Scriptures, are lacking in biblical and evangelical morality. The Europeans of the continent, who, especially in the Latin countries, obey very different rules, delight in pointing out the very evident transgressions of which the English gentleman is guilty with regard to his ideal. English hypocrisy is a subject dear to all, to the non-English moralists in all quarters of the world. It does not for all that remain less true that the attachment of the British gentleman to the Gospel gives to the English life a solid basis of morality and good conduct. The gentleman, especially if he lives in the country, will take care to frequent, as Sir Roger de Coverley already did, the village or county church. And if doubts occur to him regarding the absolute truth that his pastor preaches to him, he will keep them to himself; he will reveal them in any case only with extreme prudence. He will conform to this singular but typical sentence of John Stuart Mill: 'Let us be sceptics, but pious sceptics.' And this formula opens the door, I do not deny it, to many mummeries and even to many impostures. Man is not perfect and the gentleman is, after all, only a man.

The obligation to comport oneself and maintain one's respectability before others demands further of the gentleman that he apply to his face, in times of great emotion, a mask of impassibility. One should not let anyone see that one is suffering morally or physically. Especially no effusion in public, no embracing *coram populo*.[17] A hearty handshake and not these resounding kisses that fill the continental railway stations with sounds deemed vulgar. I shall, for my part,

---

17 In public.

never forget a spectacle that I witnessed some years before the war on the platform of a railway station of a small German town which illustrates marvellously this sentimental particularity of the British. I was coming from Berlin by train and was returning to Paris. In a station in the middle of Germany, I saw a young tearful woman board the train and sit not far from me, a German no doubt who was leaving alone. She left behind her a husband or a lover who was as certainly English as she was German. She sobbed to break your heart, publicly, without shame, while the husband or lover remained on the platform impassible in appearance, but he did not suffer less than she from this separation, perhaps he suffered more. I still see these deep and somber eyes of a brunet Englishman, enlarged by despair, and that dumb mouth twisted by a restrained anguish, that pale face. When the train stirred into motion, the German woman bent beside the door ready to throw herself out of the window, more than ever distraught with pain, whereas the man, drawing a white handkerchief from his pocket which he waved wildly, began to run behind the train, on the tracks, with a total disregard of the rules and his personal safety. He ran in this way for two hundred metres at least, like a madman without saying a word, containing the emotion that overwhelmed him. Then the train definitely took the lead and the man retraced his steps. I suppose that he was received badly by the station master, but this does not concern us. He had, in any case, shown in a most typical manner the very British self-mastery that an English gentleman retains in front of the explosive sentimentality of a German woman.

It has happened to some gentlemen, who prided themselves on being more gentlemanly than the others, to push a little farther this concern to seem insensitive to evils that afflict humanity. I have read in an American book the story, very seriously reported, of a very traditional English gentleman who went hunting on a very hot day in the company of a young clergyman. The latter shouted suddenly: 'Oh, I'm so thirsty!' Nothing more was required to elicit a reprimand from the old gentleman: 'Learn, young man, that a true gentleman is never thirsty.' And the old gentleman, drawing a dried camomile flower from his pocket, placed it on his tongue and invited his companion to do the same. This is perhaps pushing a scruple, honourable no doubt, too far. A thirst developed honestly while walking really has nothing dishonourable in it.

The gentleman is part of a discreet knighthood that is recruited without very fixed rules, spontaneously but surely. The gentleman, writes Mr. Cazamian,[18] 'believes that the quality of a man is related to his conduct.' And that is why he posits in principle that this conduct should be good. It can happen that a gentleman, who is recognised as such, is something of a sinner, but he will keep his sin to himself and his partner; he will sin behind doors, secretly. Adultery thrives in England, as elsewhere, but it is not, in this country, a native product and does not benefit from the indulgence that people grant it elsewhere. A professional seducer will not be considered a gentleman. Byron and Shelley were rakes, which is a completely different thing; that is something antipodal. Taine had already made this remark and had formulated it in a pleasantly turned sentence in the French manner: 'An Englishman in a state of adultery', he wrote, 'is miserable. His conscience torments him at the finest moment.' For the English gentleman truly worthy of the name. this fine moment is only a critical moment.

Rigorously conformist, respectful of all the rules and all the institutions, the gentleman will bow lower before the most ancient and the most sacred: the monarchy. He will love the king if it is a king who occupies the throne; he will love the queen if it is a woman who reigns over the empire. And his devotion will extend, no matter what his party, to the entire apparatus of royalty. When Queen Victoria wore the crown, English loyalty was declining. Helped by a husband of her choice, the young queen did what was necessary to reanimate it. She was able to win over to her cause all the classes of the population

---

18   Louis Cazamian (1877–1965) was a French historian of English literature.

and those virtues of which the royal couple gave the example brought back to the throne particularly the higher section of the bourgeoisie, the nursery par excellence of the gentleman. Queen Victoria and her husband have, one cannot repeat it too often, largely contributed to spreading the ideal of the gentleman in its modern form. And it is quite naturally that the sovereign on the throne and the prince consort beside her unite their efforts to make a gentleman of the young man called to reign after them. The day he began his eighteenth year, the Prince of Wales, the future Edward VII, received, along with the certificate of colonel and the Order of the Garter, a letter from his parents on 'the new life that was opening up to him.' He read in this letter that it was his duty 'to become a good man and a perfect gentleman' and that this was not so easy. The same day, all the people appointed for the education and instruction of the heir to the crown received a memorandum explaining what the royal couple understood by a perfect gentleman. The piety of Queen Victoria, the piety and the pedantry of the Prince Consort, collaborated on this text, which is so interesting for the understanding of our subject: 'The Prince of Wales', declared this document, 'must be not only a gentleman but his rank and position designate him to be the first gentleman of the country. The qualities that distinguish a gentleman are the following: *primo*, his appearance, his outfit and his clothes, *secundo*, the character of his relations with others and his manner of treating them, *tertio*, his desire to take an honourable part in the conversation or in any other occupation of the societies that he frequents and his aptitude in doing so.' The memorandum resumed then all these points, one by one, and developed them with a great wealth of admonitions that were perhaps superfluous. Was it really necessary to specify 'that a gentleman does not lounge in armchairs, does not put his hands in his pockets, and avoids also, in the choice of his clothes, the frivolity of a dandy as well as the casualness of the gamekeeper'? Did the royal couple fear that the prince royal would restore the ideal of the milords to the detriment of that of the gentleman? The chronicles report that the Prince of Wales sobbed on reading the letter enumerating all his 'duties'. Even if one is English and a prince, duty is very often, in the well-known phrase, 'that which is most boring'. However, the Prince of Wales did not profit less from all these instructions given to him. And when he grew older and when, through idleness rather than through malice, he indulged in pleasure with the ardour that we know of, he continued to observe as much as possible the principal rules of the maternal memorandum. He was always the best-dressed man, not only of his kingdom but of the two worlds. He was recognised as the arbiter of all elegance and when he forgot to button his vest to the bottom, he created a new fashion. He seemed, besides, to take pleasure in this role which suited his personality so well. His opinions had the force of a law. When he spoke, the oracle had spoken. When the Russian ambassador, Benckendorff, who was in mourning, asked him if he could attend the races, the Prince of Wales replied: 'You can go to Newmarket because one goes there in a round hat, but you will not be able to attend Derby, where one goes dressed in a top hat!'

When he came to Paris, the crown prince relaxed a bit but without ever forgetting his quality as the 'first gentleman' of the neighbouring kingdom. He was about to go to a boulevard theatre when they announced to him the death of a prince, in fact a very distant relative. Should he go to the show or not? He reflected for a moment, changed his gold cuff links for black ones and went to occupy the back seat of his loge. A solution of 'convenience', the malevolent might say. And in fact, the Prince of Wales was, as they used to say in the past, a pleasure-seeker and his concern to appear a perfect gentleman did not prevent him from entertaining himself, but he was capable also of making sacrifices to his duty as a gentleman — and to his mother. For example, he had made it a rule once, in Paris, never to go to the races on Sunday because he was only too aware of the indignation that the queen and the Puritans constituting her court would feel at it.

Polite with women, all women, friendly with his ministers, correct with his inferiors, Edward VII did not tolerate the grossness of certain great people of this world. Hohenlohe[19] recounts in his memoirs that the manners of the Bismarck family aroused his indignation. And we know to what point the entire manner of being and acting of Wilhelm II himself provoked his contemptuous jokes. Wilhelm II, like his uncle, nourished sartorial ambitions but in what a manner they were realised! Hohenlohe recounted that he seriously thought of dressing as a Roman general to inaugurate a museum of antiquities. It required the insistence of the chancellor to dissuade him from it. And when he came to the English court, what a deployment of civil and military clothes with the calculated design of dazzling the British arbiter of all elegance! The arbiter, however, burst out laughing, as soon as the emperor had left, at this display of bad taste. 'Wilhelm II', he declared often — and all England repeated it with him — 'is not a gentleman.' Wilhelm II, to whom these words were promptly reported, felt an irritation at this that was finally reflected in the relations between these two powers.

Edward VII laughed at the pretensions of his nephew to dandyism but he criticised equally severely the appearance of a French statesman, Léon Gambetta.[20] He called him 'slovenly' and no doubt he was right. But Gambetta's mind, his political judgement, did not please him less for all that. He met him privately, Galliffet[21] serving as intermediary. A conversation which took place in front of the general, who reported it, throws some instructive light on our subject. The Prince of Wales gently reproached the French statesman for keeping the French aristocracy from politics: 'Why', he asked him, 'do you

---

19 Chlodwig, Prinz zu Hohenlohe-Schillingsfürst, (1819–1901) was a German statesman who served as Foreign Minister under Bismarck in 1880 and Chancellor of Germany from 1894 to 1900.

20 Léon Gambetta (1838–1882) was a French politician who served as President of the Chamber of Deputies between 1879 and 1881 and Prime Minister of France between 1881 and 1882.

21 Gaston Alexandre, marquis de Galliffet, (1830–1909) was a French general who was made Grand Officer of the Légion d'Honneur by Gambetta in 1880.

not do as in my country, where we take what is most distinguished in industry, the sciences, letters, commerce? We make these men nobles and our nobility remains a true aristocracy.' To which Gambetta gave this response, which is, besides, little convincing: 'In your country it is still possible for some time; in ours no. The Duke de Mossy Rock would not like to mix with the Duke of Industry, the Duke of Science with the Duke of the Fine Arts. As a republic we can have only one aristocracy, that of knowledge and merit.'

There is no space to examine here to what point Gambetta's reply was pertinent. But let us observe with what fidelity the words of the Prince of Wales expressed the ideal of the English gentleman. It is there fully; it contains in its few words the secret of the English oligarchy, the secret of its duration and its services. The wool industry and the commerce with India had made the grandeur of the Buckinghams, the Salisburys, the Warwicks and the Palmerstons. Heavy industry and free trade brought to the peerage a second batch of gentlemen, well-heeled and fat: the Peels[22] and the Brasseys.[23] Then it was for the spirits to 'drown' their men, to use a bold but traditional metaphor. Where do Earl Iveagh[24] and Baron Hindlip[25] come from then? People reproached Edward VII for excessively accelerating, once he had mounted the throne, this rise of the very rich, for opening too wide the doors of the British aristocracy to Germans, Americans and

---

22 Sir Robert Peel (1788–1850) was a British Conservative politician who served as Prime Minister from 1834 to 1835 and, again, from 1841 to 1846. He was the son of a textile manufacturer.

23 Thomas Brassey, 1st Earl Brassey, (1836–1918) was a British Liberal politician who served as Governor of Victoria in Australia from 1895 to 1900. He was the son of a railway magnate.

24 Earl of Iveagh is a title created in 1919 for the businessman Edward Guinness (1847–1927), great-grandson of Arthur Guinness, founder of the Guinness brewery.

25 Baron Hindlip is a title created in 1886 for the Conservative politician Sir Henry Allsopp (1811–1887), who was director of the brewing company Samuel Allsopp and Sons.

Semites who had not yet lost their accent. But it is possible that, in increasing in this way the number of gentlemen, the king had served the Empire. The social and political machine of Great Britain is a miracle of adaptation. The fabrication of gentlemen, in a rather limited series, is a piece of the machine. Was not Edward VII, in a vein of generosity, going to one day treat as gentlemen an entire nation, still a nation of peasants whom one hardly expected to respect this name, I mean those Boers that England had had so much difficulty in bringing to their knees? 'The Boers', declared Edward VII publicly, immediately after the English victory, 'are gentlemen and we will always get along well with gentlemen.' The chroniclers of the reign think that these wise words largely contributed to making the Boers what they have become: loyal subjects of the crown.

The future Edward VII, enumerating to Gambetta the nurseries where the gentleman is grown, thought he could include literature therein. One should specify here and contradict somewhat. No, it is only with all sorts of precautions that the powers that be and public opinion resign themselves to calling gentlemen men of letters and artists. This is even a British particularity that should be mentioned. Art in France is a vocation. Is it any more than a trifle in England? In any case, it is not that essential thing, that matter of state that it is in France. And it would never have occurred to the English king to create a 'club' like the Académie française. Already in the eighteenth century, the comic playwright Congreve, when he was visited by Voltaire, who talked to him solely about literary matters, interrupted him humorously: 'Don't speak to me any more about literature, sir, speak to me as to a simple English gentleman.' So a too marked concern with literature and the quality of a gentleman did not go hand in hand in the eyes of Congreve? Oh well, no, and this sentiment has only grown. The principal matter for the Englishman is to swell his purse and much less to embellish his mind. To be honest, artists and men of letters are not very highly esteemed in England. For these marginal persons the end of the table is relegated. For the rich banker, for the rich brewer, the places of honour. Walter Scott, Byron would not have wanted to present themselves as literary professionals. In France, however, everybody is full of indulgence for the poets and the intellectuals, even if they have committed some errors. Those, ah, those!, England despises so much more heartily in that they already practise a suspect profession and the scandals in which they are involved always cause a huge sensation. With what cruelty did England not treat Oscar Wilde! And how disgusted it was when it saw him welcomed cordially in France, when it saw Paris make a success of *Salomé*! The fact is that the Frenchman is born an artist and the Englishman a sportsman. And how much more attractive are sports than the fine arts in the eyes of the Englishman! Already Julien Sorel in *Le Rouge and le Noir*[26] observed the tepidity of the English with regard to things related to the intellect. This is a tradition from which England draws more pride than it should. Disraeli, that magnificent man, had assimilated the English instincts to such a degree that he came to adore the rural gentlemen, those 'magnificent asses' as he called them, whom he admired nevertheless. And what is the work of Rudyard Kipling in its most characteristic part if not a eulogy of the British energy at the expense of the intellect, at the expense of the mind, which is too highly praised elsewhere? The individual, in the eyes of Kipling, does not count because he thinks but because he accomplishes. The intellect is most often a destructive force, thus bad. The critical spirit is essentially destructive. Analysis risks killing effort, and intellectuals, in short, play a sinister role in society. They are loquacious, cynical. They take pleasure in contemplation and conversation which are the antipodes of action, which alone counts. *The Jungle Book*, which is Kipling's finest book since he has put all of his heart into it, is in this regard very instructive. It is impossible to celebrate in a cruder manner animal life at the expense of the life of the mind. All the contempt that refractory men and intellectuals — they are the same — inspire in

---

26 *Le Rouge et le Noir* is a novel by Stendhal published in 1830.

the author Kipling has represented in his portrait of the 'Bandar-log'. The Bandar-log are a monkey people who live in the trees and whose yelps disturb the august silence of the jungle. They commit all sorts of mistakes, follies, in the name of that undisciplined imagination that they oppose to tradition. They change laws and customs all the time. Among them every truth, no sooner is it proclaimed than it is abolished. They justify themselves with this paradox: 'What the Bandar-log think now the jungle will think later.' What a stupid reasoning! The satirical aim of this portrait is striking. It is the critical spirit as an enemy of tradition that Kipling binds to the pillory in these vengeful pages that are sincere, too sincere, and very English for sure.

*

England raises gentlemen like racehorses. The stud farm par excellence of the gentleman is the public school. It is situated in the country; it is spacious, vast, airy, surrounded with flowery parks, green lawns, suitable for sports. It is perhaps, of all the inventions due to the British genius, that which does it the greatest honour. The instruction given there is that of secondary schools on the continent, but the instruction is not the principal thing there. Education goes before instruction: 'What I admire', writes Disraeli, 'in the men trained in the public schools is that they live in the open air and that they excel in athletic sports. They know only one language, they never read. It is not a complete education, but it is the best education since the Greeks.' Oh, no! It is not a complete education and perhaps it really flouts — it certainly used to flout — all advanced instruction. One does not become pale there reading, one does not train there for competitions that will make of the young man a functionary, a bigwig, a great man of letters. Tom Brown's father, in the famous novel of the same name,[27] ingenuously agrees with this: 'What final advice shall I give my son?', he wonders, 'Shall I tell him to mind his work, and say he's sent to school to make

---

27   *Tom Brown's School Days* is a novel by Thomas Hughes published in 1857. It is set in Rugby School.

himself a good scholar? Well, but he isn't sent to school for that—at any rate, not for that mainly. I don't care a straw for Greek particles, or the digamma; no more does his mother. What is he sent to school for? Well, partly because he wanted so to go. If he'll only turn out a brave, helpful, truth-telling Englishman, and a gentleman, and a Christian, that's all I want.' One may think that Tom Brown, in these conditions, is very pleased at school. He had wished to enter it (does one, by the way, see many school pupils on the continent wishing to go to school?); he lives happily there; he leaves it satisfied, conscious that he has learnt a lot. Of Greek and Latin? No, once again, but the spirit of discipline, team spirit. Tom Brown, summarising for his personal use his ideal of a schoolboy, formulates it in this manner: 'I want to be A1 at cricket and football, and all the other games, and to make my hands keep my head against any fellow, lout or gentleman ... I want to leave behind me ... the name of a fellow who never bullied a little boy, or turned his back on a big one.'

What a contrast between the sentiment of satisfaction and joy that a schoolboy's public school years leave in the heart of the English schoolboy and the mixed impressions that the continental schoolboy reports of his school! Many generations have passed between Tom Brown and the adolescents represented by Rudyard Kipling. Oh, well, Georgie, like Tom, 'was glad to be back in authority [at school] when the holidays ended.'[28] After having suffered the orders of his seniors, Georgie was elevated in his turn in the school hierarchy. And he liked to exercise his strength for the honour of the school, for the physical and moral progress of the younger schoolboys. Georgie was responsible, writes Kipling, 'for that thing called the tone of the school' and it is difficult to imagine the passionate devotion with which some boys devoted themselves to this work. This work was, besides, absolutely in accord with this cult of energy that Kipling did not stop celebrating. 'For the rest', writes Kipling, 'the school was not encouraged to dwell

---

28 Georgie is a character in Kipling's story 'The Brushwood Boy', first published in 1895.

on its emotions, but rather to keep in hard condition.' Georgie will add, some pages later, on his own authority, that 'he kept his pores open and his mouth shut.' To keep one's mouth shut is indeed an English ideal, just as to speak a lot is a Latin ideal. The latter certainly creates a more pleasant society, the former more concentrated, more reflective individuals, more inclined perhaps to action.

It is necessary, for the rest, that this special atmosphere of the factories of English gentlemen must have something very attractive and fascinating that so many foreigners were subject to its prestige. Jacques Bardoux[29] has retained an almost idyllic memory of his stay at Oxford: 'What a milieu!', he exclaims, 'and what an education full of strength and moral elevation! Poor young Frenchmen!, at the age when they are growing into men they have nothing at all. Neither on Sunday the choirs where their voices unite with those of their sisters to glorify God, nor on the other days, before their eyes, parks planted with flowers and trees, some of those old palaces whose view elevates the soul as much by their beauty as by the memories that they invoke.' England does not have conscription and universal military service. The public school and its physical exercices, which the young men engage in in conditions of strict and severe discipline give them — in an evidently pleasant way — some of those virtues that the admission into a regiment gives adolescents in the rest of Europe. Sports in the English schools is one of the most serious institutions. Its aim is to render the young men fit but also, as we have already observed, to inculcate in them a taste for rules. To act when one must, to refrain when one must, to intervene at the right moment, is a veritable science that is simple only in appearance. There exists, besides, in English sports a scrupulously observed hierarchy. Only cricket and football are considered at Eton and elsewhere as really educative sports; tennis and

---

29 Jacques Bardoux (1874–1959) was a French politician and writer who studied at Oxford University and published his Oxford memoirs as *Souvenirs d'Oxford* in 1898.

golf are merely tolerated. Practising them one does not learn either to obey or to command.

Cricket and football, these games loved by English youth, are violent exercices, football especially. In this they are in the image of the true English temperament, which is naturally rough and even brutal: 'A little Englishman', said an Englishman who was a good observer to Taine, 'is ferocious, indomitable, there is in his veins some of the blood of the Scandinavian rover.' He deserves so much more praise for having conceived the ideal of the gentleman and having realised it, but it is not without effort that he achieves this end. One knows the role that corporal punishment plays in the English schools. An object of condemnation for the sociologists and pedagogues on the continent, it is still of chief importance on the other side of the Channel. They box and they whip, they do fist-fights and wield the cane with almost as much energy today as yesterday and nothing announces the end of this fashion. Benjamin Disraeli, placed in the school of Reverend Cogan, had created, along with his young classmates, a theatrical troupe and won flattering successes. The jealousy of the great dispatched to him the sturdiest and most brutal of them: 'We do not wish to be commanded by a foreigner.' The foreigner was Disraeli, of Jewish and Italian origin. Unmoved, he landed on the face of the provoker a punch so vigorous that the big brute stretched out on the ground. Disraeli had won the match. He was no longer a foreigner. How many scenes of the same sort does one not find in the innumerable English novels where the public school life is described and celebrated! Schoolboys are everywhere belligerent. They are that in Great Britain more than elsewhere but, like team players, boxers facing boxers also obey rules. The punches are not delivered at random and the newcomer is initiated to the code of boxing with at least as much seriousness as to the secrets of its Greek version.

The corporal punishments are also a tradition, a ritual. To receive the whip is a bitter thing but not humiliating. The most illustrious gentlemen of the past passed through it: 'Essex, Sir Walter Raleigh,

Drake, Clive, Hastings, Cromwell himself. Nothing like it to teach you to dominate your passions and your emotions.' Count Kessler,[30] who spent several years in England at the end of the last century, has in his turn offered an apologia of this educative system and this testimony of a foreigner is interesting to note: 'The one among us', he writes, 'who had lied or transgressed certain essential laws whose observance constituted the gentleman — the modern incarnation of the fearless and irreproachable knight — was placed on the Index by his comrades and cited before the college of professors or, in outrageous cases, delivered to the judgement of a small number of peers, students of the higher classes, and then, according to the ritual of old England, he was made to kneel and bend over, his backside naked, on a wooden block one metre high where the victim considered it an honour to sculpt his name with a penknife during the operation.' Some strong minds, among them Winston Churchill the Paradoxical, rebelled against the persistence of this 'barbaric' custom. In spite of all their indignation they were punished. The public did not follow them. The gentlemen trained at Eton, Harrow or elsewhere do not think they were diminished for having been whipped in the past till they bled. 'And do they like to be beaten?' Is that not the price at which one becomes a true gentleman?

*

We see the powerful barricade that is erected against the revolutionary wave by the English society, of which the gentleman is in a way the efflorescence and almost the keystone. The English system forms conservative minds and that is its great merit. The sole fact of belonging to the class of gentlemen obliges the rural landowner, the owner of a fine castle or a large farm, the general or the admiral who have chosen to live in his neighbourhood, the clergyman who exercises

---

30 Harry Clemens, Graf von Kessler, (1868–1937) was a German diplomat and writer who had studied briefly at St. George's School in Ascot, which was attended by Winston Churchill too.

on both a moral tutelage that is today of course debated but real, to certain rules, certain opinions, certain customs. The king rules over the English but it is the Bible that governs them, the Bible popularised by the Puritans and interpreted by the clergy. Viewed from a distance and from this side of the Channel, Puritanism has nothing seductive about it. Observed *in situ*, in its influence on individuals, in what it has made of England, it inspires in the most sceptical, and as it were in spite of themselves, a feeling of admiration, in any case, one of respect: 'The Puritans founded England', writes Taine in his study of Carlyle, 'by the exercise of duty, by the practice of justice, by obduracy at work, by the claim of rights, by the resistance to oppression, by the repression of vice.' Tempered, humanised, adapted to circumstances, Puritanism still inspires the Church of England. It enters in a large way into this ideal of the gentleman, which the Anglican clergy contributes to defending and embodying. Sydney Smith[31] wanted people to demand of every Anglican priest the possession of a certain fortune. The Anglican clergyman, he declared, should not go to the church 'sweating and panting like the Irish priest but in a fine carriage with beautiful children in their Sunday best.' For the English, even those who only walk, fortune is not *a priori* a robbery committed at the expense of the community, the notion that tends to dominate on the continent. It is the temporal compensation granted by Providence to the industrious and practical mortal who has made of the talent given to him the use recommended by Sacred Scripture.

This tendency to look beyond oneself without hatred is evident in the peasant with regard to his pastor, it is found in the navy and prevails also in the army, these two powerful levers of English strength. During the Great War, it happened to the British soldiers as well as to the French soldiers to see the leader who led them to the fire fall, but the consequences of this were much less serious among the French than among the English. Among the former, there was always a clever

---

31 Sydney Smith (1771–1845) was an Anglican cleric and writer.

boy, whether a simple sub-officer or less, to take the place of the fallen leader. An English troop deprived of its hierarchical leader no longer had the same motivation because it obeyed more willingly an officer of mediocre competence who was a gentleman than a qualified sub-officer who was socially inferior. That being so, it is striking that the social conflicts in England do not have the same gravity as on the continent. They manifest divergent interests; they do not call into question the structure of the society. Feminism does not constitute a disadvantage for England either. The Englishman has thought it necessary to make concessions to the Englishwoman; he did that with benevolence, from a gentleman to a lady, in a chivalrous spirit, if not a gallant one, in the sense that one associates with this term elsewhere, but the gentleman has not, for all that, been dashed from his throne. His authority remains the keystone of the edifice.

We could instruct ourselves in an agreeable manner on the progress of the social ideal represented by the gentleman and on the modifications suffered by this ideal simply by taking the trouble to reread the principal works of the English novelists. All have, consciously or unconsciously, represented gentlemen, tried to describe them in their typical aspects and reinforced the national cult of which they are the object. It goes without saying that we would not be able to draw here a chart of this literature, but at random, on the basis of my memories of that which I have read, refreshed for the present circumstance, I would like to at least sketch some more or less pure characters typical of the gentleman.

In the novels of Samuel Richardson, who really created, in the middle of the eighteenth century, the modern novel in England, the gentleman is not yet that absolutely developed personage, as one says today, who ruled the fiction of the Victorian era, but already the hero of the novels of the eighteenth century tend towards the gentleman and the principal works of Richardson attest to this. His Charles Grandison is a model of all virtues, the fearless and irreproachable knight of one of the most sentimental ages, a paladin of delicate feelings and selflessness, but is he not too virtuous to be true? The historian of manners will more gladly retain the first novel of Richardson even though it did less for his reputation: *Pamela, or Virtue Rewarded*. Pamela Andrews is a common girl who, after having faithfully served her mistress, would like to leave the position that she had filled so well, but she is prevented from doing so by the son of the dead woman who has cast lascivious eyes on the maid and found her to his taste. Pamela resists, her master insists. Furious, he takes Pamela and locks her up. She still refuses. He offers her money, this money that the Englishmen and Englishwomen are supposed to like so much, but Pamela repulses with horror this new affront and her indignation extends, beyond her master, to that class of noblemen (not to be confused with gentlemen) to which her persecutor belongs: 'O how poor and mean must those actions be, and how little must they make the best of gentlemen look, when they offer such things as are unworthy of themselves, and put it into the power of their inferiors to be greater than they!' Is Pamela's tenacity perfectly disinterested? Richardson would have cursed such a cynical reader for doubting the sentiments of his heroine. Still Pamela sees her virtue richly rewarded in the end. The vile seducer, not being able to make her his mistress, makes her his wife and thus his morality, which did not deserve this name, rises to the height of the woman whom he is going to marry. He confesses at her feet his unworthiness and pleads attenuating circumstances in his own favour: 'All the education that we receive [I remind you that we are in the middle of the eighteenth century, in the age of drunk and lecherous milords] tends to make us spoiled children, tyrants, the persecutors of our women.' But the fortunate husband of Pamela will give a better example. In fact, his contact with a girl so virtuous makes him the most honest man of the land and already a perfect gentleman. 'He was known', writes Richardson, 'for his piety, his virtue, his exactness in fulfilling all the duties of a society man and of a true Christian'. He too was, in short, a precursor.

Pamela's husband is a gentleman of the period of transition. The squire of Ullathorne whom Anthony Trollope describes a century later in *Barchester Towers* marks a success and an apogee. He is less absolutely sympathetic than the Sir Roger de Coverley created by Addison but he is more strongly depicted. Henceforth the 'gentleman' rests on marble seats. He has become an institution, a power. Mr. Thorne of Ullathorne, a squire, does not have a title but he is considered more noble than many titled people. He is fifty years old; he is a bachelor. He lives in London for six weeks every year but without pleasure; he plays no role in the capital, and the squire of Ullathorne likes to be an exemplar. He is naturally the most important person in his county, more precisely in his lands, because he lives in an ancient manor that he would not exchange for a castle. This manor was in the past defended by an ancestor against an invading Norman. What a claim to glory! The Thornes of Ullathorne are also of old Saxon origin and their descendant derives more than a little pride from it. When people speak to him of a baronet, he sneers: 'Don't you know that this title exists only from James I?'[32] If one speaks to him about the Talbots,[33] he sneers once again: it is quite right if the Talbots have a right to a genealogical tree. Whereas the Thornes of Ullathorne! The beggars who wish to gain the favour of the master of Ullathorne take care to question him on the genealogy of his family. On this subject he is inexhaustible and glorious.

Contrary to Roger de Coverley, he does not despise reading. He enjoys Montaigne, Burton and the old-fashioned essayists of the seventeenth and eighteenth centuries. He goes to church, which is part of the manor, besides. He takes care of his estate and practises sports. Above all, he loves hunting, especially fox hunting. Roger de

---

32 Trollope's original is: 'Were you in your ignorance to surmise that such a one was of a good family because the head of his family was a baronet of an old date, he would open his eyes with a delightful look of affected surprise, and modestly remind you that baronetcies only dated from James I.'

33 A noted English noble family dating from the Middle Ages.

Coverley took pleasure in the slaughter of these animals. The squire of Ullathorne protects them, he prefers them to his sheep. He avoids cutting down the bushes where they seek refuge 'because that would not have been the act of a gentleman.' The squire lived happily until 1846,[34] that is, until the time when English wheat ceased to be protected and when foreign grains entered duty-free. For this heinous law Mr. Thorne of Ullathorne never pardoned the Parliament, and to think that 'the disaster entered through the Conservatives', he almost despaired of the old England.[35] Gradually, however, he reconciled himself to his fate. Fox hunting and the study of the great rural families of the Middle Ages gave him noble satisfactions. Of course, he always arrived at the conclusion that no family of this gentry that he frequented was equal to his own. And here again is a gentleman *sui generis* who is well settled.

Mr. Thorne of Ullathorne is a total snob. And it happens that gentlemen turn into snobs and are just that, but the gentleman who is made that by his moral greatness corresponds better to the ideal that was formed of him under Queen Victoria, and it is to the glorification of this type that a novel, rather mediocre at that, but one that obtained a huge success around the same time that Trollope wrote, is dedicated: *John Halifax, Gentleman*.

The author of this book is Miss Mulock,[36] to whom one owes other novels, edifying and popular, conceived in the same style, but *John Halifax* remains her principal claim to fame, a fame still relative. *John Halifax, Gentleman* is related to the Sunday school literature that

---

34 The Corn Laws, enacted between 1815 and 1846, had favoured British landowners by imposing duties on imported corn. The Laws were repealed by the Prime Minister Sir Robert Peel in 1846.

35 Trollope's original is: 'Not only must ruin come, but it must come through the apostasy of those who had been regarded as the truest of true believers. Politics in England, as a pursuit for gentlemen, must be at an end.'

36 Dinah Maria Mulock (1826–1887) was a novelist whose novels depicted Victorian middle-class life. *John Halifax, Gentleman* was published in 1856.

flourished in England more than others. And John Halifax is himself a hero of a serial novel, but *John Halifax, Gentleman* is, for that reason, no less a useful document for one who seeks to get a notion of the ideal, in tangible features, of the gentleman under the bourgeois reign of the most conventional of sovereigns. And that is why this mediocre novel deserves to be analysed briefly.

The French critic who made the French translation of this book did not fail to compare Charles Grandison and John Halifax, this Grandison 'of a democratic age'. John Halifax, who finally becomes a gentleman, is at the beginning of the narrative only a child of the street, a poor little abandoned boy who possesses only a Bible inherited from his father. He has still not known the latter. To survive he engages in the most humble trades. He begins by driving the cart containing the rabbit skins which his boss, an austere Quaker, trades in; then he is charged with handing over the revenue from these rabbit skins. He is a good person and still unselfish, it must be noted. Yes, he is the virtuous man detached from the cult of Mammon that the English are reproached for. On a tempestuous day, he rescues from the floods some real gentlemen who are drowning, but the latter, arrogant, think they reward their rescuer adequately by throwing some guineas to him. John Halifax does not pick them up and continues to stun all those who approach him with his virtue. He starts a business of his own and providence blesses him. Now he is quite comfortable. Then he falls in love with a young girl of the best society, Ursula March. She encourages John Halifax, who is as shy as he is pure, but John Halifax, sincere, mentions this barrier that separates him from the girl he loves: 'It is enough for me', declares Ursula, 'that my friends are gentlemen.' Disheartened, John Halifax replies, 'Many ... would not allow my claim to that title'. And he confesses to Ursula his low origins: 'We are not equals', he sighs, 'because you are a gentlewoman and I am a tradesman.'

A big businessman, a very big one, an industrialist producing mountains of soap or floods of liquor can be called a gentleman.

That is not the case with a modest merchant like John Halifax. Ursula March thought she was of a very free mind, quite ready to love John Halifax in spite of his 'modest' origins. On learning how much more modest these origins were than she suspected, she feels a shock. But John Halifax is going to win everything through a new deployment of unheard of virtues.

If Miss Mulock likes gentlemen, she does not like the true noblemen. Her novel attests to this very particular sentiment from one end of it to the other. A true nobleman, Mr. Brithwood, has developed a hatred for John Halifax. He provokes him to a duel, but John puts him gently in his place. Losing all self-control, the insolent nobleman then strikes the honest businessman on his face. The first instinct of John Halifax is to retaliate, but he restrains himself: 'But I am a Christian', he murmurs and he slips away. Diverse events follow from which it results finally that John Halifax is also a gentleman by birth and it is the Bible inherited from his father that provides proof of this. Then John Halifax, who is less a parvenu than a man of quality restored to his class, can marry Ursula March. A consoling end, certainly, but we must observe that Miss Mulock, as free as she considers herself of all aristocratic prejudices, did not dare to give Ursula March as husband a plebeian great only in his moral greatness. Curious evidence of a scruple that would have given occasion, if one were in the mood for it, to rather bitter remarks on the inveterate snobbism of the Englishman, whether he was, or thought he was, a democrat. A son of John Halifax declares at the end of the book: 'We are gentle folks now.' — 'We always were', replies his father. What a heartfelt cry, this reflection, which is only apparently banal!

How many types of gentlemen there would still be to describe! John Halifax is the gentleman or a type of gentleman conceivable at the beginning of a bourgeois reign when a devout queen passionate about morality occupied the throne. This era was succeeded by another (or perhaps the two eras overlap) when, under the influence of growing imperialism, England demanded of the gentleman somewhat different qualities. Kipling has embodied better than anybody for years the nationalist feeling of the British. And the ideal of the gentleman, the conflicts of duty into which a gentleman may be led, the cases of conscience that can throw a gentleman into embarrassment, hold a principal place in him. John Halifax is a civil gentleman; the gentlemen described by Kipling have, for the most part, from the school benches, something rigorously disciplined in which is reflected, to my mind, the type of life led by Kipling himself at first. During his stay in India he was in close contact with the military authority, the army. He took part, as a correspondent, in many expeditions. And here we are suddenly in touch with gentlemen of a new sort. A single piece of evidence, a single example, the very small tale called 'His Private Honour'[37] which shows what the ideal of the gentleman became when it became crystallised in the English army. It is set in India. Ouless is a young officer, very young, a novice, shy, nervous, easily carried away. His soldiers, whom he commands to exercise under a leaden sky, manœuvre badly. Exasperated and losing his self-control (a gentleman could not commit a greater error), Lieutenant Ouless strikes with his cane, tipped with silver, the soldier Ortheris. Ortheris's tunic is torn as a result. Ortheris blushes; Ouless becomes pale. He regrets his action, but how should be remedy it? The captain arrives, who does not fail to see the tear. He admonishes Ortheris, who explains the gaping tear as a result of an accident, which he had just suffered. Ouless, returning to his quarters, sinks into the most sincere despair. He is right. His conduct, observes Kipling, had been 'unbecoming an officer and a gentleman.'

Circumstances allow one to arrange everything, but how? In what English manner, specifically English manner, we shall see. Ouless, who feels guilty, takes the first pretext that appears to lead Ortheris to a hunt and, in a secluded place, the officer and the soldier explain themselves man to man. 'What would you like?' Ouless asks Ortheris

---

37 Kipling's story 'His Private Honour' was first published in 1891.

while unbuttoning his tunic. Ortheris understands and unbuttons his tunic in silence. With naked torso, face to face, the offending officer and the offended soldier engage in a merciless fist-fight. They box and box again and do not stop until their faces are bloody. They then go to a nearby stream to wash themselves and Ouless offers Ortheris — who can now accept — to pay for his tunic. Reconciled, the fighters begin to hunt together and return to their quarters at the fixed time.

A magnificent story, a typical narrative of which one would like to know the opinion of an officer of the old German army or the old Austrian army. Never would they have permitted in these countries an officer and a simple soldier who had become, through a mutual accord and for some moments, simple gentlemen, to settle their quarrel with a fist-fight. The moral beauty of the episode recounted by Kipling is, besides, incontestable. Military servitude and greatness, in an army where disciplines leaves intact the honour of a subordinate.

Augustin Filon[38] forced himself, like so many others, to define this term in some pages that he devoted in 1911 to 'Mr. Arthur Balfour, l'homme d'État gentleman'.[39] And he concludes in this manner: 'This word gentleman evokes a mode of social existence that dates from the Plantagenets[40] and attained its (relative) perfection under the Tudors,[41] that slowly atrophied under the modern influences, but whose vestiges covered England even until recently.' Filon's thesis is no doubt defensible but it is little in accord with that of the majority of the historians who have written on this subject. Filon seems to see in the gentleman the most faded and deformed image of the nobleman,

---

38 Augustin Filon (1841-1916) was a French literary critic who lived in England from 1870 and published studies of French as well as English literature and society.

39 In A. Filon, *L'Angleterre d'Édouard VII* (1911).

40 England was ruled by the French Angevin dynasty of Plantagenets from Henry II (1133-1189) to Richard III (1452-1485).

41 The Tudor dynasty ruled England from the reign of Henry VII (1457-1509) to that of Elizabeth I (1533-1603).

whereas for the majority of the unbiased Englishmen the gentleman is not descended from the nobleman but has risen to the latter, so to speak. Taine and Chevrillon[42] recognise in the reign of Victoria the golden age of the gentleman with his most acute characteristics. And I incline to think that they are right.

*

That being duly established, we must indeed declare that the ideal of the gentleman is no longer as generally in honour today as before the war. Determined adversaries have delivered crude blows and continue to do so every day. The assault in fact began before 1914, with the success of the popular masses and the petty bourgeois, awakened to what is called on the continent 'class consciousness' by the labour leaders, or even by Lloyd George and other lovers of destruction. The old values had already found enemies in the preceding century. Carlyle, who loved to fulminate wildly, had observed: 'We have for an aristocracy rapacious merchants who reduce their life to the calculation of the amounts of the revenue and of the sales and idle amateurs whose great concern is to preserve the game on their lands.'[43] But Carlyle drowned his revolutionary anathemas amongst conservative anathemas. He lashed the traditional ideal with his left hand and praised it highly with his right. Eloquent as they were, these diatribes did not have a large social reach. The novelist Thackeray exerted more influence though it should not be exaggerated. He said to Taine: 'I admire your French equality.' And his famous novel *The Book of Snobs*,[44] published in 1848, is in fact a panegyric of equality, thus a satire of the gentleman, who is by definition an aristocrat. 'One is surprised', wrote Thackeray, 'by the dimensions that lordolatry has assumed in our country. In our

---

42 André Chevrillon (1864–1957) was a nephew of Hippolyte Taine and wrote several studies of English literature.

43 This paraphrase of Carlyle is from Hippolyte Taine's *Histoire de la littérature anglaise*, Vol. V, Ch. 4, Sec 4.

44 This is a collection of satires.

country, which is said to be liberal, people are addicted to the adoration of the peerage.' All except Thackeray, whose fictional work is just a curse 'against these satanical aristocratic customs that kill natural goodness, honest friendship.' According to Thackeray, the aristocratic customs, the aspiration to become a gentleman, have also corrupted both public life and private. The gentleman courtier is servile, the country gentleman is worse. He is miserly and coarse, he beats his wife, he is always between two drinks of punch. Under the name Pitt Crowley,[45] Thackeray has sketched a hideous portrait of him that does not recall in any detail Sir Roger de Coverley or even the good squire Thorne of Ullathorne. The gentleman fallen into poverty has been treated by Thackeray with greater cruelty even than the gentleman who is well-off. His Francis Clavering[46] is more abject than his Pitt Crowley. Taine, who attached a great documentary importance to Thackeray's campaign against the hereditary and established nobility, conscientiously summarised his work in his *Histoire de la littérature anglaise*, but he cannot avoid having some substantial reservations. Taine liked literature but he was a historian. He rightly remarks that the customs, apparently detestable, described by the English novelist have not prevented England from having had a good government for a hundred and fifty years, 'whereas in a century and a half", in Taine's words, 'France has had a hundred and twenty bad governments.' Perhaps this historian judges his country with an excessive severity, that is a very French tendency, but his objection drawn from the good government of England is certainly well-founded.

Still timid under Queen Victoria, the literature hostile to the tradition already planted its revolutionary talons here and there, but conservatism was still very powerful, the love of the past very strong. The poetry of Tennyson expressed for many years the inner thoughts of Great Britain and this poetry was totally to the glory of the gentleman.

---

45 Pitt Crowley is a character in Thackeray's novel *Vanity Fair* (1848).

46 Francis Clavering is a character in Thackeray's novel *Pendennis* (1850).

Under Edward VII, there was a new more striking flowering of subversive works corresponding to the progress of the democratic parties and their success in the government. Bernard Shaw, partly Nietzschean and partly Marxist, mocks everything, demolishes everything, but if the scandal caused by his theatrical plays is great, the results are mediocre. More importance is attached to the effect of the 'emancipatory' novelists, Bennett,[47] Wells, Galsworthy: 'Now', writes Bennett, 'is dissipated this fortunate gilded, Evangelical and English fog of a world where the poor man can be virtuous and where the rich can be charitable.' Bennett expected of 'the alliance of the intellectual and the proletarian' the destruction of 'the bourgeois order' (he called bourgeois order that which Thackeray still called the aristocratic order) and its replacement by a better disorder. Wells went farther on this path, and more thoroughly, than his comrades in the struggle. He wishes to regenerate English society through science and socialism. Like Thackeray, he sees in the 'aristocratic prejudice', in snobbism, the ferments of this corruption from which English society, according to him, suffers and he attacks these errors with his sarcasms. Like Thackeray, he sees English society resting on a vast tangle of flatteries and intrigues, with each person forcing himself to rise to the top and preventing the person behind him from doing the same. An obviously erroneous conception, but primarily literary, and one which would inspire all the social novels of Wells.

Tono-Bungay[48] is perhaps the most biting satire that he directed against the old English customs. It is in any case that work of his which manifests the most vigorous talent. Very entertaining, at the beginning of the novel, is the description of a tea lasting five hours at the home of a servant working for rich and esteemed gentlemen: 'No, Miss Fison, peers of England go in before peers of the United

---

47 Arnold Bennett (1867–1931) was an English novelist with a rather democratising view of life.

48 *Tono-Bungay* is a semi-autobiographical novel by H. G. Wells published in 1909.

Kingdom, and he is merely a peer of the United Kingdom.' Another servant refuses to serve sugar, stating that people of quality no longer put it in their tea: 'They say … sugar is fatt-an-ing, nowadays.' Tono-Bungay is a drug launched by Ponderovo. It has enriched Ponderovo, who has, consequently, taken his place among the people of quality or gentlemen. Now, the entire English system is based, according to Wells, on the people of quality. Following many others, he explains England through the role that the gentleman plays there but in order to condemn the latter. Ponderovo says to George: 'It's a wonderful system this old British system, George. It's staid and stable and yet it has a place for new men. We come up and take our places. It's almost expected. We take a hand. That's where our Democracy differs from America. Over there a man succeeds; all he gets is money. Here there's a system open to every one'.

What would Mr. Wells say if the system were not open to everybody? He would detest it even more. As it is, he abhors it and perhaps he is angrier with the democrats for complying with it than with the aristocrats for defending it. Wells does not have enough insults for the 'imbecile puffism' of a manure merchant who, 'after having dirtied the innocence of the peasants with his false wealth', buys himself with silver the title of baron. To which Mr Firmin Roz,[49] who has judiciously analysed and passed these English novelists through a severe critical scrutiny, both literary and social, objects not without reason: 'However, this is how England has progressed.' We shall add: progressed in a healthy manner, certainly to its advantage. Wells' manure merchant has shown that energy without which a society is damned to an imminent decadence: 'He will bring his qualities', writes Mr. Firmin Roz, 'to the society which he aspires to enter and the latter will give him some others.' It is on this exchange of good procedures, which has become the *system* but a system that is equal to many others,

---

49 Firmin Roz (1866–1957) was a French historian and literary critic, one of whose works was *Le roman anglais contemporain* (1912, 'The Contemporary English Novel').

that is better than many others, that the English society is based. The survival of the system in Great Britain, when all the systems on the continent are crumbling, proves its solidity and justifies its duration.

All Englishmen are imbued with it and even, unconsciously, those who attack it. I have named Galsworthy[50] among the adversaries of the gentleman, but this detractor of the system happened to celebrate it magnificently. The proof of this is a novella published eight years after the war, called *The Man Who Kept His Form*. The hero of this tale is called Miles Ruding. He has failed in life but with what dignity! From the school benches he showed himself distant and secretive, but generous: 'He never showed his feelings', writes Galsworthy, 'yet he never seemed trying to hide them, as I used always to be.' On leaving school, Miles Ruding could not restrain a tear, but he experienced so much humiliation on account of it that he pretended that had 'a grit in his eye' and 'began to pull the eyelid down in a manner which did not deceive me in the least.' Poor, he went away to earn his livelihood as a planter in Vancouver. He lived on a modest ranch, alone, with some Chinese servants who adored him because he was good and fair: 'He shaved every day, had his cold tub every morning ... He didn't precisely dress for dinner, but he washed.' When war breaks out, he is no longer young but, a good patriot, he dyes his hair and enrols. When the war is over, he returns to Vancouver but he no longer has the strength to put his ranch back into order. He sells it at a very low price and settles in London, where he hopes, as an old soldier, to find some work, but they want only young people now. Reduced to extreme poverty, he becomes a chauffeur but does not want to be pitied: 'This isn't a bad life in good weather', he declares. The author tries in vain to come to his aid. Miles Ruding refuses all help. And the novella ends with this observation of Galsworthy: 'I saw him with the cigarette between his lips ... Very still he sat — symbol of that lost cause, gentility.' Galsworthy's narrative is indeed something of a funeral oration, but

---

50 John Galsworthy (1867–1933) was an English novelist and playwright noted for his series of novels called *The Forsyte Saga* (1922).

a funeral oration from which an emotional sympathy is not absent. The *littérateurs* may well climb to an assault on the old English edifice and the old English Ideal; they will have difficulty in demolishing it. The novelist Lawrence was able recently to join the chorus also and attack the gentleman; the system resists and one can only congratulate England on it.

Better even than the Mediterranean peoples, direct heirs of Athens and Rome, England has appropriated the Greek ideal and the Roman ideal and has perpetuated them by adapting them to a Christian society. Like the British Empire from which he emerges, the British individual is a continuous creation. He practises, within the framework of the state, the cult of the personality. Politics, in his view, must not suffocate the human being for the benefit of a God or a king but make him serve both to the degree to which it is just while retaining his independence. Just as the Greek ideal of the time of Pericles smashed the Asiatic ideal of theocratic servitude and statist autocracy, the English ideal, since the dawn of the modern age, combats the false democracy based on a sordid egalitarianism and blind complacence with regard to the masses. The Greece of Marathon, of Thermopylae, of Salamis, finds its pendant in the England of the Magna Carta,[51] of the Protestant opposition, of the war against the Invincible Armada, of Puritanism, and the Habeas Corpus Act.[52] The liberty of the subject or of the citizen has not been better defended anywhere than in Great Britain against the assaults of absolute monarchy, on the one hand, and of the demagogic state, on the other. The continent, in this regard, could learn lessons from the big island. That there may be in this very obvious phenomenon a certain deliberate imitation of the Greeks and the Romans, an aspiration to the Athenian καλός κἀγαθός and to the *civis romanus*, is probable. What is taught and especially what

---

51 The Magna Carta was issued by King John in 1215 to ensure the rights of the Church and the barons in the English kingdom.

52 The Habeas Corpus Act was passed in 1679 under King Charles II to ensure that no person is imprisoned unlawfully without a court appearance of the accused.

was taught before the war most carefully in the public schools, where the English leaders are trained, was the Greek and Latin humanities. There certainly enters into the ideal of the gentleman some of those moral elements of which was formed the ideal of the Greek noble in body and mind and of the Roman proud of his human liberty and of his quality as a citizen of an already universal empire. *Civis romanus sum*, it is with an identical pride that the British subject displays his titles and qualities today. And these two prides, the ancient and the modern, resemble each other strongly. They have allowed the two empires to accomplish astonishing achievements. The Englishman of today, like the Roman of the past, has the very clear consciousness of belonging to an aristocracy or quite simply to one of those elites by means of which alone the chosen peoples accomplish their destiny.

*

In a private session in Geneva, during the first sessions of the League of Nations, was discussed the future of European culture. One of the persons addressing Sir Austen Chamberlain[53] asked him, not without malice, if the level of the studies had risen in the public schools after the war. Sir Austen was of too fine a mind not to guess the ulterior motive of the interrogator. He replied coldly: 'I agree that the studies are not very advanced at Eton and Harrow but perfect gentlemen are still formed there and we appreciate the gentleman.' And there are people — and not the least important — who maintain that the ideal of the gentleman is in decline and that this survival of an aristocratic ideal in an age where equality is of prime importance does not accord with anything anymore. Everything leads us to believe that that is a false view. The gentleman as a hero was at his pinnacle during the war. One did not yell out one's patriotism in the English ranks, the English having a horror of everything that is yelled out, but the patriotism that the stuffy tranquillity of the preceding period had numbed was

---

53 Sir Joseph Austen Chamberlain (1863–1937) was a British statesman who served as Secretary of State for Foreign Affairs from 1924 to 1929.

awakened and inspired a thousand heroic actions. Then, when victory was won, the English gentleman adduced his code of honour to help Germany, which was finally defeated, to raise itself up. It is even permitted to think that he showed himself at that time more of a gentleman than was politic, but the Englishman is constituted thus and his entire conduct on the morrow of the hostilities proves the survival of this curious mixture of chivalry and utilitarianism of which he has been moulded through the centuries. The programme of the public schools, they say, has been modernised. At the school and outside it, the fetishism of respectability and of all that was meant by it under Queen Victoria has been attenuated. They have become less snobbish and more 'social', to use the fashionable term. To reconcile the permanent respect of the individual with the collective interests, such would be the ideal that the gentleman of today proposes to himself, but on the whole his prestige remains and it is a writer already cited, Mr. Cazamian, a scrupulous depictor of British customs after the war, who proclaims it: 'In spite of everything', he writes, 'the education of the youth in the ruling classes remains guided by this ideal'. A declaration confirmed by the English themselves. A committee of social and political studies, which met for a while in Rue d'Ulm in Paris, debated between Englishmen and Frenchmen, just after the war, this problem of the conflicts arisen in Great Britain from the clash of tradition and novelties: 'In spite of appearances', declared an Englishman present at the debate, 'in spite of the successes of the Labour Party in Parliament, the ideal of the gentleman dominates today the social life and even the political life of England.'

Let us accept that as an omen. The guarantee of stability provided by this assurance is too consistent with the fundamental truths recommended in this book for us not to note it here with satisfaction.

VI

WHAT CONCLUSION DO WE DRAW FROM THE PRECEDING?

THE PHILOSOPHER-HISTORIAN Carlyle posited that if humanity lives for men, it lives only through great men. It is the great man, the hero, who puts men on the path of progress, often defending it with their bodies. Contrary to this theory, Karl Marx and his disciples see the determining factor of history in the obscure instincts which they divinise. The hero, the so-called hero, thinks that he leads the people; on closer consideration, he is led by them. He thinks that he acts; in fact he is acted on by massive and murky forces infinitely more powerful than the individual who is apparently the most energetic and strong. In an age like ours, when the masses have become predominant, it is naturally the latter theory that prevails. It is nevertheless radically false and the voyage through the centuries and the elites that we have just accomplished seems to us suited to demonstrate its falseness.

Historical experience proves much rather that civilisation, which is never a unanimous work (the level at which it holds itself prevents it from being that), is not more necessarily the work of great men. It is quite especially difficult to impute to the great men of the West the most brilliant periods of Western civilisation. The great man has something immoderate and excessive whereas the Western genius, considered in its most noble creations, always contains something measured, tempered, balanced. Western civilisation is much rather the fact of these elites whom we have rapidly reviewed, who crystallise in some way the European genius in its most significant and most admirable moments. Heroes prepare the way for elites. We owe to them the prosperity and the stability that will allow the elites to form themselves and to give their all, but their role is limited to that, magnificent though it is and very useful! It is when Louis XIV reigned, not when Napoleon I reigned, that the French civilisation, in its aspect of literary flowering and in its classical discipline, reached its apogee. The great man is subject to errors. He is sometimes, in spite of himself, more destructive than constructive. The elite, in which the responsibilities are divided, is less likely to commit injustices and faults. As long as the spirit that presided at its formation lasts, it plays its role, which is both glorious and profitable. People talk of the century of Pericles and the century of Louis XIV. These terms are justified but they must be explained. Pericles would not have written the chronicles of Thucydides or composed the dramas of Sophocles, but it is his personal policy that permitted the flowering of these masterpieces. Similarly, we cannot imagine Louis XIV composing a play of Racine's or a funeral oration of Bossuet's, but his reign and his court were necessary to produce this Pléiade of incomparable authors whose renown is one with his. It required his taste, his love of greatness and beauty, to give birth to this manner of being and thinking, of speaking and living that ensures to France of the classical period a place of honour among Western civilisations.

A civilisation is therefore more the work of elites than that of great men and it is a pity, really, to have to repeat this fundamental truth in opposition to the theoreticians of totalitarian or Bolshevist demagogy. The prince of Greek philosophers, Plato, already affirmed what we affirm here again against the modern errors. What Plato calls divine men is quite simply what we call the elite beings and nobody has ever defined them better: 'One always finds', observes Plato, 'among the masses some divine men, few in number in fact, whose company is of an inestimable value. The citizens who live under a good government must walk in the footsteps of these men who have preserved themselves from corruption and look for them on land and sea, partly to affirm what is wise in the laws of their land, partly to rectify that which is arranged defectively in it.' (*Laws,* Bk. XII)

The best historians and the best sociologists have all fully agreed with this interpretation in the course of the centuries. They have always saluted in the elite the instrument of progress and the indispensable factor of an authentic civilisation. Taine, who liked to borrow his terms of comparison and his social formulas from the animal and vegetable world, wrote in his book on the Revolution[1] these striking lines: 'In a forest, the few thousands of fine trees, the three or four hundred thousand ancient and new saplings of the reserve, contain more useful or precious wood than the twenty or thirty million shrubs or briars. Likewise, if a society has lived long under a justice and a police system that are rather correct, almost all the assets of the secular civilisation are found in its notable figures, and, on the whole, such was the condition of French society in 1789.' The French Revolution is, in Taine's view, a collection of facts where the misdeeds, alas, predominate, but it is more especially the worst of misdeeds, the revolt of the masses against the elite, a gruesome contest between uncouth and greedy men and a wealthy minority of cultivated minds forgetful, as it happened, of its duties that partially deserved its fate through its faults. Elites too get worn out in time and when they stop enriching themselves spiritually and materially through a sustained effort, constant work, a renovation coming from the absorption of the best popular elements, they suffer the fate of all aristocracies, they degenerate and disappear. Up to the present, they have always been like the phoenix, which is reborn from its ashes, but today, this time, their fate seems to be more

---

1   The second, third and fourth parts (1878–83) of Taine's *Origines de la France contemporaine* deal with *La Révolution* ('The Origins of Modern France').

seriously threatened than ever. It is the principle of elites itself that is being smashed; it is the legitimacy of their function that is contested.

All modern life seems made to ensure the triumph of the majority against the eminent individual, who is already suspect on account of the fact that he is above the sad average. One does not see one of those historic elites, the glory of Europe, whose physiognomies we have sketched, arising today even in an embryonic form. At most, an elite exists in England, which is not to say that it survives.

A sociologist of a remarkable originality who wrote at the turn of the century books full of substance, this Gustave Le Bon already mentioned in the introduction to this book, has provided on the relations between the masses and the elite a treatise full of prophetic visions that the present state of the world confirms in an astonishing manner. This book Gustave Le Bon had entitled *La Psychologie des foules*, but it is indeed the masses that he means by the crowds. People have tried since then to differentiate between these two terms, but the differences that they have posited seem quite subtle. If there is a divergence between a crowd and the masses, it is supported on a fragile basis, but it is not at all essential. And one can apply to the politicised masses of today almost everything that Gustave Le Bon observes on the subject of the crowds of yesterday. His conclusion is not less antigregarious than that of Taine and it is with an equal fervour that he pleads in favour of the elite and claims for it, in a well-constructed society, the role of shepherd: 'One cannot contest', he writes, 'that civilisations have been the work of a small minority of superior minds constituting the tip of a pyramid whose stages widen in direct proportion to the decrease of the intellectual value representing the lower strata of a nation. Assuredly, it is not on the suffrage of inferior elements having for themselves only numbers that the greatness of a civilisation depends.

Gustave Le Bon, who composed his *Psychologie des Foules* before the Great War, was already worried about the fate that the imminent future was going to reserve for the elites. What would he think of this today? The elites depicted or sketched in the different chapters of my book at least offer, as I indicated in my introduction, some common traits from which one can deduce the indispensable conditions for their success and their influence. The members of these great elites, ranked in the course of the ages, were naturally inclined to what is beautiful and good. They were free spirits with generous hearts. They adhered most often, either by birth or as a consequence of some work that was rewarded, to a certain level of material life that was infinitely propitious, no matter what one may have claimed, to the development of intelligence, to its elevation, its refinement, its transmission from one generation to another. They ensured with equal care the satisfactions of their bodies and the aspirations of their souls. They attached a great value to balance, the fruit of reason and reasoning. The French seventeenth century is so perfect only because it combined in its elite rationalism and spirituality.

The man of the people rarely comes straightaway to such a state of mind. *Stages* are necessary. And it seems that social duty consisted not so much in calling the masses to offices that they are incapable of fulfilling well as in preparing individual ascents, in facilitating through prudent measure those passages from one class to another. They may enlarge the segments but must avoid breaking them. Downgradings are desirable, indispensable but problematic. An elite solicited haphazardly, an elite formed of random elements, collected by chance is only a false elite. It seems — and I insist — that modern democracy is not aware of this danger.

The great misfortune of the contemporary world is the prestige of the socialist Revolution, it is the influence exerted by the spirit of subversion, by the egalitarian folly and nominally by the Russian Revolution, this victory of the East over the West. We see before our eyes an ideology winning whose principles are strictly incompatible with the norms of the civilised societies whence issued the elites described above. Everything leads us to believe, unfortunately, that the Russian Revolution is going to play in Europe in the twentieth century the role of the French Revolution in the nineteenth century. If the latter, after spreading, sank very quickly into the cult of the masses, it was not less individualistic in its principle, in its fundamental aspiration. It proclaimed the Rights of Man, and the Rights of Man, observed honestly, would have favoured the rise of new elites. The idea did not occur to the theoreticians — who remained reasonable — of this effervescent epoch that one could confide the destinies of a great nation to the lowest and least educated part of society: to the proletariat. The poorest and the most uncultivated class is worthy of regard. It is the duty of the superior classes to strive to alleviate its condition but nothing designates it to command.

It is to Tsarist Russia that we owe this folly, a folly in decline but that only waits to be revived elsewhere. Russia did not have any elite. One found there landowners and merchants but in no way comparable, in terms of intellectual development and of refinement of social sense, to the great historic elites of old Europe. The aristocracy and bourgeoisie did not represent in the eyes of the Russian people, when it swept away the Tsarist society, anything respectable, anything that deserved to be conserved. This intellectual situation created ripples. Europe will not heal unless it returns to the elites and restores the hierarchies to honour. Some writers, in the full maturity of their talent, who acquired great renown since the success of Bolshevism, are aware of this and fight the good fight. Among these is, in France, Mr. Georges Duhamel,[2] whose scientific training gives a special authority and who tries valiantly to demonstrate the need that I affirm here: 'What one should not stop saying', wrote the author of the *Chronique des Pasquier*, 'in the present confusion of ideas, doctrines and parties, is that the entire effort of a healthy nation, provided with good institutions and well-governed, tends to constitute elites, that is, an intellectual aristocracy whose function is to conserve and increase the treasury of knowledge, to administer the country, to make laws, to administer justice, to ensure the security of the nation, to prevent

---

2   Georges Duhamel (1884–1966) was a French novelist noted for his ten-volume *La Chronique des Pasquier* (1933–45).

or heal illnesses, to direct the work of the masses in the workshops and factories, to compose works of art, to write history and to keep accounts.' This belief is so dear to Mr. Georges Duhamel's heart that he proclaimed it once again in his acceptance speech at the Académie française. It is this that inspired in him the best passages of this fine speech. Elites are necessary, affirmed Mr. Duhamel once again, and he added this, which, on the lips of a writer so little suspected of fetishism with regard to the past, assumed an extreme importance: elites are formed only in a reverence for tradition; one forges a propitious future only in respect and love for the past.

In celebrating the old elites, in showing the initiating and fertilising role that they played, does one not do a charitable work?

*

One should repulse the Asiatic or Eurasian current; one should repulse Communism and Bolshevism; one should return to humanism, to its ideal, its methods.

Humanism is the continuous and constant awareness of humanity. It invites us to know ourselves better; it invites us to love our neighbour better. It is at once the child of Plato and of Jesus Christ. It re-establishes man in his dignity; it gives him the knowledge of his duties. Between the past and the present, it constructs a solid and safe bridge.

We owe to Athens the chronologically first of the historic elites of whom Europe has conserved a memory. And, far from having exhausted its virtue, classical humanism is still a salutary example. In what antiquity has bequeathed to us the West possesses a treasure, its own treasure. Let us be inspired by this incomparable subject! Humanism is nothing but a method commensurate to man to know himself and to perfect himself; it is γνῶθι σεαυτόν and *Homo sum et nihil humani a me alienum puto*,[3] it is also — harsh recall to reality but

---

3   A quote from Terence's comedy *Heauton Timorumenos*, meaning 'I am a man and nothing human is alien to me.'

how opportune, how justified! — *Humanum vivit genus paucis*.[4] Many are called and few are chosen, the vocation of the masses is to engender elites. It is not to put themselves in their place.

Humanism has changed somewhat in nature in favour of new currents that have been traversing the world for a century. In its origin, humanism was oriented solely to literary studies. Born in the fifteenth and sixteenth centuries from this vast spiritual movement directed against the mediaeval routine, against a theology that was bogged down and a scholastic philosophy, humanism in its cradle was revolutionary whereas today it is conservative. Perhaps it favoured rhetoric and the rhetoricians, perhaps humanism and this Classicism that it encouraged produced, more than was necessary, fine speakers distinguished by their talent for intellectual gymnastics, often mediocre in their scientific culture. Humanism today is no longer opposed to science. On the contrary, it presupposes it. And true humanism is henceforth a temple resting on two pillars: literary culture and scientific culture. A real elite can no longer be imagined without these two robust bases.

It is interesting, but disappointing also, to observe the attitude adopted by the different Western nations with regard to the humanities and humanism. The results of such an inquiry show the distortion of this ideal, the shakiness of this discipline. And through this is partly explained the decline, the stagnation, the present deficiency of the elites worthy of this name. Italy, just after the war, was the first in the West to turn its back on humanism. And yet, was it not the Italian Renaissance which restored humanism to honour in the past in its ideal form celebrated by the Roman authors, capable of reconciling the respect of the personality to the service of the public good? The Renaissance had rendered to the individual his prestige when such an operation had become the condition of redemption itself for the West. The return to antiquity freed the human being, released energies that

---

[4] A sentence uttered by Caesar in Lucan's *Pharsalia*, Bk. V, meaning 'The human species lives by virtue of a few men.'

had been suppressed for a long time, created splendid elites. It seems that Fascism trifles with the elite. Certainly, one must praise Italy for having freed itself from orientalising Bolshevism, but one counts on its very sure political instinct not to divinise the state in order to redeem the individual: 'The century in which we are', writes Mussolini, 'is the collective century and consequently the century of the state.' In ancient Rome, the state was strong but the individual was respected. The present stage is no doubt in Italy only a stage. In a consolidated, reassured, peaceful Italy, the notion of elites, which was so enduring and fruitful in this country, will rise again to the surface and assume once again its high significance.

In Germany, the other totalitarian state, humanism is clearly suspect. Already Wilhelm II, influenced by the Pan-Germanists and their nonsense, viewed it with suspicion on account of its Greek and Latin source. Hitlerism sacrifices much more to the exclusive and jealous idols of Pan-Germanism. Nothing less in accord with humanism than this 'racist' ideal predominant today in Germany and this frivolous cult of the gods of Valhalla set up against Christianity. The theoreticians of the Swastika reproach in the Gospel of Christ its Jewish origin, but Christianity, where Hellenism is amalgamated with Judaism, has given to the nations of the West a moral law and an ideal of love that have not been surpassed and to which illustrious elites have adapted. Turned against Hellenism and Romanism, the Third Reich seeks its law in its own tradition. It also exalts the state, an all-powerful state, at the expense of the individual. And the notion of an elite has become as alien and even hostile to it as the notion of humanism. What a pity!

Fortunately, things are not the same in France and in England. A certain school of French historians strives, in fact, to reduce to the minimum the contribution of Hellenism and Latinism to the formation of French civilisation, but Hellenism and Latinism have entered the blood of France to such an extent, the prestige of Classicism and the elites that it engendered remains so strong in this country that they try more to hoard its advantages for the benefit of the masses than to suppress them radically. The notion of the state can, there too, fascinate the masses; the collective can prevail over the individual; the word 'elite' may emit, in the mind of the demagogues, some trace of a guilty aristocracy — but humanism is so much a part of the French patrimony that throwing it out of the door one would only condemn oneself to seeing it re-enter through the window. Mr. Charles Maurras[5] concurs on this point with Mr. Georges Duhamel. Both of them fight for elites because they are the rungs on which the peoples elevate themselves. They alone, in times of crisis, maintain the cult of the mind. Defining 'intellectual art', of which we owe the formula to Hellenism combined with Latinism, Mr. Charles Maurras writes: 'The Roman, the Carthaginian, the French, the German — if they feel they have a strong vitality to defend, to spread, to perpetuate — run naturally to the school of the masters who teach the means by which man immortalises himself.' We owe to Greece, Maurras further observes, 'humanity, or everything that the traditions of our arts and of our mind have allowed to survive of that which is human.' And it was the role of the elites, he concludes, to relay, through the course of the centuries, from one to another, the torch of this lifesaving and redeeming culture.

How instructive it is to see the English people, this English people that a wonderful intuition always directed so surely through all sorts of pitfalls, affirming today with more strength than ever its allegiance to the Western ideal forged in the past on the resounding anvils of ancient Greece and Rome! Mr. André Joussain[6] writes, in his fine book on the *Psychologie des masses*, that in England, 'the preponderance of the elites and more or less pronounced submission of the masses to the elites have placed this country in shelter against the evils resulting from the preponderance of the masses.' Would it not be by virtue

---

5   Charles Maurras (1868–1952) was a French monarchist and anti-parliamentarist who was a leading figure of the Action française movement.

6   André Joussain (1880–1969) was a French thinker and novelist whose *Psychologie des masses* was published in 1937.

of a just instinct that the English, faithful to their elites, intend also to preserve this classical humanism which they have made the very foundation of their instruction in their large schools? Having reached the end of my study, I can only repeat in this regard what I announced in my introduction. The Englishman of yesterday and today, this Englishman of an era where the humanities were hardly attacked, claimed to adhere less precisely to Athens and Rome. Tennyson still said: 'Saxon and Norman and Dane we are.'[7] Since the world war which brought them back to the continent, the English Hellenise and Romanise once again. Speaking in 1926 as Prime Minister, before the Classical Association, of which he was president, Mr. Stanley Baldwin[8] paid homage to classical literature in these terms: 'To be an Englishman, native of a country which was an integral part of the Roman Empire for a period as long as from the Reformation until this present night, and to be ignorant of the history of that Empire, is to be without that sense of perspective in viewing both the change of events and their day-to-day reactions which is essential to see our national life and to see it whole … It was not for nothing that Western Europe was forged on the anvil of Rome, and who can say how much we owe to those long years of Roman law, Roman discipline, Roman faith, and partnership in a common Empire? During the first four centuries of the present era Roman thought and Roman manners imposed themselves upon our island and made themselves a home here.'[9]

What lofty views in this generous speech! Does it not seem that Western civilisation can count on a nation where the Prime Minister attributes to the successful mixture of humanism and Liberalism, as well as to the elites formed by this mixture, the high style of British culture and its prestige in the world? This presence of a good side of

---

7   From Alfred, Lord Tennyson's ode to Princess Alexandra, 'A Welcome to Alexandra' (1863).

8   Stanley Baldwin, 1st Earl Baldwin, (1867–1947) was a British Conservative statesman who served as Prime Minister three times between 1923 and 1937.

9   'The Classics' in *On England, and Other Addresses* (1926).

the barricade compensates for other betrayals, which one would like to hope are temporary. Nietzsche asked in a moment of discouragement: 'Have we learnt something from what the Greeks taught to their youth? Have we learnt to move with beauty and pride like them, to excel in sports, in wrestling, in boxing like them?' Are the English not authorised to reply to these questions, keeping all proportion and taking into account the sombre needs of the century, that they did their best to revive and maintain the *kalokagathia* and that their loyalty to the ideal of the gentleman shows, at the very least, their persistent faith in the benefit of an elite in the Greek style of the past?

Humanism is, besides, incorporated into all of Western civilisation and constitutes such an integral part of its patrimony, even among the Germanic peoples, whatever they may claim, even among the Slavs, even though they rebel, that the most zealous partisans of the masses and of their domination have recently attempted to integrate humanism into their philosophy and their programme, but they have called it Neo-Humanism to differentiate it from the other and have built it on shaky foundations. Neo-Humanism was for a long time fashionable, in September 1934, at certain congresses of Soviet writers to which went a number of foreign authors coming from the 'rotten West'. One thought for a moment that one could come to an agreement at least on certain essential principles. Recalling these memorable days, Mme. Hélène Iswolsky[10] writes that they thought 'they were breathing a freer air in a gentler climate.' It almost seemed as if the materialism dear to the Bolshevist revolutionaries (what would Dostoyevsky have thought of them?) melted somewhat in contact with some honest people come from Europe, all imbued with a Christian spirit, but the poet Surkov[11] abruptly curtailed a debate that was wandering and declared what one should think of humanism or Neo-Humanism: 'In the course of this

---

10 Hélène Iswolsky (1896–1975) was a Russian aristocrat and anti-Communist who was briefly married, in 1931, to the Baron Roman Fyodorovich von Ungern-Sternberg, the anti-Communist general of the Russian Civil War.

11 Alexey Surkov (1899–1983) was a Soviet poet and literary critic.

congress', he said, 'a word that even here inspired defiance and even hostility has acquired civic rights, that is the word humanism. Our young writers, however, forget the fourth element of humanism, that which is expressed in the austere but beautiful idea of hatred.' Does one see the humanists of the West, the true; does one see the most typical members of those elites whom we have described and who are the best that the Western spirit has produced in its most generous outbursts, affirming in this way the educative and ennobling value of hatred? Humanism and Bolshevism are in fact incompatible. Elites and Bolshevism scream to be uncoupled. The tragedy of the West threatened by barbarian Eurasia continues.

Some great minds who have remained optimistic strive to communicate to us their hope. I have quoted Nietzsche, disgusted by the spectacle of sheep-like men, keeping nevertheless his faith in the superman. In a less apocalyptic region, a great philosopher who has nothing of the visionary about him and who, consequently, deserves to be heard so much more, Mr. Bergson,[12] shows that he is also preoccupied with the problem of a necessary elite. During the international congress of philosophy that was held in Paris for the 1937 Exposition, which he had to preside over, he sent to this assembly a message of an admirable elevation of thought, a true spiritual testament. Mr. Bergson did not cast a hypocritical and prudish veil 'on the disproportion that has become monstrous between the body and the soul of the human species'; he confirmed the disorder but formulated the hope of seeing humanity, instructed by its experiences, return one day or another to balance, to rules, to health. Far from rendering man brutal, mechanism will finally liberate him. Earning their livelihood easily, human beings will have leisure. Reasonable and wise, he will use it to cultivate his mind: 'In number', wrote Mr. Bergson in his message, 'and especially in valour the elites will be reinforced.' For the moment

---

12 Henri-Louis Bergson (1859–1941) was a French philosopher who countered the mechanistic philosophy, psychology and anthropology of his time with his emphases on intuition and continuous creation.

one does not ask so much of them and it is enough for us that the elites are maintained. Let us draw from the memory and the contemplation of those elites to which the West owes all its prestige the will and the strength to fight so that this idea will not perish. On the little known and abandoned altar let us make the flame burn.

BIBLIOGRAPHY

Foreword

Bertrand-Barraud, D. *L'Elite et ses rappôrts naturels avec l'État et la nation*, Paris, 1929.

Bourget, Paul *Essais de psychologie contemporaine*, Paris, 1890.

Delhorbe, Florian 'L'Abétissement', *Le Mois*, no. 36.

Dumont-Wilden, L. *L'Esprit européen*, Paris, 1936.

Gaillard, Gaston *Péril jaune ou péril blanc*, Paris, 1937.

Heyraud, Charles *La grande faute. Le problème des élites*, Paris, 1929.

Iswolsky, Hélène 'La tradition communautaire russe', *Esprit*, 1 January, 1935.

L'homme 1936 en Russie soviétique, Paris, n.d.

Johannes, W. *Herr Jean Jaurès und Nietzsche*, Cologne, 1905.

Key, Ellen *L'Individualisme*, Paris, n.d.

Kidd, Benjamin *Principles of Western Civilisation*, London, 1902.

Launay, Louis de *La fin d'un monde et le monde nouveau*, Paris, 1934.

Le Chatelier, Henry *La formation des élites* (speech made at Mulhouse, 14 January 1928).

Lichtenberger, H. *La philosophie de Nietzsche*, Paris, 1898.

Maeterlinck, Maurice *La vie des termites*, Paris, 1927.

Mautner, Wilhelm *Der Bolschewismus*, Berlin, 1920.

Mussolini, Benito *Le fascisme. Doctrines et institution*, Paris, 1933.

Pichon, Alfred *Théorie de l'élite*, Paris, 1906.

Sieburg, F. *Défense du nationalisme allemand*, Paris, 1933.

Spencer, Herbert *L'individu contre l'État*, Paris, 1885.

Spengler, Oswald *Der Untergang des Abendlandes,* Munich, 1920.

Spenlé, J. (ed.) 'Nietzsche médiateur spirituel entre la France et l'Allemagne', *Mercure de France*, 2 June, 1937.

Rousiers, Paul de 'La formation de l'élite dans la société moderne'. *Bibliotheque de la science sociale*, October, 1912.

Rouzic, Louis *L'Élite*, Paris, 1922.

I. The Handsome and Good Athenian

Aristotle *La Morale*, tr. Barthélmy Saint-Hilaire, Paris, 1856.

Bertrand, L. *Le livre de la Méditerranée*, Paris, 1911.

Burckhardt, Jakob *Griechische Kulturgeschichte*, 4 vols., Berlin, 1898.

Chaignet, A. (ed.) *Histoire de la psychologie des Grecs*, Paris, 1892.

Cherbuliez, V. *A propos d'un cheval: Causeries athéniennes*, Paris, 1860.

Cloché, P. *La civilisation athénienne*, Paris, 1927.

Croiset, A. *Les démocraties antiques*, Paris, 1911.

Dantu, G. *Opinions et critiques sur le mouvement politique et intellectuel à Athènes*, Paris, 1907.

Fustel de Coulanges *La Cité antique*, Paris, 1903.

Girard, J. *Des caractères de l'Atticisme*, Paris, 1854.

Glotz, G. *La Cité grecque*, Paris, 1928.

Gomez-Carillo, E. *La Grèce éternelle*, Paris, 1909.

Gréard, O. *De la morale de Plutarque*, Paris, 1866.

Kessler, Harry, Graf von *Gesichter und Zeiten*, Berlin, 1935.

Laberthonnière, L. *Le réalisme chrétien et l'idéalisme grec*, Paris, 1904.

Labroue, E. *Athènes sous Périclès*, Limoges, n.d.

Mahaffy, Rev. J.-Paul *Social Life in Greece*, London, 1875.

Maurras, Charles *Anthinéa: d'Athènes à Florence*, Paris, 1912.

Monceaux, P. *La Grèce avant Alexandre*, Paris, 1892.

Phaliès *Études historiques et philosophiques sur les civilisations*, Paris, n.d.

Plutarch *Les vies des hommes illustres*, tr. G. Amyot, Paris, 1926.

Puech, A. *Ce qu'il faut connaître de la Grèce antique*, Paris, 1928.

Renan, E. *Prière sur l'Acropole*, Paris, 1899.

Ridder, A. de *L'idée de la mort en Grèce à l'époque antique*, Paris, 1896.

Sophocles *Tragédies*, tr. M. Artaud, Paris, 1845.

Taine, H. *Essais de critique et d'histoire*, Paris, 1892.

II. The Roman Citizen

Boissier, G. *Cicéron et ses amis*, Paris, 1884.
Bossuet *Discours sur l'histoire universelle*, 2 vols., Paris, 1885.
Bouché-Leclercq *Manuel des institutions romaines*, Paris, 1931.
Carcopino, J. *Points de vue sur l'impérialisme romain*, Paris, 1934.
Chapot, V. *Le monde romain*, Paris, 1927.
Duruy, V. *Histoire des Romains*, Paris, 1879.
Ferrero, G. *Grandeur et décadence des Romains*, Paris, 1904.
Gibbon, E. *Aperçus historiques sur le droit romain*, Paris, 1821.
Grenier, A. *Le génie romain dans la religion, la pensée et l'art*, Paris, 1925.
Homo, Léon *Les institutions politiques romaines*, Paris, 1927.
La civilisation romaine, Paris, 1930.
Houssaye, Henry *Athènes, Rome, Paris*, 1879.
Kurth, G. *Caton l'Ancien*, Bruges, 1872.
Machiavelli *Sur la première décade de Tite-Livy*, Paris, 1851.
Montesquieu *De l'esprit des lois*, 5 vols., Paris, 1803.
De la grandeur des Romains et de leur décadence, Paris, 1882.
Renan, E. *Saint Paul*, Paris, 1869.
Rousseau, J.-J. *Le contrat social*, Paris, 1881.
Roux, G. *La leçon de César*, Paris, 1932.
Showerman, Grant *Eternal Rome*, Newhaven, 1924.
Titus Livy *Histoire romaine*, Paris, 1934.
Wells, H. G. *Esquisse de l'histoire universelle*, Paris, 1925.

III. The Renaissance Man

Burckhardt, Jakob *La civilisation en Italie au temps de la Renaissance*, 2 vols., Paris, 1906.
Burdach, K. *Reformation, Renaissance, Humanismus*, Berlin, 1918.
Cassirer, E. *Individuum und Kosmos in der Philosophie der Renaissance*, Leipzig, 1927.
Castiglione, Baldassare *Le parfait courtisan*, Paris, 1690.
Delaborde *La vie de Benvenuto Cellini*, Paris, 1881.
Demogeot *Histoire de la littérature française*, Paris, 1889.
Finzi, G. *Pétrarque*, Paris, 1906.

Gautier, L. *La chevalerie*, Paris, 1884.

Gebhart, E. *La Renaissance*, Paris, 1914.

Gleichen-Russwurm *Die Sonne der Renaissance*, Stuttgart, 1921.

Gobineau, Arthur, Comte de *La Renaissance*, Paris, 1877.

Lemonnier, H. *Les origines des temps modernes et la Renaissance*, Paris, 1890.

Mabilleau, L. *Étude historique sur la philosophie de la Renaissance*, Paris, 1881.

Nisard, D. *Études sur la Renaissance*, Paris, 1855.

Pater, Walter *La Renaissance*, Paris, 1917.

Sabrié, J.-B. *De l'humanisme au rationalisme. Pierre Charron*, Paris, 1913.

Séailles, G. *Léonard de Vinci*, Paris, 1892.

Strauss, D.-F. *Ulrich von Hutten*, Leipzig, 1858.

Thévenet, A. de *L'Italie au XVIe siècle*, Paris, 1877.

Voigt, G. *Die Wiederbelebung des klassischen Alterthums*, 2 vols., Berlin, 1880.

Yriarte, Charles *Un condotierre au XVe siècle. S. Malatesta*, Paris, 1882.

IV. The French gentleman

Aynard, G. *Le bourgeois français*, Paris, 1934.

Bouglé, Bréhier, Delacroix and Parodi *Du sage antique au citoyen moderne*, Paris, 1921.

Brunetière, F. *Histoire de la littérature*, vol. 3, Paris, 1898.

Canoba, G. *Molière moraliste*, Paris, 1901.

Caraccioli, Marquis de *La religion de l'honnête homme*, Paris, 1766.

Faguet, É. *XVIIe siècle. Études littéraires*, Paris, 1890.

Faret, Le sieur *L'honnête homme ou l'art de plaire à la cour*, Yverdon, 1649.

Jeudon, L. *La morale de l'honneur*, Paris, 1911.

La Bruyère *Les Caractères*, Paris, 1883.

Méré, Chevalier de *Œuvres*, ed. C. M. Boudhors, Paris, 1930.

Œuvres posthumes, La Haye, 1701.

Molé, Mathieu *Mémoires*, Paris, 1885.

Pascal, Blaise *Pensées*, ed. Léon Brunschvicg, Paris, 1904.

Pilon, E. *La vie de famille au XVIIIe siècle*, Paris, 1928.

Le Rapin *Mémoires*, 3 vols., Paris, 1865.

Roederer, P.-L. *Mémoire pour servir à l'histoire de la société polie en France*, Paris, 1835.

Sainte-Beuve *Port-Royal*, Paris, 1867.

Étude sur La Bruyère, Paris, n.d.

Étude sur le chevalier de Méré ou l'honnête homme au XVIIe siècle, Paris, n.d.

Taine, H. *Vie et opinions de M. Frédéric Thomas Graindorge*, Paris, 1914.

Terraillon, E. *L'honneur, sentiment et principe moral*, Paris, 1912.

Voltaire *Siècle de Louis XIV*, Paris, 1914.

V. The English gentleman

Bardoux, J. *Victoria I, Edouard VII, George V*, Paris, 1911.

Souvenirs d'Oxford, Coulommiers, 1898.

Chevrillon, A. *Kipling*, Paris, 1936.

Demolins (ed.) *A quoi tient la supériorité des Anglo-Saxons*, Paris, n.d.

Descamps, P. 'La hiérarchie des classes en Angleterre', Bibliotheque de la Science sociale, October, 1911.

Filon, A. *L'Angleterre d'Edouard VII*, Paris, 1911.

Fleury, J.-A. *Histoire d'Angleterre*, Paris, 1890.

Goss, E. (ed.) *The French Moralists*, London, 1918.

Halévy, E. *Histoire du peuple anglais au XIXe siècle*, Paris, 1912.

Izoulet, J. *La Cité moderne*, Paris, 1894.

Jesse, William *The Life of George Brummel*, 2 vols., New York, 1886.

Kessler, Comte de *Souvenirs d'un Européen*, Paris, 1936.

Leclerc, M. *Les professions et la société en Angleterre*, Paris, 1894.

Lectures of the Comité national d'études sociales et politiques, Paris, 19 December, 1927.

Maurois, A. *La vie de Disraeli*, Paris, 1927.

Edouard VII et son temps, Paris, 1933.

Mulock, Dinah Maria *John Halifax, Gentleman*, Paris, 1863.

Pineau, 1916. G. 'La noblesse anglaise' (doctoral thesis), Paris, 1911.

Ransome, A. *Oscar Wilde*, Paris, 1914.

Roz, F. *Le roman anglais contemporain*, Paris, 1912.

The Spectator, 'Sir Roger de Coverley', London, 1850.

Strachey, Lytton *La reine Victoria*, Paris, 1923.

Landmarks in French Literature, London, 1923.

Suarès, A. *Angleterre*, Paris, 1916.

Taine, Hippolyte *Notes sur L'Angleterre*, Paris, 1872.

Histoire de la littérature anglaise, Paris, 1905.

VI. What conclusion do we draw from the preceding?

Bergson, Henri *Les deux sources de la morale et de la religion*, Paris, 1932.

Bossuet *Discours sur l'histoire universelle*, 2 vols., Paris, 1885.

Carlyle, Thomas *Les héros, le culte des héros et l'héroique dans l'histoire*, Paris, 1898.

Chardon, Henri *Les deux forces. Le nombre. L'Élite*, Paris, 1921.

Daniel-Rops *Tournant de la France*, Paris, n.d.

Faguet, E. *Le culte de l'incompétence*, Paris, 1910.

Gaultier, P. *Leçons morales de la guerre*, Paris, 1919.

Hitler, Adolf *Mein Kampf*, Munich, 1930.

Iswolsky, H. *L'homme 1936 en Russie soviétique*, Paris, n.d.

Joussain, A. *Psychologie des masses*, Paris, 1937.

Keyserling, Hermann, Graf von *Das Spektrum Europas*, Heidelberg, 1928.

Kornis, J. 'Humanisme et politique mondiale', *Nouvelle Revue de Hongrie*, July 1937.

Le Bon, Gustave *Psychologie des foules*, Paris, 1895.

Maurras, Charles *Dictionnaire politique et critique*, Paris, 1933.

Ortega y Gasset *La rebelión de las masas*, Madrid, 1933.

Rousiers, P. de *L'élite dans la société moderne*, Paris, 1914.

Taine, Hippolyte *Les origines de la France contemporaine*, vol. 8, Paris, 1921.

OTHER BOOKS PUBLISHED BY ARKTOS

Sri Dharma Pravartaka Acharya	*The Dharma Manifesto*
Joakim Andersen	*Rising from the Ruins*
Winston C. Banks	*Excessive Immigration*
Alain de Benoist	*Beyond Human Rights*
	Carl Schmitt Today
	The Indo-Europeans
	Manifesto for a European Renaissance
	On the Brink of the Abyss
	The Problem of Democracy
	Runes and the Origins of Writing
	View from the Right (vol. 1–3)
Arthur Moeller van den Bruck	*Germany's Third Empire*
Matt Battaglioli	*The Consequences of Equality*
Kerry Bolton	*The Perversion of Normality*
	Revolution from Above
	Yockey: A Fascist Odyssey
Isac Boman	*Money Power*
Charles William Dailey	*The Serpent Symbol in Tradition*
Ricardo Duchesne	*Faustian Man in a Multicultural Age*
Alexander Dugin	*Ethnos and Society*
	Ethnosociology
	Eurasian Mission
	The Fourth Political Theory
	The Great Awakening vs the Great Reset
	Last War of the World-Island
	Political Platonism
	Putin vs Putin
	The Rise of the Fourth Political Theory
	The Theory of a Multipolar World
Edward Dutton	*Race Differences in Ethnocentrism*
Mark Dyal	*Hated and Proud*
Clare Ellis	*The Blackening of Europe*
Koenraad Elst	*Return of the Swastika*
Julius Evola	*The Bow and the Club*
	Fascism Viewed from the Right
	A Handbook for Right-Wing Youth
	Metaphysics of Power
	Metaphysics of War
	The Myth of the Blood
	Notes on the Third Reich
	The Path of Cinnabar
	Recognitions
	A Traditionalist Confronts Fascism

OTHER BOOKS PUBLISHED BY ARKTOS

GUILLAUME FAYE	*Archeofuturism*
	Archeofuturism 2.0
	The Colonisation of Europe
	Convergence of Catastrophes
	Ethnic Apocalypse
	A Global Coup
	Prelude to War
	Sex and Deviance
	Understanding Islam
	Why We Fight
DANIEL S. FORREST	*Suprahumanism*
ANDREW FRASER	*Dissident Dispatches*
	Reinventing Aristocracy in the Age of Woke Capital
	The WASP Question
GÉNÉRATION IDENTITAIRE	*We are Generation Identity*
PETER GOODCHILD	*The Taxi Driver from Baghdad*
	The Western Path
PAUL GOTTFRIED	*War and Democracy*
PETR HAMPL	*Breached Enclosure*
PORUS HOMI HAVEWALA	*The Saga of the Aryan Race*
LARS HOLGER HOLM	*Hiding in Broad Daylight*
	Homo Maximus
	Incidents of Travel in Latin America
	The Owls of Afrasiab
RICHARD HOUCK	*Liberalism Unmasked*
A. J. ILLINGWORTH	*Political Justice*
ALEXANDER JACOB	*De Naturae Natura*
JASON REZA JORJANI	*Closer Encounters*
	Faustian Futurist
	Iranian Leviathan
	Lovers of Sophia
	Novel Folklore
	Prometheism
	Prometheus and Atlas
	Uber Man
	World State of Emergency
HENRIK JONASSON	*Sigmund*
VINCENT JOYCE	*The Long Goodbye*
RUUBEN KAALEP & AUGUST MEISTER	*Rebirth of Europe*
RODERICK KAINE	*Smart and SeXy*
PETER KING	*Here and Now*
	Keeping Things Close

OTHER BOOKS PUBLISHED BY ARKTOS

	On Modern Manners
James Kirkpatrick	*Conservatism Inc.*
Ludwig Klages	*The Biocentric Worldview*
	Cosmogonic Reflections
Andrew Korybko	*Hybrid Wars*
Pierre Krebs	*Guillaume Faye: Truths & Tributes*
	Fighting for the Essence
Julien Langella	*Catholic and Identitarian*
John Bruce Leonard	*The New Prometheans*
Stephen Pax Leonard	*The Ideology of Failure*
	Travels in Cultural Nihilism
William S. Lind	*Reforging Excalibur*
	Retroculture
Pentti Linkola	*Can Life Prevail?*
H. P. Lovecraft	*The Conservative*
Norman Lowell	*Imperium Europa*
Richard Lynn	*Sex Differences in Intelligence*
John MacLugash	*The Return of the Solar King*
Charles Maurras	*The Future of the Intelligentsia &*
	For a French Awakening
John Harmon McElroy	*Agitprop in America*
Michael O'Meara	*Guillaume Faye and the Battle of Europe*
	New Culture, New Right
Michael Millerman	*Beginning with Heidegger*
Brian Anse Patrick	*The NRA and the Media*
	Rise of the Anti-Media
	The Ten Commandments of Propaganda
	Zombology
Tito Perdue	*The Bent Pyramid*
	Journey to a Location
	Lee
	Morning Crafts
	Philip
	The Sweet-Scented Manuscript
	William's House (vol. 1–4)
John K. Press	*The True West vs the Zombie Apocalypse*
Raido	*A Handbook of Traditional Living* (vol. 1–2)
Claire Rae Randall	*The War on Gender*
Steven J. Rosen	*The Agni and the Ecstasy*
	The Jedi in the Lotus
Richard Rudgley	*Barbarians*

OTHER BOOKS PUBLISHED BY ARKTOS

	Essential Substances
	Wildest Dreams
Ernst von Salomon	*It Cannot Be Stormed*
	The Outlaws
Werner Sombart	*Traders and Heroes*
Piero San Giorgio	*CBRN*
	Giuseppe
	Survive the Economic Collapse
Sri Sri Ravi Shankar	*Celebrating Silence*
	Know Your Child
	Management Mantras
	Patanjali Yoga Sutras
	Secrets of Relationships
George T. Shaw (ed.)	*A Fair Hearing*
Fenek Solère	*Kraal*
	Reconquista
Oswald Spengler	*The Decline of the West*
	Man and Technics
Richard Storey	*The Uniqueness of Western Law*
Tomislav Sunic	*Against Democracy and Equality*
	Homo Americanus
	Postmortem Report
	Titans are in Town
Askr Svarte	*Gods in the Abyss*
Hans-Jürgen Syberberg	*On the Fortunes and Misfortunes of Art in Post-War Germany*
Abir Taha	*Defining Terrorism*
	The Epic of Arya (2nd ed.)
	Nietzsche's Coming God, or the Redemption of the Divine
	Verses of Light
Jean Thiriart	*Europe: An Empire of 400 Million*
Bal Gangadhar Tilak	*The Arctic Home in the Vedas*
Dominique Venner	*For a Positive Critique*
	The Shock of History
Hans Vogel	*How Europe Became American*
Markus Willinger	*A Europe of Nations*
	Generation Identity
Alexander Wolfheze	*Alba Rosa*
	Rupes Nigra

www.ingramcontent.com/pod-product-compliance
Lightning Source LLC
Chambersburg PA
CBHW032222080426
42735CB00008B/678